D0811314

£ 1-00.
25/4/97.

TRESCO

ENGLAND'S ISLAND OF

FLOWERS

RONALD KING

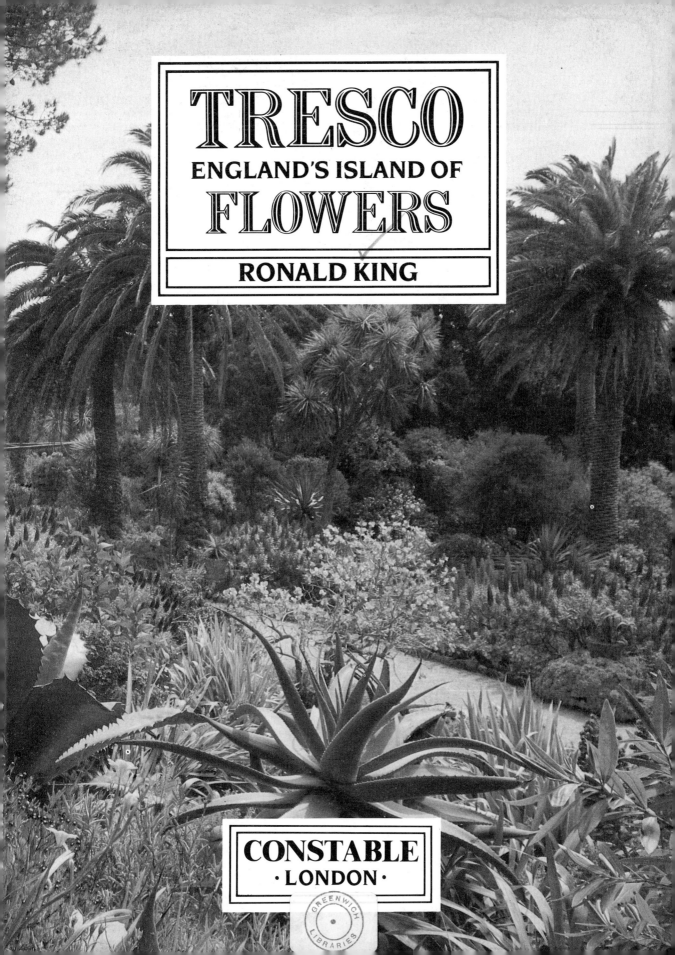

TRESCO

ENGLAND'S ISLAND OF

FLOWERS

RONALD KING

CONSTABLE
· LONDON ·

Tresco: England's Island of Flowers was conceived, edited and
designed by Thames Head Limited, Avening, Tetbury,
Gloucestershire, Great Britain

Editorial director
Martin Marix Evans

Editors
Stephanie Mullins and Alison Goldingham

Consultant editor
Sandra Raphael

Design director
David Playne

Art editor
Barry Chadwick

Designers
Nick Allen, Tracey Arnold, Heather Church, Tony De Saulles,
Nick Hand and Philip Evans

First published 1985
Constable & Company Limited
10 Orange Street
London WC2H 7EG

Published simultaneously in the USA by
Salem House Limited

Text ©Ronald King 1985
Paintings by Frances le Marchant and Gwen Dorrien Smith
©Robert Dorrien Smith 1985
Design ©Thames Head Limited 1985

King, Ronald, 1914-
Tresco: England's island of flowers
1. Tresco Abbey Gardens
I. Title
580'.74'442379 QK73.G72T/

ISBN: 0-09-466170-7

Typesetting by SP Typesetting, Birmingham
Reproduction by Redsend Limited, Birmingham
Printed in Great Britain by
Purnell & Sons Limited, Paulton

CONTENTS

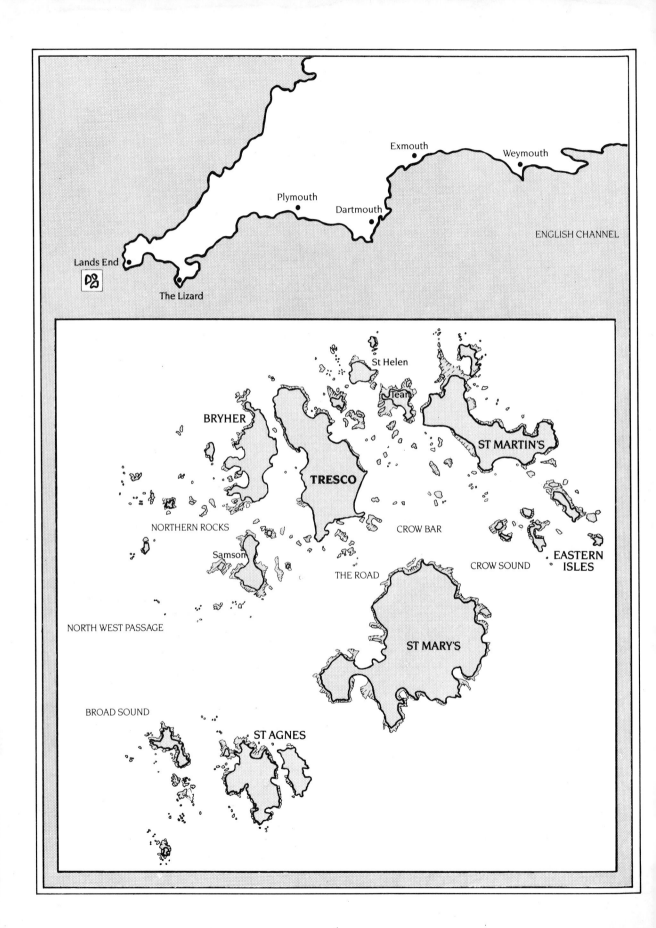

Exmouth

Weymouth

Plymouth

Dartmouth

ENGLISH CHANNEL

Lands End

The Lizard

St Helen

Tean

BRYHER

ST MARTIN'S

TRESCO

NORTHERN ROCKS

CROW BAR

Samson

EASTERN
ISLES

CROW SOUND

THE ROAD

NORTH WEST PASSAGE

ST MARY'S

BROAD SOUND

ST AGNES

THE SCILLY ISLES

INTRODUCTION

The Isles of Scilly are an archipelago located at 49°56°N and 6°18°W. They comprise an oval group eleven miles in length from Bishop Rock in the west to Hanjague in the east and a little over five miles from Scilly Rock in the north to Peninnis Head on St. Mary's in the south. Five of the islands are inhabited and there are some forty smaller islands which, although uninhabited, are large enough to carry green vegetation. The remainder are rocks, around 150 of which have their own names. All stand on a shallow shelf, most of the sea between the islands being less than two fathoms (i.e., about twelve feet) deep. The water is dark blue in colour, being free from plankton and silt.

The larger islands of Scilly are flat-topped masses of granite which were originally dome-shaped (technically, granite 'laccoliths'), the upper parts having been cut off by marine denudation. The highest point is only 165 feet above sea level so that the islands in general present a low profile. In all the higher parts, the granite is at the surface, or covered only by very shallow soil; and all the sea-washed rocks are granite. The 'carns', or rocky hillocks, which are such a feature of the coastal scenery, are also of granite.

Much of the visual charm of Scilly arises from this granite, which is whiter, more sparkling and softer than the rock of Land's End. It contains muscovite and biotite, which are white and dark mica respectively: orthoclase, which is a kind of felspar: and quartz, which is a form of silica (silicon oxide): with other minerals. There are two main types of the granite, a coarse-grained sort with porphyritic crystals of felspar, and a finer kind which is non-porphyritic. The finer type is less common than the coarse-grained. When it decomposes, the granite breaks down into fragments which form the 'head' or 'rab' found in quantities on the larger islands; finally it degenerates into a white sand which has blown all over the islands. There is more sand than the existing islands could have produced, and much must have come from land that is now submerged. The small cultivated fields of Scilly are found in the 'head' or sandy areas.

Scilly has been separated from Cornwall for at least 300,000 years, but until quite recent times the land must have been higher in relation to the sea than it is at present, as there are many sites of former human occupation now submerged. Remains of this kind found on the tiny uninhabited eastern island of Nornour have been dated as late as the fourth century A.D. Some land has been lost within living memory. The present islands have very rocky coasts and there are many reefs.

The climate of the Isles is described as mild and equable, the mean monthly temperature ranging from 7°C to 17°C (45° to 63°F), but this is not the whole story. High temperatures are, indeed, like frosts, uncommon. Although 28°C (82°F) has been recorded, the *Scillonian* magazine once described a temperature of 22°C (72°F) as 'almost unbearable'. Severe winter spells are also rare, but –4°C (25°F) has been reached. These are the bare facts, but they tell you little about the soul of Scilly, which is as variable as a chameleon.

THE HAPPY ISLES

CHAPTER I

. . . my purpose holds
To sail beyond the sunset, and the baths
Of all the western stars, until I die.
It may be that the gulfs will wash us down: It may be we shall reach the Happy Isles . . .
Ulysses Tennyson

The books about Scilly speak in rhapsody of calm weather, of the light airs of a summer afternoon, when the blue of the sky is reflected in the bluest of water, and the profound peace and silence is broken only by the gentle lapping of the ripples against the rocks. It is difficult, they tell us, to imagine a more beautiful place. Scilly might be an island paradise of the South Seas, or Tennyson's land of the Lotos-Eaters: '. . . a land in which it seemed always afternoon . . .a land where all things always seem'd the same!' A land where time glides by and

Scilly calm by Cicely Dorrien Smith 1906

9

nothing ever changes, or a 'Land of Heart's Desire' where the fortunate inhabitants bask in a surfeit of pleasure and the visitor feels that he could remain there contentedly for ever. This is Scilly, seductive and charming, like a beautiful woman anxious to please; and it is, indeed, hard to withstand its blandishments, or believe that it could ever be different. But even on such days of quiet and calm a subtle change can occur which may bring disaster to the mariner. Imperceptibly, the smile vanishes, the fog drifts in from the sea, and wisps of swirling ghostly mist conceal the islands and their reefs and rocks, which become a fearful hazard because they are now hidden from sight. Then, frequently, in summer or winter, a further change takes place, and the contrast with the previous scene of sunlit calm, is so marked as to be almost unbelievable.

For much of the year, the British Isles lie squarely in the track of the North Atlantic depressions that form as atmospheric disturbances along the east-west line of the surface of discontinuity between the Polar maritime air to the north and the milder southern air warmed up by the Gulf Stream. In the summer, with the slow warming of the water from the increased sunshine, the line itself moves north, but in any season these depressions, rotating anti-clockwise like great wheels a thousand miles wide, can travel fast on their track from west to east along the line, carrying much water vapour in the great masses of cloud that form as fronts wihin them. Almost the first part of the British Isles to feel the impact of these depressions is the archipelago of Scilly.

The approach of these storms is heralded by the appearance of wisps of high cirrus cloud, 'mare's tails'; and at the same time a wind begins to whisper between the rocks. As time passes, the clouds lower and thicken, rain begins to fall and the wind rises, until, with the clouds seeming just to clear the cliff tops, the rain drives almost horizontally, so that in the worst of such storms trying to walk through it is like trying to advance against a wall of solid water. From the time the cirrus first appears to the onset of the worst of the tempest is no more than five or six hours. Listen to the words of a native of the Isles, Clive Mumford, describing the scene during one of these storms in his *Portrait of the Isles of Scilly*:

'. . . the so-tranquil scene is soon to be one of rare savagery. The waters of St. Mary's Sound become a heaving, protesting mass, and the lagoon-like surface of the Roadstead a cauldron as huge waves roll in from the west through Broad Sound in an ugly breaking line from Bishop to Mincarlo. All around Scilly the Atlantic builds up to thunder against the granite bulwarks of the islands and funnels into the narrow channels sending spray leaping hundreds of feet upwards. All hell seems let loose. No longer is the sea a friendly, deep blue; now it is a forbidding green and black. The salt flung up on to the cliffs by the breakers is carried into the heart of the islands by the winds and is a constant taste on every lip. Car doors are encrusted by the salt, wind-blown sand scythes blindingly down street and across foreshore . . .'

The winds in these storms are usually of the order of fifty to eighty miles per hour, but can be much greater. In 1954 the anemometer on Round Island registered a wind velocity of 110 m.p.h. before it broke. In the same storm Bishop Rock Lighthouse saw seas racing past the window ninety feet up in the tower.

The balmy weather in which one has basked in Scilly during the afternoon may thus have changed by dusk into a howling gale raising tremendous and

angry seas over the formidable rocks. The vegetation has to withstand the impact of winds which, unimpeded by any obstacle, have been gathering strength over more than two thousand miles of sea. The soul of Scilly is, therefore, a tempestuous one, its peace often broken by sudden and violent rages. So treacherous a climate has bred a bold and hardy race; without such characteristics survival would have been impossible.

Scilly storm by Cicely Dorrien Smith

The time of the first arrival of men in Scilly is a matter of conjecture. Nothing has been found which could suggest the presence of inhabitants earlier than those who left solid and lasting memorials—the megalithic tombs of the type called 'entrance graves'. The makers of these tombs are generally thought to have come to the islands from Brittany during the Bronze Age (c. 1900—500 B.C.), their ancestors having originally come from the Mediterranean. There are about fifty of these graves, which has led some to suggest that the Isles of Scilly were the Isles of the Dead referred to by ancient authors, since the number of graves seems too large for the population of so comparatively small an area, (when it is considered that the rest of the whole of mainland England and Wales contains only two hundred). While the islands may certainly have been used for the burial of the dead from elsewhere, it must be borne in mind that the large number of tombs may also be accounted for because it includes burials from the land now submerged. The tombs are always found in high situations and thus were not drowned when the land was inundated; they therefore represent a population much greater than that which now exists on the reduced area.

Ancient authors tell of the voyages of the Phoenicians to obtain tin from the British Isles. Several, such as Herodotus and Strabo, relate that the tin was obtained from a group of islands which they call the Cassiterides; this has led many, beginning with William Camden in the time of Elizabeth I, to identify the classical Cassiterides with the Isles of Scilly, because much tin has been mined in adjacent Cornwall. The difficulty about this theory is that it was on the mainland that the tin was mined, the amount found in Scilly itself being so little that it could never have supported an export industry. Nevertheless, it is possible that there were workings on the land now submerged. The case has been slightly strengthened by the finding in 1948 at Par Beach on St. Martin's of a Romano-British hut containing pottery of the third and fourth centuries A.D. together with pieces of casserite (tin ore). The identification of Scilly with the ancient Cassiterides therefore remains a possibility.

The earliest literary reference to Scilly occurs in the late Roman writer Sulpicius Severus (c A.D. 400). He speaks of *Sylina insula*, describing this island as lying beyond or beside Britain, and records that in 384 the Bishops Instantius and Tiberianus were banished there for heresy by the Emperor Magnus Maximus. Relics of the Romans have been found on several islands. A Roman altar discovered on St. Mary's is preserved at Tresco Abbey.

For several centuries following the departure of the Romans in the early fifth century, there is no reference to Scilly except in legend. That of King Arthur is particularly attached to the Isles of Scilly because the sunken land between Scilly and Cornwall has been traditionally supposed to be the lost land of Lyonesse, associated with the defeat and death of Arthur at the hands of Mordred. As Tennyson wrote in *Morte d'Arthur*:

'. . . all day long the noise of battle roll'd
Among the mountains by the winter sea,
Until King Arthur's table, man by man,
Had fallen in Lyonesse about their lord . . .'

If there was a real prince with the Latin name Artorius, who fought and held power, dispensing justice for a little space in those dark centuries after the Romans went, it may have been here, between Scilly and Cornwall, that he also went down into the darkness, to become only a doubtful memory.

The Vikings, those fearless sea-wanderers who ranged far afield from their Scandinavian homeland, certainly knew and visited Scilly and some may very well have settled there, as there are fair-haired, fair-skinned natives of St. Martin's today who, from their colouring, could well be their descendants.

According to the 'Saga' of Olaf Tryggveson, written down by Snorri Sturluson in the thirteenth century, this famous king, after ravaging the coasts of western England, Scotland and France for some four years happened on this group of peaceful islands in the year 993 and paused there for a rest and to careen his ships. As the story is told, this visit had momentous consequences for western Europe for he there found St. Elidius (also spelt Lide or Ilid), a Celtic hermit of holy life, who had great influence on him. When he moved on to Tresco he was met by 'a famous abbot, head of a great cloister', the Benedictines having settled in Scilly in 938. Here he received further instruction and was baptized in

the Christian faith. After several years in Scilly, King Olaf returned to Scandinavia a changed man, turning his sword to the task of stamping out the religion of Odin and establishing Christianity in its place. St. Elidius gave his name to the island on which he lived, and this became corrupted in course of time to St. Helen's, where remains both of his buildings and his tomb have been found.

In the first part of the twelfth century King Henry I granted a charter to the Benedictine monastery at Tavistock in Devon which gave to the abbot of that foundation 'all the churches of Sully with their appurtenances', and in 1200 King John granted to the settlement 'tythe and three acres of assart land in the Forest of Guffer.' Where this was is not known and the 'Forest' could, in fact, have been on land now under the sea; there is also a possibility that it could have been on Tresco, because Augustus Smith found large tree stumps there when he arrived as Lord Proprietor of the Scilly Isles in the 1830s.

The Tavistock monks had a certain amount of secular as well as spiritual authority over the islands but they were unable to control the piracy, which flourished unchecked, the islands becoming a favourite haunt of freebooters from France, Spain and elsewhere along the western European coasts, including Cornwall itself. The lawless men of every kind who found a refuge on the islands kept the few islanders and the monks in constant fear. Measures were taken to deter them. In 1209, for example, on Ascension Day, no less than 112 pirates are said to have been beheaded on Tresco. The monastic establishment could not, however, flourish in this unpropitious atmosphere, although it struggled on for a long time. Long before the dissolution of the monasteries, which brought it to an end in 1538, it had fallen on very evil times, with its buildings already in decay and its monks desperate for help which rarely came.

The Duchy of Cornwall was created in 1337 to endow the Black Prince and included in its control the Isles of Scilly, though the Prince can have drawn little from them. Previously, the Earls of Cornwall, and from 1337 the Dukes, who nominally possessed the Isles, were represented there by the Blanchminster family, the first of whom had married the heiress of a governor appointed by Henry III. This man's son, Ralph Blanchminster, was empowered by Edward I to embattle Ennor Castle. The Blanchminsters connived with the pirates, however, as did the lesser inhabitants, who naturally found it politic to remain on the right side of them. According to the *Victoria County History of Cornwall*, on one occasion: 'William le Poer, coroner of Scilly' (the King's local representative) 'went to Tresco to enquire into a wreck and to take charge of the salved cargo. He was seized and imprisoned by a mob, the ringleader being the prior of St. Nicholas' (the head, under the abbot of Tavistock, of the local monks). 'He bought his freedom and a subsequent enquiry showed that the men-at-arms and their leader, who garrisoned the islands were the principal offenders.' Later in the Middle Ages other families succeeded the Blanchminsters but conditions remained unchanged, and in such circumstances law-abiding people left Scilly, which became a wasted land.

The antiquary John Leland described Scilly in the 1530s. He noted in his 'Itinerary', using an old name for Tresco, that 'Iniscaw longid to Tavestoke, and ther was a poor celle of monkes of Tavestoke. Sum caulle this Trescaw, it is the biggest of the islettes, in cumpace a 6 miles or more.' and in another note, using yet another

name for Tresco, he adds: 'In the biggest isle (cawled S.Nicholas Isle) of the Scylleys ys a lytle pyle or fortres, and a paroch chyrche that a monke of Tavestoke yn peace doth serve as a membre to Tavestoke abbay. Ther be yn that paroch about a lx. howseholdes:

In Queen Elizabeth I's time control of the Isles passed to the Godolphin family. In 1571 Francis Godolphin leased the islands from the Queen for thirty-seven years (to 1608), paying £20 annual rent. For the first time Scilly had an administrator prepared to exert himself. John Leland, thirty-six years before, had written that: 'Few men be glad to inhabitte these islettes, for al the plenty' (he had commented on the exceptional corn fertility of St. Mary's) 'for robbers by the sea that take their catail (cattle) by force. The robbers be Frenchmen and Spaniards:

A comment made by Francis Godolphin himself, in 1579, eight years after he had taken his lease, showed that, in spite of his efforts, conditions had not yet improved: There are now not a hundred men but more women and children: the tillable ground does not find half of them bread. Only the islands whereon are fortifications (St.Mary's and Tresco) are inhabited . . . ' Nevertheless, he persevered. Plots were made available to tenants and eventually people began to return to the islands and new workers were attracted there for whom employment was found. They had a hard task to make their way in a territory which Francis himself had described as 'a bushment of briers and a refuge for pirates that range.'

There was at this time no means of defending the Isles, Ennor Castle on St. Mary's having fallen into disrepair and fortifications that had been put up in Edward VI's time being of little use. The Queen was alive to the situation, fearing that the hated Spaniards might seize Scilly and use it as a base to harass England. She told Godolphin to provide new fortifications and showed the strength of her fear by seeing 'despite her notorious parsimony' that he got the money for the project. In 1593-94 Star Castle, still standing today and in use as a hotel, was built on St. Mary's. Constructed from the local granite for less than £1,000, it was made in the form of an eight-pointed star, hence its name, and was surrounded by a moat. It proved effective, warning off both Spaniards and pirates, perhaps to the detriment of the mainland, as the Spaniards raided and sacked Mousehole and Penzance in 1595.

The new settlers attracted by Godolphin's policy had an impact on the racial characteristics of the population of the islands. Before the influx, people of the Isles were still largely Celtic, had Cornish names (by Tre, Pol and Pen, you can tell the Cornish men) and called the isles, rocks and other places by Celtic names. The adventurers and pirates had, over the years, somewhat modified the Celtic strain and Godolphin's immigrants carried this anglicizing process still further. Today, with further influxes since, the English strain has almost overwhelmed the Celtic and, with other admixtures, produced what can only be fairly described as a mongrel population. Lest Scilly be offended by this term, it should be remembered that mixing of the genes in breeding produces a strong and sturdy stock!

When the Civil War broke out in the mid-seventeenth century, Scilly under the Godolphins was staunchly Royalist. Prince Charles (later Charles II) fled to Star Castle in 1646 but after six weeks continued his flight to Jersey and

ultimately to France. Shortly afterwards, Scilly was captured by the Roundheads, who remained until 1648. As soon as they had left, the Isles boldly declared themselves again for the King and from them a Royalist leader, Sir John Grenville, and his Cavaliers carried on a sea campaign against Parliamentary shipping, getting their supplies of ammunition and food partly from this source and partly from France. Action by Sir John's men against a Dutch ship in 1651 brought the famous Admiral Van Tromp with twelve ships against them. This news roused Parliament to action, since the capture of Scilly by the Dutch, thus giving that enemy a base from which to attack England, was unthinkable. A fleet which was being assembled at Plymouth for the West Indies, together with a military force of 2,000 men, was diverted with the double objective of staving off the Dutch threat and reducing Scilly to obedience.

The history of what happened next is confused, but the Dutch realised that they could not obtain their objective and left the scene, allowing Parliament to turn its attention to Scilly. There were large numbers of experienced Royalist soldiers in the Isles, with a high proportion of officers; these comprised a formidable force that on level terms would perhaps have deterred the Parliamentary attackers (made up of twenty ships and nine companies of foot soldiers) from attacking them. Sir John Grenville's troops were, however, short of food supplies, and lacked both water and munitions. After five weeks they were forced to give up, but not until after they had given a good account of themselves.

The island of Tresco was involved in the severest of the fighting, resisting two abortive attempts to carry it. An officer of the Parliamentary land forces, Joseph Leveck, compiled, in vindication of the proceedings of those forces, 'A true accompt of the late reducement of the Isles of Scilly; published in regard of the many false and scandalous reports, touching that service (1651)'. The story is lengthy, but since it shows proceedings of almost monumental ineptitude, and concerns Tresco, it is here included in full.

'After we of the Parliamentary forces had laid at sea from Saturday, April 12, till Thursday, the 17th, in the morning betimes (each officer having received orders overnight) we boated our soldiers, intending to gain a landing place upon Triscoe .... But the quicknesse of the Tyde had set our boats so much to the Eastwards out of the way, and the fearful Pilots directing another course among the Rocks, we were necessitated to set all forward towards Old Grimsby Harbour .... Our Boats, being all of them exceedingly cramd with men and many of them very slenderly accomplished for such a service, rowed exceedingly heavily and could not by any means be brought to row close one with another, and some were set fast upon the rocks for want of water'.

This was a fine beginning. The boats were filled with ignorant landlubbers squashed tightly together. No wonder some boats ran aground! The officers took the only sensible course:

'... Orders were given that the Boates should stop under a Rock until they came up altogether that we might joyntly set upon the work.'

However it all went wrong again:

'But in the progress the Pilots and many of the Rowers (who were taken up in the West Country, very backward to the Service) misguided our headmost boats to a

little island called Northworthal, standing in the entrance to Old Grimsby Harbour and within half-a-musket shot of Triscoe and so situate as none save those who were acquainted could know whether it were part of Triscow or not.'

It seems very unlikely that any of the Scilly pilots would not have known that the tiny island of Northwethel was not Tresco! It is a hundred to one that they were doing their best to turn the attack into a farce. The commander of the expedition seems to have had his doubts, too, but what could he do? He was wholly at the mercy of the local men. His own West Country yokels were as ignorant as he was of the topography of the islands.

'To this place the timerous or treacherous Pilots directed, affirming once and again that it was Triscoe, and when Major Bawden replyed he was doubtful of it (in regard he discovered none of the enemy coming down to oppose the landing), one Nants (accounted the most knowing Pilot of and for the place) affirmed resolutely (upon his life) that it was Triscoe, whereupon three Companies presently landed, but the mistake prevented the landing of many more, yet not without some disorder upon our business.'

Nants (Nance) was a brave man to take such a risk, since as 'the most knowing pilot', it is impossible to imagine that he was not well aware that the place was not Tresco. The farce continued:

'Notwithstanding which and that the Tyde and opportunity might not be lost, orders were given that the rest of the Boats should row on into the Bay where we intended to land; but our foremost Boats were again misguided and unadvisedly made for that part of the Island nearest to hand, occasioned the rather, I suppose, for that the Enemy had there drawn down a Body of Muskateers and fired much upon our Boats, with whom our men desired to be doing, but the place proved craggy and inaccessible, so that we could not land.'

Now they had got themselves into a real pickle:

'Here was hot firing between our men and the Enemy (the Rocky shore being the only Interponent). They had a sufficient advantage against us, having the Rocks for their shelter, and our men so thick crowded in their open Boats as many of them could not make use of their Arms. Indeed it was a miracle of mercy that we lost not many men there. If any of our Boats had been foundered, all the men must needs have been lost, for every Boat was so exceedingly full . . .'

Jos Leveck now has a delicate and reluctant admission to make: some of the Parliamentary forces ran away:

'Now to be plain, where the Boats drew somewhere near and the great, small and case shot flew about to some purpose, and the danger must be looked in the face (for I believe we endured about 70 great shot besides muskets in abundance), many of the Boats, instead of rowing forward into the Bay, turned the helm and rowed backward and aside from the Business. And notwithstanding Lt-Col Clark struggled all he could to draw them on, earnestly calling to one and commanding another to follow him with their Boats, yet would neither commands nor threats persuade them to observance, but do what he could they rowed off.'

Leveck takes the opportunity to have a crack at an officer he dislikes:

'Capt Dover may please to remember that he, among others, was called to—yea, and commanded to upon pain of death—follow on with his Boat. What his

answer was and how carefully observed cannot be unknown to himself, nor yet to others, for I am sure his Boat rowed off and came no nearer.'

It was now decided that what had happened so far was enough for one day and the attack was called off.

'After some time spent, I think neer half an hour, in this perilous yet successless manner, we withdrew to Northworthal, the little island where our Boats were first misguided.

'Three Companies were left upon Northworthal to keep the Enemy busy, and the rest were landed on an adjacent island called Tean, from whence we had a better discovery of the Enemy's shore. The place yielded but little fresh water, which through the number of our men was soon troubled and made unfit to drink, which, together with the want of provisions and the raw constitution of our men, newly come on shore, made this cold night's lodging the more irksome and comfortless.'

The morning of the following day opened unpleasantly, but the commander was able to improve the men's situation:

'The next day, April 18th, the Enemy spent some great shot at us which fell among some of our tents and brake them, but did no further harm.

'We laboured to get some provisions ashore (which could not be suddenly done, our ships riding at that distance), for want of which our men were indeed distressed, and some where upon murmured even to discontent, repining at the condition of the service thay were to undergo upon such faint terms. But through a supply of victual and careful regard of Lt-Col Clark all were put into an exact posture in order to make a second attempt.'

The raw troops which had taken part in the first day's assault obviously needed stiffening, and action was taken to effect this:

'To which end Capt. Hatsel and Capt. Smith were sent aboard Admiral Blake to desire that the Boats and Rowers who would stick more resolutely to their oars, might be sent to us, which he did.

'And that we might be better besteaded in our landing, he moreover appointed 150 or 200 seamen (who were better acquainted with Marine Affairs) to attempt with us under the conduct of Capt. Morrice.'

They now made their plan:

'Upon consultation we resolved (it being judged best) to storm the Enemy by night, and to that end had in this daytime carefully observed how to direct our course to the place we intended for landing (which was about three quarters of a mile and interrupted with many rocks on the way). For now we became our own Pilots.'

The plan was put into action:

'We boated our men (having drawn off those three companies from North-worthal) in the dark of the evening and left there only some 80 men to Alarum and Arouse the Enemy in that quarter while we fell on and between 11 and 12 of the Clock at Night set forward (the Seamen's Boats being head-most) at which time it pleased God it was very calm, so that the Enemy's Frigates, whom we doubted might injure us in our passage (being thereto designed) and do most prejudice, could not come up to do us any harm, though they spent some great shot at us.

'We made fires on Tean as if we had continued there, the smoke thereof was blown towards the enemy which somewhat obscured our passage. Yet the Enemy

discovered us when we came about half way over and took an Alarum and ere we attained the shore fired many Ordnance upon us which did no hurt.

The Boats came up for the most part roundly together, and put to the Shore where the Enemy disputed our landing with stout resistance insomuch that the Seamen were forced back into the water, yet our men charged them resolutely, even to club-musket, and through the Blessing of God worsted them, killed upon the place one Captain and some 12 or 14 others took prisoners 167 and 4 Captains, the rest fled and none had escaped had we been better acquainted with the Island.'

And now appears Jos Leveck's true reason for writing the account. He thought that credit for the attack's success, which should by right have gone to the soldiery, had instead been given to the seamen: he sought, therefore, to give a truer picture.

'And now what reason is for some to write and report that the Seamen did all the work. That they alone gained the landing place. That they did the main work undervaluing and declaring the service of the Soldiery let all men judge . . .'

When Tresco capitulated in 1651, the fall of St. Mary's became inevitable. Cromwell's Castle was built on Tresco and guns were set up on Carn Near which prevented supplies getting through to the Royalists in St. Mary's. Allowed to march out with honour, many of Sir John Grenville's men went to Ireland, but some stayed in Scilly and settled there. Sir John himself received much honour from Charles II at the Restoration in 1660, among other things being made Earl of Bath and High Steward of the Duchy of Cornwall. A new Sir Francis Godolphin, grandson of the first, assumed control of the Isles.

Cromwell's castle

AUGUSTUS THE EMPEROR

CHAPTER II

His ready speech flow'd fair and free,
In phrase of gentlest courtesy;
Yet seem'd that tone, and gesture bland,
Less used to sue, than to command.
The Lady of the Lake Sir Walter Scott

The plight of the Scillonians, which had deteriorated over the years, did not improve with the advent of Charles II. Nothing was done for them by the government. The Godolphins, with more important commitments elsewhere than in virtually worthless Scilly, were for most of the time absentee landlords.

The islands continued to be a menace to shipping and in 1707 occurred one of the greatest sea disasters of all time. A British squadron under Sir Clowdisley Shovell, returning from an expedition against Toulon, was wrecked on the Scillies on 22nd October of that year. His ship, the *Association*, sank immediately, with the loss of 800 men, and three other ships were also lost, bringing the total of those drowned to the region of 2,000. Nevertheless, in spite of the treacherous nature of its rocks and seas, the poverty of its inhabitants, and its treeless nature, Scilly had a beauty of its own which some observers and inhabitants were beginning to appreciate.

A manuscript of the seventeenth century entitled *Some Memorialls toward Natural History of the Sylly Islands* notes that there was 'not so much as a shrubb, except Brambles, Furzes, Broom and Holly, and these never grew above four feet high. Nor is there in all these islands one Tree . . .'

Robert Heath, who was an officer engineer on St. Mary's in 1744 wrote that: 'Beheld at a distance the islands appear like so many high banks in the water. But the rocks about these islands, especially those to the westward, appear off at sea like old castles and churches.'

The need to do something to provide shelter for crops induced three residents of St. Mary's who signed themselves 'J.B.', 'S.M.' and 'M.C.' to raise the matter in the *Gentleman's Magazine* in May 1757:

'Our islands lie greatly exposed to every wind, and particularly to the south, the west and the south-west; and in storms the wind blows the spray of the sea over our grounds, which very often destroys our young tender plants and herbs, and ruins our crops, because they have no shelter afforded them by high hills or lofty trees, to keep off this spray; and our stone hedges (or walls) are but low. In dry windy weather also

the sand is so much blown over our grounds, as makes them considerably more barren than they would otherwise be.

We should therefore be greatly obliged to any person who would faithfully inform us, what trees will grow on both our sandy and our rocky shores, will bear the spray of the sea, and rise so high, and grow so thick, as to preserve the neighbouring grounds from both these inconveniencies. And we flatter ourselves that any gentlemen who live near the sea coast in *Great Britain*, and have made exact and careful observations what trees succeed best, in such a soil, and such an exposure as ours is, will be so good as to communicate them to you; and we hope that you will indulge us so far, as to publish them in one of your Magazines before next autumn. We also desire, that they would inform us of the easiest and quickest methods of raising such trees and whether the seeds should be sowed at first in a distinct nursery, or in the places where they are to grow, because we cannot afford any considerable expense.

We have been told, that the juniper, firr, holly, and cedar, will bear the spray of the seas, and also the blowing of the sand; but we should be glad to be well assured of the truth of it. But as the juniper and holly are only shrubs, they may indeed serve to screen and defend the lower parts, but must have other trees intermixed with them, that will grow higher, that the sand and spray may

be better stopped; and if the firr and cedar will suit our soil and exposure, we should be glad to know what sorts of them will answer best'.

This elicited the following reply:

'Acquaint your correspondent in St. Mary's Island, that there are two trees, one of higher, the other of lower growth, perfectly suited to his purpose: they are the *sycamore* and *sallow thorne*. A plantation of sycamores at 50 feet asunder, with three sallow thorns between every two of them, will make a tall thick fence, perfectly securing the adjacent lands; and they are both trees that will grow better near the sea than anywhere else. J.H'.

The sallow thorn is better known to us as *sea buckthorn* (*Hippophae rhamnoides*), a seaside shrub with orange berries.

William Borlase, a famous eighteenth-century Cornish historian who wrote an authoritative book on the Isles, added another comment on their beauty:

'These islets and rocks edge this Sound in an extremely pretty and different manner from anything I have seen before. The sides of these little islands continue their greenness to the brim of the water, where they are either surrounded by rocks of different shapes which start up here and there as you advance, like so many enchanted castles, or by a verge of sand of the brightest colour. The sea, having eaten away passages between these hillocks, forms several pretty pools and lakes, and the crags which kept their stations, intercepted and so numerous that the whole seemed but one large grotesque rockwork'.

The Godolphin line failed in 1785 and the Lord Proprietorship, as it was called, passed to Thomas Osborne, fourth Duke of Leeds, who had married a Godolphin. But the new Lord Proprietor continued, like his predecessors, as an absentee landlord, governing through a 'Council of Twelve', headed by his hired steward, to run affairs in his absence. These local administrators were often unprincipled and their actions very questionable. Sir Francis Godolphin disbanded one Council . . . 'on account of their not duly administering Justice according to their Oath, and punishing all offenders without Partiality, and encouraging Vice instead of preventing it'.

The islanders lived by cultivating small strips of land, and by fishing and piloting. The land was, however, held on short leases, which gave the tenants a feeling of insecurity and removed any incentive to improve a holding. Rye, barley, wheat, 'pillas' and potatoes were grown. Pillas is a primitive oat (*Avena nuda*). Some sheep, cattle and pigs were reared, and between 1684 and 1835, kelp burning for the production of soda and potash helped to augment the income of the islanders. Fish was also dried for export. These pursuits did not produce for most of them more than a bare subsistence, so they turned to smuggling to ameliorate their hard lot. The Preventive Service became more and more efficient, however, so this source of profit was gradually cut off. The restrictions brought about by the Napoleonic Wars still further hampered the islanders' activities. And a further blow, amounting, in fact, to a disaster, came when Scilly's traditional immunity from the payment of salt tax was brought to an end in around 1809.

The Reverend Richard Warner wrote in his *Tour Through Cornwall*, that

'Each cottager on an average is wont to lay in about a thousand fish for winter use. The quantity of salt necessary is about seven pounds to a hundred fish. Till the late rise in the duty of that article, salt might be procured at 1½d. per lb., and the whole stock cured at the expense of 8s.9d. But *tempora mutantur*: salt is now increased to 4d. per lb., and a thousand fish cannot be cured under £1.3s. 4d., a sum of unattainable magnitude to a poor man who gets only 6s. or, at most, 7s. per week for his labour.'

An eyewitness wrote in the *West Briton* on 25th June 1812, about Scilly that:

'The situation of the poorer inhabitants here during the last winter was truly distressing. These persons are chiefly dependent for their support in winter upon the fish caught and cured by them during the summer months, but such has been the pressure of the times, even upon these poor islanders, that they have been unable to purchase the salt necessary for curing their summer's catching and, there being no market to which they could have resource, their sufferings have in consequence been very alarming.'

A.K. Hamilton Jenkin adds, in his *Cornwall and Its People* (1945):

'So desperate, indeed, was their plight, that the matter at length came to the ears of the Bishop of Exeter, who "most humanely" laid their case before the Lords of the Treasury. These, in turn, gave orders for a quantity of salt to be shipped from Penzance, free of duty, in quantities not exceeding half a bushel to each person. But for this timely intervention it appears certain that many of the inhabitants must have died of actual starvation during the ensuing winter.'

In 1813 a person who was afterwards to be a great help in providing plants for the garden on Tresco visited the Isles. William Jackson Hooker, then a young man but afterwards Sir William and Director of the Royal Botanic Gardens, Kew from 1841 to 1865, wrote to his future father-in-law, Dawson Turner of Yarmouth, from St. Mary's on April 27th 1813 giving his impressions of Scilly. His letter does not add anything to our knowledge of the Isles and is not therefore included but is of interest because of the later connection.

Farming on Scilly was becoming increasingly uneconomic because the system of inheritance divided the land up into ever smaller and smaller parcels. Land for which there were no heirs was sold off in lots, so that a single owner might have several plots widely separated from one another and virtually

impossible to operate as a unit. The position deteriorated year by year and desperate appeals were sent to the mainland. The following, for example, was despatched in 1818 to Robert Peel (the future Prime Minister), then MP for Oxford University.

'We, the undersigned, inhabitants of one of the Scilly Isles, humbly beg permission, once more, to lay before you, Sir, a statement of our distress praying that you will be pleased to use your influence on behalf of ourselves and our starving families. In reply to your kind enquiry "What can be done for you?" permit us to say we are in want of everything; and if some assistance is not afforded, hunger will soon remove us to a situation where human help can be of no avail. Do not leave us to perish for lack of bread.'

Some money was collected as a result of these piteous cries, £9,000 being contributed in all; food and clothes were also provided and distributed around the islands.

In 1820 a fish cellar was built on Tresco with government aid at a cost of some thousands of pounds, the intention being to establish an industry for the curing and storage of pilchards. Two new fourteen-ton fishing boats were also provided and money found to repair the islanders' own vessels. All the ancillary equipment required to operate the industry, huts and other gear, was also supplied. The venture flourished for a short time but after a year or so it had to be abandoned because the price of pilchards was too low for it to pay its way.

The condition of the islanders became worse and the attitude of some visitors was far from sympathetic. James Silk Buckingham, MP for Sheffield (1823-37), wrote that:

'Nothing could be conceived more primitive than the state of society among which we were now thrown. The town of St. Mary's had a Governor, two clergymen, three doctors, two lawyers, several merchants, who were all smuggling; the rest were mere tradesmen, shopkeepers and boatmen, who lived partly by fishing, still more by smuggling, and worst of all, it was said, by visiting wrecked vessels and helping themselves freely to whatever could be saved from destruction.'

It does not seem to have crossed Buckingham's mind that the Duke of Leeds, the absentee landlord, may have had some responsibility for the situation, and also the government: nor did he recognize that the islanders, to make even the meagre living which he observed, were driven to smuggle because those in a position to help them failed to do so.

The Duke of Leeds, in fact, finding the Isles becoming an increasingly irksome possession, decided in 1831 not to renew his lease, and the Isles reverted to the Duchy of Cornwall. The first act of its Council was to send their surveyor to Scilly to enquire into the state of affairs. He found something near chaos. The Duke of Leeds' agent had let many rents fall into arrears far beyond recovery. Indeed, the poverty was such that he probably had no option. Another matter out of control was the building of houses, which had been put up at random without proper agreements. A new agent, appointed by the Duchy, was instructed to raise rents. In the circumstances, this was a measure so cruel and gauche that it seems almost unbelievable!

Indeed it caused a hatred of the Duchy so intense that it lasted for many

years. The initial indignation was such that letters were even sent to the King about it.

One of the things that caused the administration difficulty was the number of tenants with the same names. Clive Mumford writes: 'On Tresco, for example, there were sixteen Jenkinses, ten Nichollses, seven Penders and nine Ellises. In order to differentiate, he had to use the person's nickname, as well as his proper name, in his report, and one can imagine the amazement of the senior Duchy officials in London when faced with such picturesque soubriquets as Billy Chad, Treacle Breeches, Aunt Polly Cunder, Long Tom, Nancy Dango, Cap'n Jack, Tailor Isaac, Long John, Rachel Mungy, Sammer Dagger and Dreamer'.

With the withdrawal of the Duke, the Twelve Men, 'His Grace's Council', were disbanded, with no regrets on the part of the islanders. There now being no machinery to administer affairs, a public meeting was held which appointed Overseers for the Poor and set up a select vestry of thirty-four persons with responsibility for roads, health, sanitation and similar matters. The other inhabited islands, being now made separate parishes from St. Mary's, set up their own vestries.

At this juncture a new face came on the scene. Those who had been tempted to identify Scilly with the ancient Isles of the Blest, the Hesperides, or the Happy Isles, had so far had little to justify their notion which, indeed, in the face of the prevailing distress, seemed a cruel travesty of the truth. With the coming of Augustus Smith, however, a new era opened during which conditions were changed so much that, within a short time, the title of 'The Happy Isles' might well be applied to them.

Augustus Smith's family stemmed on one side from Thomas Smith, mercer, of Nottingham, and had its origins in the remote country parish of Titheby, nine miles east of the city. Thomas had laid the foundations of the family fortune which, through banking, eventually endowed Augustus' father, James Smith, with Ashlyns, a comfortable country house standing in a well laid-out park on the London side of the Chilterns, near Berkhamsted. James Smith, a quiet man, lost his first wife in childbirth within ten months of their marriage, shortly before Ashlyns came into his possession in 1801. Two years later he married Mary Isabella Pechell, daughter of a neighbour, Augustus Pechell, and in 1804 their son, named Augustus after his grandfather, was born in a rented house in Harley Street, London.

The Pechells were of French extraction, having been driven out of France after the Revocation of the Edict of Nantes in 1685 and, as refugees, had had a colourful history, most of the men being soldiers until Augustus Pechell's father achieved a baronetcy. Augustus Smith grew up to love the Pechell side of his family and devoted much more time to them than to his paternal relations.

His father James Smith strengthened his position by acquiring additional landed property in Hertfordshire and Buckinghamshire. As son of a rich man Augustus could have lived, if he had wished, the life of a landed gentleman. He passed through Harrow and Christ Church, Oxford and arrived in the fashionable world in 1826, being taken into society by his cousin George Pechell, who had married a daughter of Lord de la Zouche. The vacuities of this world had,

however, little appeal for him. They bored him, and he was impelled to find some more serious occupation. Beneath the level of high society he saw a great mass of the common people struggling under the follies of his class and the hopeless victims of injustice and wastefulness. Around Ashlyns, set in farming country, pauperism was rampant.

Since the 1790s the practice had spread of supplementing agricultural wages from the poor rate. This policy had, over the years, tended severely to depress wages, while providing totally inadequate support for the unemployed. The farmer turned his labourers off at the end of the harvest so that they and their families had no recourse but to the meagre dole from the rate, which pressed hardly on the poor householder who had to find his share of it. A more efficient system for hopelessly and progressively depressing the rural poor it would be hard to find.

Within a few months Augustus was voicing the opinion at parish meetings in his locality that these evils could be remedied to everyone's advantage if people only had the will to do it. Those who opposed him, and many did, found themselves up against a force with which they had to reckon seriously. Once his mind was made up, Augustus would not be deterred: he drove like a tank through their arguments and eventually convinced people that there was something in what he said.

Eventually select vestries were set up to deal with parish business, and very practical results followed, as parish management was brought into line with the proposals (1834) of the central government's Poor Law Commission, the rates dropping from eight shillings in the pound to three shillings.

From his parish activities, which brought him in close contact with the very poor, Augustus derived a solid and unshakeable conviction that providing children with a good education would be a great help towards solving their problems because it would give them the means to help themselves. He had to fight battles against the entrenched Anglican clergy to get his will around Ashlyns, but get it he did. The detail of this would be out of place in this book, but it is a splendid story told elsewhere.

The obstacles thrown in his way at Ashlyns and the continued criticism convinced Augustus that, if he were to put his theories about self-improvement of the poor into practice, he would have to find somewhere free of such obstruction: a region so poor and derelict that it had no attraction for the sort of people who were opposing him. He would not need to give up his work about Ashlyns, but could always spend part of the year there fostering his schemes, while his main work was pursued elsewhere. In 1831 he heard by chance that the Duke of Leeds was giving up his lease of Scilly. It occurred to him on hearing this news that this might be the very place for which he was looking, as the dreadful state of the Isles was well known.

He got into touch with the Duchy of Cornwall but was at first deterred because HM Woods and Forests claimed the Isles as Crown property and a wrangle between the Departments followed. He turned his attention to Ireland as another possibility and spent some time there; but when, a few months later, the Duchy of Cornwall told him that the legal complications had been resolved in

their favour and they were prepared to negotiate with him, he jumped at the chance. The first thing he did was to get a copy of a report on the Isles compiled for the Duchy by Edward Driver, its surveyor, and brother of George Neale Driver, who had subsequently gone there as the Duchy's agent and was still trying to sort out the various rent and tenancy questions. The report was entitled *On the Present State of the Scilly Islands*; when he had finished reading the sorry tale of a population sinking into famine and despair, Augustus decided to go to the Isles and see for himself the state of affairs.

The young Augustus Smith

No advance publicity was given to his coming and those who saw him on the way must have wondered what his business was in the Isles. Someone who noticed him in Penzance while on his journey wrote long afterwards in the *Cornish Telegraph* that his appearance had something of the naval officer about it, perhaps because of the short jacket that he wore, which was: 'a skirtless coat that bore no naval buttons or ornament. Above the middle height, lithe in figure, firm in step, upright in carriage, with well-cut handsome features, a face so closely shaven as to leave only small 'mutton-chop' whiskers, and an eye—cold, grey, observant, he looked as if he had been accustomed to command or was born to be ruler. While his very demeanour bespoke drill and discipline, there was nothing of hauteur about him . . . .His gentlemanly address was prepossessing'.

He made his first voyage on a rough and windy day, and it is unlikely that he enjoyed it as, despite his nautical appearance, he was only a moderate sailor.

The arrival of such a figure in their midst with no ostensible object must have roused in the islanders considerable apprehension that, whatever it was that he was after, it boded no good to them. The persistence of his enquiries—for he questioned everyone with whom he came into contact—must have heightened the impression that he was prying into their affairs for some unpleasant purpose. No one seems to have connected him with the Lord Proprietorship, though he must have had long talks with General Smythe, the Lieutenant-Governor, (an

army appointee who exercised the Lord Proprietor's military authority) with W.J.Johns, son of the former agent of the Duke of Leeds, and who afterwards became agent for Augustus himself, and with George Driver, the Duchy's agent.

The only place he saw with any pretence to prosperity or comfortable living was St. Mary's, which was concerned with shipping and the profitable early potato trade. But even that island showed many signs of being run down: the dilapidated courthouse and prison, the pitiful little ill-attended SPCK school, the inadequate roads which were in abominable condition, the unkempt farms and hovels and the neglected land. Children of school age were running wild, and idle young men lounged about with no occupation. Everywhere Augustus received an impression of ignorance and hopeless incompetence. When he went to the other inhabited islands, Tresco, Bryher, St. Agnes and St. Martin's, he saw a picture that was, if anything, worse. But he saw something else also, which made a deep and lasting impression on him. The Isles, in spite of the lack of elevation, with only coarse grass, bracken and stunted thorn growing on them were, even without trees, beautiful. Here could be built an island kingdom such as he desired, in which his ideas could be tested. If his theories were found to work, the starving population would learn how to live and prosper, and the forlorn islands now under his gaze would become idyllic. It was an objective for which it was well worth fighting. He went away determined to take the lease if he could get it.

How much Augustus guessed then what might be done in the way of ornamental planting we do not know. Possibly it was no more at this stage than the idea that, if he could get some trees to grow, he might then be able to make a garden in their shelter to set off and ornament the house which he would have to build.

Augustus returned to the mainland and the Scillonians began to forget about him. He duly signed the lease and became the new Lord Proprietor. News filtered down to Scilly that they had a new chief, and speculation endowed him with all sorts of attributes, all to the advantage of the islanders. Even when they found that he bore the undistinguished name of Smith and was the nautical-looking gentleman who had quizzed them, they were not too disappointed. He had money and represented to them an end to the insecurity that had reigned since the Duke of Leeds had relinquished his lease. The new lease ran from 21st November 1834, for a term of 99 years or three lives, for the trivial rent of £40 per year; but Augustus had to pay a fine of £20,000 and undertake to spend another £5,000 on improvements in the first six years. He also undertook to pay the stipends of the islands' clergy.

By a coincidence, Parliament at this time had taken action which was to be of advantage to Augustus. The absence hitherto of any kind of legal jurisdiction within the Isles had been a serious disadvantage and this was now remedied. The Lord Proprietor was given power to appoint Justices of the Peace to enforce the law. Augustus immediately took advice on possible candidates and proceeded with the appointments.

The new Lord Proprietor, as almost his first act, communicated to his agent Johns his 'Benthamite' views on the general good being more important than that of the individual, and that there would be no yielding to sentiment.

Those who would make no attempt to improve their standard of living when given the opportunity to do so, would be required to go elsewhere. Only the old would be exempt. When Johns passed on this information it raised doubts in the mind of many, and gloom and apprehension settled over the Isles.

In this atmosphere the Scillonians watched Augustus arrive and settle in with fear and worry. He had four main planks in his programme: a good education for all the children, an end to the sub-division of holdings, the eradication of smuggling, and the provision of work as an alternative means of subsistence. He began by visiting personally every holding. As each came under his penetrating scrutiny the islanders' last faint hopes died and they waited for the axe to fall. They had not long to endure. A notice was put up informing any tenant who sub-let his farms that, unless he could show good reason, his tenancy would be terminated on 11th October 1835. The new broom had begun to sweep.

In the meantime, where could the new Lord Proprietor live? He intended to be a resident Lord Proprietor, the first in history. He took a temporary residence in Hugh Town on St. Mary's and began to look around. His choice finally fell, not on St. Mary's as had probably been expected, but on the neighbouring island of Tresco. Here were the old Priory ruins where grew the narcissi probably first planted by the monks; and from the Priory there was a wonderful view over the sea to the other islands. Here, too, were the interesting fortress relics of old wars and, a great asset to any gentleman's estate, a freshwater lake. Augustus soon made up his mind and began to build just above the ruins of the Priory on a site that looked down over the slope to the sea, a slope which he saw could be terraced as a garden, while the back part of the island could remain in its wild state. In the winter of 1835, however, he suffered a sad blow. His second sister Paulina, fifteen years old, caught a chill while visiting him on St. Mary's and died. It is easy for us, protected by antibiotics and other life-saving drugs, to forget that death in youth and the loss of much-loved children was an ever-present fact of family life, up to and even beyond the Second World War.

Other troubles crowded in on him during his first years. The inhabitants of Tresco were recalcitrant and some refused to obey his wishes; workers building his new property struck for more pay, his new chaplain was more interested in

View of the Scilly Isles from St. Mary's by W.J. Hooker

ferreting than conducting funerals (the islands were full of rabbits), the storms were particularly bad, the roof of his new house being in danger of being ripped off before it was finished, and there were, as usual, a number of wrecks. The hardy islanders, while doing sterling work as rescuers, profited much from these and, although Augustus got his agent Johns to try to persuade the younger men, who mostly hung about the islands idling their time away between wrecks, to join the navy, he had little success. A nasty blow was an attack on his new house by vandals, probably some of these young idlers; they broke the windows and did other damage.

There was much other work to be done in establishing himself on Tresco. A home farm had to be brought into being with adequate pastures, cottages erected for workers, covers provided for game, and communicating roads constructed. The making of the roadway to link Old Grimsby Harbour with the house was a major task. The road passed along the shore, turned inland across the fields and climbed upwards along the side of a rocky hill before reaching its destination. Although Augustus soon laid out in his mind's eye where the various parts of the farm would be, and how the garden terraces would be made, the work could be done only by stages, and would take years to bring to fruition. Looking at the land at the beginning, he saw only a wind-swept upland covered by brambles and a close-growing mat of furze. It needed considerable imagination to envisage what the landscape might be like when he had carried out his plan.

One problem at the beginning was to devise a way in which seedlings could be protected when small. He could not begin to plant until he had mastered this difficulty. At length it occurred to him that planting gorse, which was stiff and wind-resistant, might well be the answer. As he walked about he scattered gorse seed brought from the mainland and was gratified to find that it not only established itself surprisingly quickly but was as effective a barrier as he had hoped. Sure now that they would survive their early years, he had to face the second stage, how to protect the seedlings as they grew larger. In this, whether he knew it or not, he took a leaf out of William Borlase's book, *Observations on the Ancient and Present State of the Islands of Scilly*, published in 1756. Borlase recommended the planting of 'shelters of Elder, Dutch Elm, Sycamore, and the like, in clumps and hedgerows,' for he had noticed that 'everything which rises not above the hedges' did very well. Augustus set elm, sycamore, oak and poplar on the lee side of the hill behind the house, both to provide shelter and to afford game cover. The very first planting of all was around the well.

Closer still to the house he built a sheltering wall, and began to stock his garden, at first, of course, laying out only a comparatively small area near the house. Although he had many friends who would send him seeds and cuttings, the process of stocking was necessarily slow in the early years. Seeds and plants of the kind with which he wished to furnish his garden were most of them too tender to be grown outdoors on the mainland, and had to come from private gardens or nurserymen who cultivated them in glasshouses. No doubt he also obtained some from persons who travelled overseas. The plants he did get and the seeds which germinated throve in the equable climate and the sunny southern aspect of the gardens.

These years in which he was providing a house for himself and beginning to develop the garden, clearing away the furze and carrying or blasting away unwanted rocks to make his farm and fashion his terraces, were also years in which he was enforcing his will on the people of Scilly as to how they should live in order to prosper. It was like administering beneficial medicine to an unwilling patient who had no faith in its efficacy. Re-adjusting the tenants' boundaries so that their holdings were rationalized into viable units was, he knew, a vital step before any further real progress could be made. He made it a rule that only one member of a family could succeed to a tenancy. Younger sons and daughters would have to go elsewhere to make their own way in the world. Helped by his other major step, the provision of a good compulsory education for every child, forty years before such a measure became law on the mainland, in newly-stablished or revitalized schools, the enforced exiles were well-equipped to succeed. However the enforcement of the system of regular daily attendance at school on families whose children had hitherto wandered free as air and sneered at education, required a great deal of personal attention both to ensure good teaching and to maintain attendance. The parents complained of the school fee; a penny a week was charged for attendance, twopence if a child was absent without good cause. Playing truant carried the risk, particularly on Tresco, of being confronted by the tall threatening figure of the Lord Proprietor, with his stout stick, prying into every cottage and corner to haul out the defaulters and drag them to school. But Augustus' determination paid off, many of the pupils returning afterwards to acknowledge the advantage their education had given them in the world. Some people already above school age when Augustus arrived voluntarily came and sat in with the children to make up the deficiencies in their knowledge. Of those who went to sea, most rose to be officers and many became masters or captains. So far as the garden was concerned, there was a considerable pay-off in after years because many of those who had only reluctantly attended school brought back plants from the countries they visited.

Augustus put into force other unpopular measures. Only in very exceptional circumstances was a tenant allowed to sub-let his land or take in lodgers. Failure to conform was followed by a notice to quit. Further, no young couple were permitted to marry until they had a house to occupy. Augustus also stopped the wasteful paring off of turf as fuel. He built a public bakery where the women could do their baking at his expense; but it fell into disuse because the women preferred to use their own ovens, which they found would burn dried seaweed. A steam flour mill was also provided where corn was ground free of charge and coal was imported from South Wales and sold cheaply to tenants or given away to the old. He also curbed smuggling, giving an undertaking, after the owners of two of the principal pilot-cutters had been imprisoned in Bodmin that, if the authorities would release the men and give them back their boats, any tenant of his would in future be ejected without mercy if caught smuggling.

All these actions, designed for their good, did not impress the ungrateful Scillonians, but excited resentment. They particularly objected to the limitation of access to lands on Tresco, now become the Lord Proprietor's private demesne, but over which they had hitherto wandered freely. They simply ignored the

restrictions, except when his men were in sight, and carried on as before, cutting turf, collecting, firing and gathering blackberries in defiance of the orders of the 'Governor', as they called him.

At this stage they felt only the restrictions of his new rules, and could not sense the prosperity coming. His return after each absence at Ashlyns was greeted with gloom, but they had no escape if they wished to remain on the islands. J.G. Uren, a Cornishman and post-office official at Penzance, who later knew Scilly well, summed it up: 'In all things relating to the government of the islands, his rule was absolute and his word the law . . . To oppose 'the Governor' . . . spelt ostracism and deportation; the man or woman became a pariah, no one dare shelter them or give them a meal's meat'.

As part of the terms of his lease Augustus built a new church on St. Mary's, laying the foundation stone on 31st October 1836. At the same time he began the other work to which he was committed by the lease, the building of a pier on St. Mary's at which sizeable ships could berth. The original contractor backed out after a year, and the terrible winter of 1837-38 undid much of the work already done, but the pier was completed in 1839.

The works on Tresco had provided employment there and created a permanent need for more workers. Now the new pier brought ample employment to St. Mary's, not only in dealing with the shipping and the cargoes, but to ancillary trades such as those, for example, concerned with building the new houses for which the increased affluence of the islanders created a demand. As conditions improved on these larger islands, Augustus took the others one by one and applied the same treatment so that, by the mid-1840s, the whole of Scilly had moved into a new era. But this did not improve his popularity: rather the reverse. The Scillonians could not stomach his arbitrary methods. Where he found slovenliness and a refusal to cooperate which could not be overcome by advice or admonition, he acted ruthlessly. The 'offenders' were advised to leave the islands, and those who would not go of their own free will were evicted. At one time the flow of paupers from Scilly to Penzance reached a stage where it caused embarrassment to the mainland authorities.

Sometimes his iron methods got him into difficulty. Old Mrs. Webber of Samson was proficient in the black arts and one day apparently laid a spell on Augustus as he left her after warning her that her family would have to go. As he went to get into his boat he found he could not do so. He was rooted to the spot, unable to stir a limb, and his men, no matter how they pushed and pulled, could not move him until at last, at the boatmen's entreaties, the old lady relented. The only suitable comment on this story is that of Hamlet when he saw his father's ghost 'There are more things in heaven and earth, Horatio, than are dreamt of in your philosophy'.

Another incident might have had more serious consequences. He was set on, on St. Agnes, by a band of young ruffians who overpowered him, tied him up in a sail and left him in the path of the incoming tide. But they finally thought better of it and cut his ropes and fled before the water got to him. It is, however, indicative of the malice to which his stern rule gave rise.

Augustus not only had enemies within his own realm, but was also at

loggerheads with others without. It took him from 1837 to 1848 to get the Post Office to agree to a postal service for Scilly, even though the contract finally signed with the St. Mary's Shipping Company to carry the mails cost only £150 per year. After the death (1837) of King William IV, under whom there had been an easygoing relationship with the Duchy of Cornwall, the advent of Queen Victoria brought a new regime which entirely disregarded the money and effort which Augustus had sunk in the Isles, and tried to screw every penny it could out of him.

Admittedly the rent he paid the Duchy of £40 per year was small; but Augustus had turned a starving rabble of hopeless people into a thriving, prosperous and industrious community which, in hidden returns, was of immense indirect financial benefit, if the penny-pinching politicians, following the lead of Prince Albert as Lord Warden, had had the sense to see it. Augustus was also concerned about the terms of his lease of three lives which could in some circumstances have meant that his family would lose all after his death. In his continual battle with an unsympathetic Duchy, he must often have been tempted, in a moment of wrath, to give up and leave the islands. To compensate, however, he had a lot of personal friends whom he delighted to invite to his new house on Tresco, into which he moved in 1838. Thereafter he never spent less than eight months of the year there. He could never give it up. He enjoyed it so much, and felt that he would be letting the people down whom he was helping to raise themselves if he abandoned them.

AUGUSTUS THE PLANTSMAN

CHAPTER III

Trees did grow and plants did spring . . .
Richard Barnfield (1574-1627)

One of Augustus' friends was Lady Sophia Tower, granddaughter of a famous horticulturist, Lady Amelia Hume, who, through the connection of her husband, Sir Abraham Hume, with the East India Company, had established a well-known garden of exotics from the Orient, camellias, paeonies, chrysanthemums and the like, at Wormleybury, in Hertfordshire. There were other gardeners in the family and it was natural, therefore, for Lady Sophia, familiar with many great estates, herself to enjoy exotic plants and the company of a man who enjoyed growing them. Augustus had tried to get the Towers to come to Scilly in 1845, but it was 1847 before they actually made the journey. At that time the Great Western Railway had reached only as far as Totnes in Devon. From there the rest of the trip took them several days, and they were unfortunate enough to encounter a gale on their sea crossing, which took fifteen hours. They arrived at the Abbey at two o'clock in the morning, to be dosed by Augustus with vermicelli soup before tackling their mutton chops. Augustus had great faith in the power of vermicelli soup to settle queasy stomachs.

The Towers greatly enjoyed themselves. The pleasure of their visit was enhanced because, by a coincidence, the Queen and Prince Albert were travelling by sea to Scotland at the same time. Thick weather in the Channel having delayed them, the Royal couple decided to spend an extra night on their journey, anchoring in Scilly on their way between Dartmouth and Milford Haven. The Queen expressed a desire to land on St. Mary's, and made an excursion to Star Castle in Augustus' pony carriage. Apart from the Queen not being entirely herself because of sea-sickness, the visit was a huge success. Lady Sophia gained more than the pleasure of the Royal visit, however, from her holiday, because she fell in love with Scilly. The active outdoor life suited her, and she painted views of the Isles, some of which

Lady Sophia Tower

were lithographed, including one of the Abbey, which she painted on a later visit in 1848. Another of her pictures showed the new lighthouse on Bishop Rock in course of erection. She did not then know it, but this was to be one of the few records of that first building on the Rock. It was totally destroyed by a tremendous storm on the night of 5th February 1850. As her family grew up they became visitors to Tresco on their own account, and were often there.

Although Augustus did not keep Sophia's letters, which ranged over twenty-five years, she kept his, and after his death had a selection printed. These sometimes mention the garden, so that we get an occasional glimpse of it as the years go on. Before the first of these occurs, however, there is another pointer to the progress of the garden. Augustus had succeeded in establishing a number of species, and had begun to get an idea of what would grow well on Tresco. One genus had particularly flourished, the mesembryanthemums, which were fleshy, low-growing South African plants,

LIGHTHOUSE IN COURSE OF ERECTION ON THE BISHOP ROCK, as it appeared, previous to its total destruction in the terrific storm on the night of the 5th of February 1850.

and now an idea struck him. The Royal Botanic Gardens at Kew had become a state garden in 1841. Under the direction of Sir William Jackson Hooker tremendous progress had been made, both in the provision of buildings such as the Palm House, completed in 1848, and in the extension of the plant collections. Augustus and Sir William had a mutual friend; Augustus, wrote to the latter on 22nd July 1849, in the formal style of the time:

'On a former visit to the Gardens' (Kew) 'the sight of a house full of mesembryanthemums excited his' (Augustus') 'admiration and cupidity and his friend Sir Charles Lemon had been kind enough in consequence to furnish him with a letter of introduction to Sir William, as he' (Augustus) 'is very desirous to obtain some cuttings of some of the varieties which he saw there. These plants grow most admirably with him in the islands of Scilly, which has induced him to collect what specimens he can, as they flourish there in the open air all the year round or at least with very little protection. These plants not being much in vogue or procurable in general at nursery gardens induces him to apply to Sir William Hooker if it should be in his power to furnish him with a few slips to assist his collection.'

Sir William was able to oblige and Augustus wrote to him again on 25th October 1849, giving directions as to how the consignment should be sent, adding:

'. . . Though unwilling to give so much trouble he would be glad to have the name attached to each cutting, and he adds a list of those he has already to save what trouble he can in this respect. He hopes Sir William will one day venture over to see how this tribe of plants flourish in this climate.'

When the mesembryanthemums arrived Augustus wrote again on 13th November 1849. The letter is of interest because it refers to a plant called 'Tapac'. This may have been the Falkland tussock grass, which it was hoped could prove a useful fodder grass on Scilly.

'. . . The "Tapac" I have tried but without success several times, having had my attention drawn to it some years ago by your description of its merit. I was inclined to believe it would have succeeded here from the luxuriance with which the *Veronica* or *Crassula decussata* vulgo Box Myrtle flourishes here, standing if planted in good soil the extreme exposure to the violence of the winds. On my finding that this plant had come from the Falkland Islands, any plants coming from thence I was in hopes would answer . . . I obtained a large parcel of seed direct through the Governor but not a grain of it condescended to germinate. I have had seed also given me by other parties who have succeeded in growing it, but equally without effect. I propose now, however, procuring a few plants as a friend of mine has just written to me to say that it is growing luxuriantly in Orkney where it is to be seen 8 feet high.'

Unfortunately the Kew record of 'Outwards' despatch does not show the names of the individual mesembryanthemum species sent, but merely notes that the cuttings totalled eighty in all.

On 9th May 1850 Augustus wrote to Lady Sophia telling her among other things about the mesembryanthemums:

Tresco Abbey by Lady Sophia Tower 1849

'Scilly is very gay, and still more so, could you take a walk in my garden, though the winds have played sad havoc there of late, breaking and shrivelling the ixias and sparaxises, and mesembryanthemums most cruelly; of these last I have now two of the great large-leaved ones in flower, one being a beautiful yellow, and the other a purple, both as large as Adelaide's face. I am now hammering at the rocks beneath my study windows to extend my mesembryanthemum plantations; this is slow work, and can only be carried on under the master's own eye.'

Again, in another letter he sent to her on 27th September 1850, he writes:

'My gardens are very brilliant, particularly the fuchsias and mesembryan-themums; at present, the Guernsey lilies, lately imported from a Mr. Luff at Guernsey, are pre-eminent; they are very handsome, but are nothing to the "Bella Donnas" (now better known as *amaryllis*) as to making a show in the garden.'

With the exception of the fuchsias and chrysanthemums, too well known to require comment, the plants mentioned in these letters are all South African in origin, the ixias and sparaxis being floriferous and attractive bulbous species, while the Guernsey lily (*Nerine sarniensis*) and the belladonna lily, also bulbous, are larger and, particularly the latter, more flamboyant.

On 2nd August 1851, another consignment was sent to Augustus from Kew, this time recorded there as '28 greenhouse plants', but again with no list showing the names of the species sent. Receipt of these plants was acknowledged by Augustus on 25th August 1851. He mentions in his letter that he 'found the *Hydrangea quercifolia* in full bloom in my garden. It has been there in the border for some years, but has never flowered before.'

As there is no letter from Augustus requesting this consignment, it seems likely that it was sent as a result of a visit made by him to Sir William at Kew, which he had promised in his letter of 13th November 1849 above. The tender *Hydrangea* mentioned is a shrub about five or six feet high, with white flowers and large, handsomely scalloped leaves, which comes from Florida.

Christmas the same year saw him at Marazion in Cornwall. On 24th December 1851, he wrote:

'I had a spanking passage over on Monday before a fine north-west half-gale, and stay here for Christmas with my friend Cole. My garden was left in high beauty, the *Clianthus* just bursting into flower, and the *Acacia lophantha* (*Albizia lophantha*) also covered with yellow blossoms.'

Clianthus, the glory pea, glory vine or parrot's bill, is a striking shrubby or climbing genus from Australia and New Zealand, with brilliant red and black or scarlet flowers. *Acacia lophantha* (*Albizia lophantha*) is a very distinctive yellow-flowered Australian shrub.

During 1851 Augustus was busy with a search for a new schoolmaster and clergyman. The search produced Charles Allen, whom he found so satisfactory that he eventually made him his steward and installed him at Star Castle on St. Mary's, where he remained for the rest of his life. As the years went on, Augustus was drawn more and more into public life. He acted, for example, as arbitrator for the allocation of salvage money from the San Giorgio, a Sicilian vessel, which had been brought in from fifty miles out at sea by a number of the Scilly cutters, a feat which took them six days. He was also involved in some difficult cases

concerning emigrant ships in the Scilly roadstead: these were often leaky, ill-found vessels not properly manned. In 1849 he accepted an invitation from Truro Liberals to fight one of the two Truro Parliamentary seats at the next election, which came up in July, 1852. In spite of the pressure, he still had time for his garden. He wrote to Lady Sophia on 3rd June 1852, just before the polling day, telling her:

'It has been very cold and wet here of late . . . My garden is, notwithstanding, very resplendent; the first blow of my geraniums is over and the second beginning. The irises have been very beautiful, as also the ixias. I have been bringing the Long Walk part of the way in due form as it is to remain, where most of my rarities are planted, and have also been proceeding with the Mesmerism' (*mesembryanthemum*) 'garden on the rock on the east side; these have been and are most magnificent; both the large yellow and purple have been covered with big flowers; the Box Myrtle is particularly full, such as I never saw before, being covered with bloom, many bushes looking as if powdered with snow'.

Four months later, on 27th September 1852, he wrote again:

'We have had a sharp touch of Easterly wind lately; it has, however, been wonderfully fine, and my garden is looking splendid in consequence. I have had a great triumph as' (to) 'the Guernsey Lilies, which are never said to flower twice except in Guernsey, and last year not one of them showed the least signs of bloom; this year, however, they have shot up long thin necks and are now quite in perfection.'

Presuming on the previously favourable reception of his requests, he again solicited help from Sir William Hooker at Kew, writing on 14th August 1853 from his London address at 1, Eaton Square, where he had a lodging much frequented by the Towers.

'On looking over your mesembryanthemum collection I made a list of all those I had not got and should be much obliged for slips of any you can spare me of these varieties. You will observe by the list of desiderata that all the best sorts are not among them, having these already and flourishing most vigorously. I also have many varieties you do not appear to have and shall venture to send you a few specimens, particularly some of which I am anxious to know the right names.

I have added the names of some other plants, which I could not help jotting down as I walked about yesterday—*L'appétit vient en mangeant* and your former kindness I fear has rather whetted mine, particularly when I get among plants from Australia, New Zealand and the Cape. Many you gave me before, to be sure, have perished, but so many have survived, and are growing so kindly, that further experiments are not only warranted, but full of interest.'

This letter seems to have put Sir William's back up. Quite clearly he could not allow Kew to be used as a reservoir of plants for Tresco whenever Augustus wanted to augment his collections, Augustus offering a few cuttings in return mainly because he wanted to know their names. Sir William must have written a fairly peremptory refusal of the request, because Augustus' next letter, sent on 2nd September 1853, was an apology:

'I am sorry you should have misapprehended, as I think you have done, the application that I ventured to have made to you for plants, or that I should have expressed myself, as to have drawn from you the letter which I have just received . . .

I have only to beg you will accept my apologies in the spirit in which they are offered and consider the application with which I had troubled you, as never having been made.'

This exchange cut off further contact between Tresco and Kew for a number of years.

During the next two or three years Augustus was in demand in another connection. He had acquired a reputation as an interesting lecturer, giving talks, among other things, on ghosts and on the Crimea, the Crimean War having broken out in 1854. His sister Frances ('Fanny') had married Major Thomas le Marchant of the 5th Dragoons in 1846; Thomas was serving in the Crimea, so the latter subject had a family interest. Then, in March 1857, the government fell, there was a general election and Augustus was returned to Parliament as a Liberal member for Truro. Much of the animosity against him in Scilly had begun to die down as people came to see that his measures were producing prosperity for the Isles; and he was given a splendid welcome when he returned there from his victory. The demands of Parliament impinged on his time and he saw somewhat less of his garden, but the letters to Lady Sophia continued. On 3rd September 1857, he wrote:

Tresco Abbey Gardens by Gwendoline Dorrien Smith

'On Saturday was wafted over and landed on these shores in 4½ hours. The aloe was conspicuous even on landing, being backed from that point by the greenhouse roof; it has grown but little of late, and is not as tall as I had expected, being under 30 feet; it is now coming into perfection, the flowers just bursting. The garden is looking everywhere very gay, but immensely overgrown: I know not where I shall pack my treasures in future'.

A few weeks later, on 20th November 1857, he uttered a cry from the heart:

' . . . So many of my rarities are in bloom and beauty that I am in despair at being summoned away, not to return, I opine, till Easter; my Pampas Grass is flourishing, but did not flower; my Fuchsia dominiana is doing well out of doors, and is now in blossom; many of the mesmerisms are also in full beauty'.

Fuchsia dominiana is a garden hybrid raised by the Veitch Nursery in 1852.

At the beginning of 1858 Augustus had more to report to Lady Sophia, including a building operation: he was always busy with some change of this kind. There was also more progress in the construction of the garden. On 3rd January 1858, he wrote:

'This gentle winter has not been unfelt in my garden, which is a blaze of blossoms wondrous to behold; the Veronica andersonii, correas, fuchsias, genistas and above all Acacia lophantha are covered with flowers; one of the last particularly, not less than twelve feet high and as many broad, along the Long Walk, is a perfect picture; the sedums also, with their large yellow pyramids of bloom, each nearly as big as my lamp papers, are very ornamental—the plant I mean is that the leaves of which are like a green rose, or house leek; some have not less than twenty great ceres on them. The geraniums, of course, are as yet all green, and a certain set of mesmerisms are also in flower; I am now very busy converting the verandah into stone, which will fully occupy me the month I have to spend here. The upper terrace is also intended to progress so as to be open for loungers in August; it is to be the chief feature of the gardens, and will, I fear, rather make the lower alleys, especially the Long Walk, not a little jealous . . .'

The sedums referred to are probably the plants now called Aeonium, which are still a prominent feature of the garden. Veronica andersonii is a small half-hardy evergreen shrub of hybrid origin with bluish-violet flowers. The correas are very floriferous evergreen Australian shrubs, and the genistas are yellow-flowered whins or furzes. On 1st June 1858, he wrote again:

'My garden is a blaze of blossom, especially as to geraniums; more than usual survived last winter, and the whole bed of 'Unique' especially, and other sorts are one mass of flower; among other curiosities are two bunches of sweet peas. The Dracaena indivisa is fast advancing to perfection; the flower is not very conspicuous, but a mass of white feathery stems crowning the summit of the plant; the blossom is white . . . '

Dracaena indivisa (Cordyline indivisa) is a decorative palm-like plant with dark green, graceful, pendent, tapering leaves three to four feet long.

The completion of the top terrace in the summer of 1858, 300 yards long, with spectacular views, looking down over the whole garden, was a notable advance. The figurehead of S.S.Thames, which had been wrecked on Jacky's Rock in 1841, had already been installed on the rocky eminence at the head of the flights of steps which lead down to the Long Walk below. This figurehead is now

popularly called 'Neptune' but is, of course, intended to represent Old Father Thames. Little by little, the garden as it exists today was coming into being, at least in plan.

The old sailing cutter *Ariadne* which the St. Mary's Shipping Company had used for traffic to and from the mainland, and in which Augustus had made many passages, was sold for use as a cargo ship in 1858 and replaced by the paddle steamer *Little Western*, which eliminated the long tedious journeys which were often caused by bad weather. With the extension of the Great Western Railway to Penzance in April 1859, Scilly suddenly became much more easily accessible and many more sightseers began to visit the Isles. Among them was Joseph Hooker, afterwards Sir Joseph Hooker, son of Sir William Hooker of Kew, who says in Volume 98 of *Curtis's Botanical Magazine*, issued in 1872:

View from the top terrace in Augustus Smith's time

'I had the pleasure of visiting the gardens (on Tresco) about fifteen years ago with my late friends Professor Harvey of Dublin and Veitch' **(the grandfather of the founder of the firm)** 'when we were all astonished and delighted with the luxuriance and variety, especially of the Cape and Australian vegetation they displayed.'

This visit doubtless did much to bring Tresco and Kew together again as Joseph Hooker, when he succeeded his father as Director of Kew in 1865, resumed relations with Augustus.

A letter to Lady Sophia on 14th October 1859, records the establishment of another section of the garden:

' . . . The garden is looking very well, and the new district called Australia, though still in the rough, has some very brilliant productions, particularly of the *Aralia* tribe, acacias and cassias. The Palm also looks well, all the better for his outdoor residence; the border along the upper terrace is not behindhand. The new orchard and vegetable garden look pretty well . . .'

Nearly two years elapse before the garden is again mentioned in Augustus' correspondence with Lady Sophia. Then, on 9th June 1861, he writes:

'I have grand botanical promises which I must announce . . . Two aloes have announced themselves to be in an interesting situation, which even their crinolines can no longer disguise from the world; these are the great variegated aloe in front of the Abbey which exhibited some queer little symptoms last year, and the large green aloe in the Wall Garden, near the one that flowered before. In addition to these, the *Phormium tenax* is going to do likewise. Now I rather think this is a rare event, and the *Metrosideros floribunda* still more so, at least I have had it many years without any attempt being made at blossoms; it is a very pretty evergreen shrub, and was in the Hop Garden, but lately moved to Australia, which probably is the cause of this new movement . . . Seven of the beschornerias have also shot up their blazing red stems . . .'

Phormium tenax is the New Zealand flax, a fine-looking plant with very distinct long, erect, sword-like leaves and large dull red or yellow flowers. *Metrosideros floribunda* (*Angophora intermedia*) from Australia, has white flowers with yellow stamens. Beschornerias are evergreen succulents from Mexico which throw up long stalks bearing greenish-red flowers.

The next comment, made in a letter to Lady Sophia dated 14th September 1861, is of considerable interest because it reveals Augustus' attitude to the increasing number of sightseers coming to the Isles:

'The gardens are looking very well and are made a mighty fuss about by visitors, it appears, being a little out of the usual rut and their contents rather peculiar. They are now invaded by excursionists, which would be a bore, did they not really seem to enjoy themselves and appreciate the place and its peculiarities; some fifty were here this week in a body, from all parts of the kingdom, of which a few are really learned in plants, to Chivers' great satisfaction; the Scotch, he says, are the most intelligent, as shown by their questions and observations; the Cornish the least so, and who, when he points out some botanical rarity, answer, "Well, that's not so good as a cabbage".

Augustus Smith in his role as Grand Master of the Cornish Freemasons

Six months later, on 25th April 1862, he was writing:

'The garden is looking very well, with a crowd of cinerarias in flower in the open air, such as I have never seen here before: . . . the plants never seem to have suffered less than this winter. Among other rarities that have survived is the *Mandevilla suaveolens*. The *Pitcaimia* is an extraordinary-looking affair, with its spikes now above nine feet from the ground; from appearances some weeks will elapse probably before the flower expands; there

are six stems; the proper name I believe to be *Puya*, a native of Chile . . .'

Mandevilla suaveolens, the Chilean jasmine, is a tall, climbing, South American shrub bearing white, or creamy-white, very fragrant flowers, often in great profusion. The *Pitcairnia*, or *Puya*, which Augustus later calls *Puya chilensis*, from South America, throws up long flower stalks of greenish-yellow flowers. Towards the end of the year, on 14th December 1862, Augustus wrote:

'. . . All the garden is now green and flowery, particularly with Veronicas and the *Sparmannia africana*, which has been in full bloom since October, and does not seem tired of putting on its best . . .'

Sparmannia africana, from South Africa, is African hemp, which grows to a height of ten to twenty feet, and bears white flowers with showy barren stamens, yellow with purple tips.

Augustus was President of the Royal Institution of Cornwall. In 1863 another local honour came his way: an enthusiastic Freemason, he was in that year installed as Provincial Grand Master for Cornwall.

His letter of 6th December 1864, to Lady Sophia, reveals more plants in his collection:

'We have had heavy gales, but very intermittent, with beautiful fine sunny calm weather and seas intermixed; the thermometer has never descended lower than 39°F, and that only once for a few hours. I have had some beautiful Australian plants in flower, particularly *Hakea suaveolens*, which seems to be quite hardy; the polygalas are also full of blossom, and become quite an important feature.'

Hakea suaveolens is a sweet-smelling evergreen Australian shrub with white flowers. *Polygala* is a large genus; Augustus seems to have grown some of the species with more showy flowers.

As the election of 1865 approached, Augustus decided that he would not stand again for Parliament. On Tuesday, 25th July, Tresco had a visit from the Prince of Wales, afterwards Edward VII, which went off very well, the Prince asking for a photograph of Augustus, which was duly provided. In October his nephew, Thomas Algernon Smith Dorrien, came to visit him on Tresco for the first time; he had just been gazetted to the 10th Hussars. His father, Colonel Smith Dorrien, had stayed at Tresco, but his mother had a lifelong antipathy to Augustus, and 'Algy' was the only one of her sons and daughters ever to visit their uncle.

On 1st January 1866, Kew received from Augustus seeds of *Dracaena indivisa* (*Cordyline indivisa*) ripened at Tresco, inaugurating the new era of more cordial relations between Kew and Tresco now that Sir Joseph had become Director. On 6th January seeds of *Mandevilla suaveolens* also arrived at Kew from Tresco. A fortnight later, on 19th January, Augustus wrote to Lady Sophia letting her know that a large number of the trees he had been establishing in shelter belts had been blown down. These included the holm oak (*Quercus ilex*), the Monterey cypress (*Cupressus macrocarpa*) and the Monterey pine (*Pinus insignia*), now *P. radiata*.

'A gale from N. and N.E. is very rare, but very destructive when it does come. Of the firs covering the hillside between the Abbey and the farm (which I was flattering myself might soon have been mistaken for the Forest of Guffaer spoken of in some old deeds) at least a third have been more or less displaced, many completely

uprooted, particularly towards the farm end, where they were largest and thickest. But for the grandeur óf the devastation, I could almost have cried.'

In February 1866, Ashlyns became a seat of trouble and Augustus was involved in a dispute with Lord Brownlow about Berkamsted Common. Quite arbitrarily and without warning Lord Brownlow enclosed 600 acres of the Common with 'strong, high iron railings'. He had, however, chosen the

Beschorneria yuccoides

wrong opponent. On the night of 5th-6th March, Augustus sent 120 navvies from Euston in a special train to Tring Station, from whence they marched three miles to the Common, set to work, and by seven o'clock in the morning had uprooted the railings, rolled them into neat piles and departed. The ensuing legal wrangle was vexatious to Augustus and cost him a good deal of money but four years later, early in 1870, the verdict was given in his favour, and the Commoners' rights were saved.

On 16th March 1866, thirty-five mesembryanthemum cuttings were dispatched from Kew to Tresco, the receipt of which must have greatly pleased Augustus, with whom these plants, as will have become obvious, were a special favourite. No list of the species sent has survived. On 11th May Kew received from Tresco a plant of *Beschorneria yuccoides*, an attractive species with bright pendent green flowers within rich rosy-red bracts. Augustus followed this up with two plants of *Dracaena* (species not recorded) which arrived at Kew on 21st May. Shortly afterwards Augustus wrote to Lady Sophia complaining that the wet weather was delaying the flowering of some plants:

'There has been a cold east wind with a good deal of rain. My garden is therefore very slow in recovering its good looks, and appears very *seedy* and like an invalid: the *Puya*, however, shows one stem for flower, but no aloe as yet: both *Chamaerops excelsa* and *C.humilis* are throwing out large buds; as for dracaenas and beschornerias, I have a forest of both already in full blossom.'

The *Chamaerops* were two palms. *C.excelsa*, subsequently known as *Trachycarpus fortunei*, was a recent introduction, having been brought from China by Robert Fortune in 1849. *C.humilis* is the fan palm indigenous to southern Europe.

In August 1866 Lady Sophia and some of her children, including her seventeen-year-old golden-haired daughter Edith came to stay with Augustus. Arriving at the same time was Algy Smith Dorrien, the first occasion probably when he and Edith met on the way to Tresco. But we are in danger of getting in advance of our story and must leave them there, drinking, as usual after the sea crossing, some of Augustus' vermicelli soup.

A further despatch from Kew to Tresco was made on 19th October 1866. It comprised *Retinospora pisifera* (*Chamaecyparis pisifera*), a conifer from Japan, two plants of *Fourcroya* (or *Furcraea*) *longaeva*, a splendid agave-like plant from Mexico which bears a stalk of white flowers thirty to forty feet long, and '70 greenhouse

plants'. No list of plants included in the last item has been retained but presumably there were a number of different species. The generosity of this action contrasts with the attitude shown by Sir William Hooker on the earlier occasion recorded above (page 37).

The winter of 1866-67 brought very bad weather to Scilly, of which Augustus gave an account to Lady Sophia on 24th January 1867:

'What weather! Wet, wet, wet, after snow, snow, snow and frost, frost, frost; the two latter I brought with me twelve days back. The islands were all white, having about three inches depth of snow, which was renewed from time to time, as much melted, the frost not being at all severe, indeed the thermometer was never below 28°F, and generally stood at 30°F.

Abutilon vitifolium

But the weather did not seem to make much difference to the garden, as two months later, on 21st March 1867, he was able to say:

'My garden is gay with bulbs and other flowers . . . .'

Two months later still, on 14th May 1867, Augustus repaid some of his debt to Kew, which received from him on that day six plants of *Beschorneria yuccoides*, eighteen plants of *Dracaena australis* (*Cordyline australis*) a New Zealand tree bearing its leaves in tufts with large clusters of fragrant creamy-white flowers, and two of *Abutilon vitifolium*, a fine tree-like shrub from Chile bearing large cupped porcelain-blue flowers in May. With this, the exchange with Kew ceased for a time.

Augustus' sister Fanny, Mrs. Frances Isabella le Marchant, now began to spend some of her time painting the Abbey and its gardens, and the flowers which grew in it, leaving an invaluable record of Augustus' creation. The first dated paintings are scenes, entitled respectively 'Tresco Abbey from the East', 'Tresco Abbey from the South', 'Abbey Road, 1867' and 'In the Gardens', all of which she executed in September 1867.

Over a year went by before the garden is mentioned again in a letter to Lady Sophia. In his letter of 10th May 1868, Augustus said:

'The *Puya chilensis* now just in high beauty . . . .My garden besides can boast many great beauties, particularly as to beschornerias and mesembryanthemums: these are at least a month earlier than usual, owing no doubt to the dry season.'

View of Tresco Abbey from the north

The continued hot weather began to get him down. On 10th July he wrote:

'This guinea-fowl and mesembryanthemum summer is as much as I can support with the assistance of real marine breezes. We are getting terribly burnt up; but have had some heavy dew . . . .'

Fanny was painting again in the garden in September, 1868, this time recording the view along The Long Walk, which she painted on 12th September, and 'Tresco Abbey from the North', also painted in September. Later in September, while riding along the shore, Augustus' mare shied at some seals and threw him. For a man of his weight this was a serious accident and it took him several weeks to recover. Although there seemed to be no permanent damage, the fall may have weakened him somewhat, with consequences later.

A year later, on 15th September 1869, writing to Lady Sophia, he again showed concern about the weather:

'We have been visited by a very severe fit of equinox. I never saw the foliage so damaged by any storm before, just as if it had been struck by a hot blast; all my flowering aloes, alas, are snapped right off, just below the first flowering branch, except one small one that was too dwarf to be noticed by the gale . . . .I once had the silver tree you saw at General Huyshe's; its botanical name is *Leucadendron argenteum*'.

Leucadendron argenteum is a short-lived South African tree, allied to the showy proteas, with very beautiful silvery foliage. There is a fine specimen in the garden at the present time.

Early in 1870 Augustus had another fall from his horse but though his limbs were very bruised he was not apparently shaken so much in body as on the previous occasion. Nevertheless, the fall cannot have left him entirely unscathed and, indeed, his friends began to see a change in him. Fanny was again at Tresco in September 1870, executing seven paintings during the month. All except one, a painting of 'Carn Near: the Sandhills', are scenes around the Abbey itself. They are 'Entrance Gateway, Tresco Abbey' (the gateway that takes the visitor into the outer court); 'Entrance, Tresco Abbey' (the archway leading into the forecourt of the Abbey); 'The Steps Walk: Aloes in Bloom'; 'Ruins of the Old Abbey'; 'Tresco Abbey from Penzance Road' and 'Tresco Abbey from the West'.

Augustus wrote to Lady Sophia on 12th May 1871 telling her that the mesembryanthemums were

' . . . promising to be very fine this year, and seem to be forwarder than usual, the large purple being already one grand blaze of beauty'.

At the beginning of July he had a slight stroke, which affected his speech and the movement of his right hand; but he recovered a little as time went on. On November 27th 1871, Kew received from him a clump of *Schizostylis coccinea*, the crimson flat or Kaffir lily, a South African plant with long-lasting showy red flowers produced in autumn, which had been introduced as recently as 1864. The next day Kew sent off to Tresco '62 species of temperate plants', of which again no list remains. Augustus responded to this gift by sending to Kew on 4th December fourteen plants of *Musschia wollastonii* and a packet of seeds of this plant, a yellow-flowered introduction from Madeira in 1857. There were also two packets of

seed in the consignment recorded as having been received 'without names'. In addition to these he sent 'mesembryanthemums and other succulents in flower', of which there is no list.

Kew sent Augustus another consignment of plants on 18th January 1872; of this the list has survived. Included were *Astelia cunninghamii* ; two species of *Carmichaelia*, a New Zealand evergreen shrub; two species of *Dianella*, *D.caerulea*, a very ornamental blue-flowered plant from New South Wales, and *D.tasmanica* from Tasmania, a similarly ornamental, rigid, grassy-leaved plant with pale blue flowers followed by bright blue berries which hang on the plant for a very long time; *Doryanthes excelsa*, a tall plant from New South Wales with very brilliant scarlet flowers at the top of a stalk nearly twenty feet high; *Frenela rhomboides* and *F.ventenatii*, which appear to be synonyms for *Callitris calcarata*, the black cypress pine, a useful timber tree from Australia; *Jubaea spectabilis*, the Chilean honey palm, which grows into a large tree sixty feet high; and *Rhapis flabelliformis* (*R.excelsa*), the ground rattan cane, a low-growing palm from the Far East. A month later Augustus sent to Kew, on 17th February 1872, seeds of *Dracaena erythrorachis* (*Cordyline banksii*), a New Zealand shrub, the veins of whose long leaves are green, red or yellowish.

Augustus continued to follow his various interests through the spring and early summer, spending much time in London, from which, in June, he was itching to get away. But on his way back to Scilly he developed a severe feverish cold which by the time he reached St. Austell, had developed into pneumonia. He moved to Plymouth but became worse, and died soon after midnight on 31st July 1872.

The death of the 'Emperor' as Edith Tower still called him in a letter written just before he died, left a huge gap. His friends could not believe that his kind and commanding presence was gone, and that they would never see him again. It took a while for things to sort themselves out; gradually the pain and loss receded, in Scilly the 'ship of Tresco' righted itself, and a new helmsman took the wheel.

Carn Near: the Sandhills

Top Terrace

Cyprus Rockery

Middle Terrace

Toy Greenhouse

Higher Australia

Long Walk

Aloe Walk

Lower Australia

East Orchard

Tree Ferns

Bamboos

TRESCO
ABBEY
GARDENS

THE GARDEN MATURES

CHAPTER IV

Father Neptune

Neptune Steps

Mexico

Old Abbey

West Rockery

Lighthouse Walk

Where are those starry woods? O might I wander there,
Among the flowers, which in that heavenly air
Bloom the year long.
Nightingales Robert Bridges

On 24th August 1872, a few weeks after the death of Augustus, the *Gardener's Chronicle* published a list of plants growing in the Abbey garden, excluding ephemeral plants. There are a number of misspellings in the list and some of the species mentioned have not been identifiable with a modern plant. The misspellings have been corrected, and the names of species against which there is a query are included as shown in the original, without comment. The list totalled 111 species in all, of seventy-four genera. Of these almost half have been described already or will be described later as they appear in paintings. The remainder comprised two species of *Abutilon*, *A.bedfordianum* from Brazil, whose yellow flowers are streaked with red lines and *A.venosum*, whose unusually large orange flowers have red-brown veins; *Acacia melanoxylon*, the blackwood acacia from Australia, a valuable timber tree; *Adenandra uniflora*, a small South African shrub with large flowers white inside but pink outside; several species of aloe, unnamed, which are probably American *Agave*, there being confusion between the two in those times; and five species of *Aralia*, *A.sieboldii* (*Fatsia japonica*), a large late-flowering evergreen with milky-white flowers, *A.quinquefolia* (*Panax quinquefolius*), the well-known ginseng, *A.trifolia* and *A.crassifolia*, which appear to be synonyms for *Pseudopanax crassifolius*, an evergreen tree from New Zealand, and *A.papyrifera* (*Fatsia papyrifera*), a small tree native to China and Formosa whose shoots are filled with white pith from which Chinese rice paper is made.

The list also included three species of *Araucaria*, *A.bidwilli*, the bunya-bunya or Moreton Island pine and *A.excelsa*, the Norfolk Island pine, both from Australia, and *A.brasiliensis* (*A.angustifolia*) the Parana pine from South America; the handsome shrubby grass *Arundinaria falcata*, a bamboo from the Himalayas; *Brachyglottis repanda*, a large evergreen shrub from New Zealand with shining dark green leaves felted underneath and greenish-white flowers; *Calendula japonica*, two species of *Chrysanthemum*, *C.frutescens*, the shrubby Paris daisy and *C.trifurcatum*, a yellow daisy with slender divided leaves; *Cineraria arborea*, the slender tree-like *Cordyline rubra*, of garden origin; and four species of *Cordia*, *C.alba*, the 'jackwood' from South America, *C.ferruginea* from Mexico, *C.rubra* (*C.myxa*), a deciduous tree about forty feet tall bearing white flowers in clusters, native from India to Australia, and *C.speciosa* (*C.sebestena*), the 'geiger' tree, a large West Indian shrub with flowers varying from orange to dull scarlet, and white fragrant edible fruit.

The list continued with five species of the South African genus *Crassula*, fleshy shrubs or herbs, the scarlet or carmine *C.coccinea*, a shrub from Table Mountain, with green leathery leaves in four ranks, the prostrate *C.jasminea* (*Rochea jasminea*) with leaves crowded along the stem and white jasmine-like flowers turning pink, the winter-flowering *C.lactea* from Natal and the Transvaal, a shrubby plant with thick stems, woody at the base, and white showy flowers, *C.orbicularis*, a stemless rosette with white flowers from Cape Province and *C.portulacea* (*C.argentea*) a largish shrub with pink flowers, also from Cape Province; the graceful weeping

Cupressus funebris, the 'mourning cypress' from north-east China;

Dactylis caespitosa (*Poa flabellata*), a grass from the Falkland Islands and Cape Horn; *Dammara australis* (*Agathis australis*), the famous kauri pine from New Zealand; *Eugenia ugni* (*Myrtus ugni*) the Chilean guava, a moderate-sized shrub with white flowers, tinged rose, followed by blue-black juicy fruits; *Eurybia purpurea*: the large Australian tree *Eucalyptus robusta* (*E.multiflora*) and its relative *E.saligna*, whose leaves are narrower than those of most of the other species in the genus; and the large New Zealand shrub *Griselinia littoralis*.

Also in the list were the big-leaved *Gunnera scabra* (*Gunnera chilensis*), a fine specimen plant for large gardens, from Chile; *Hedychium flavum*, a handsome herbaceous plant with bright orange flowers, from Nepal: *Hydrangea involucrata*, a shrub with whity-bluish or pinkish flowers, from Japan; *Lardizabala biternata*, a purple-flowered climber from Chile; *Lomatia aromatica*; *Myrtus trinervus* (*Rhodamnia trinervia*) a tall shrub with white flowers from India, Malaysia and Australia; *Olea europaea*, the wild olive; two species of prickly pear, *Opuntia cylindrica* with small inconspicuous scarlet flowers from Peru, and *O.exuviata* (probably *O.imbricata*) a very spiny tree-like species with large purple flowers; *Oxylobium calycinum*; *Philadelphus mexicanus* with creamy-white flowers from Mexico; and *Plumbago capensis*, a pale-blue-flowered climber from South Africa.

The list concludes with three species of *Podocarpus*, *P.asplenifolia*, *P.chilensis* (probably *P.chilinus*) a large tree from Chile, and *P.ferrugineus*, the 'miro', a large New Zealand timber tree with bright red seeds; *Prostanthera lasianthos*, a tall tree-like shrub with fragrant white flowers tinged with purple from Australia called the Victorian dogwood; *Quercus glabra* (*Lithocarpus glabra*), the Japanese oak, a small evergreen tree from east China and Japan; *Swammerdamia antennaria* (*Helichrysum antennaria*), a medium-sized shrub from Tasmania with pale greenish-white flowers; *Tasmannia aromatica* (*Drimys aromatica*), a large very aromatic shrub also from Tasmania, called 'Winter's bark': and six species of *Veronica*, *V.andersonii* a garden hybrid, *V.decussata* (*V.elliptica*) a large evergreen shrub or small tree with fragrant white flowers marked with purple lines, from the southern hemisphere, *V.lindleyana*, *V.salicifolia*, a large willow-leaved New Zealand shrub with bluish-purple or white flowers, *V.speciosa* a small shrub with deep reddish-purple or blue-purple flowers, also from New Zealand, and *V.variegata* a variegated tufted perennial with pale blue flowers forming glossy-leaved mats.

This was the garden as Augustus had left it. The question was, who was to run it now he was gone, and would his work be continued? Augustus had left no legitimate offspring. His brother, Robert Algernon Smith, had married Mary Ann Drever in 1843. Her grandfather Thomas Dorrien outlived all his children and Mary Ann thus became heiress to his fortune. His will provided that any male coming into possession of his fortune must take the name of Dorrien and, married women not being able in those days to hold property, Mary Ann's husband Robert Algernon added Dorrien to his name and became the first Smith Dorrien.

Robert Algernon and Mary Ann had five sons, one of whom, Thomas Algernon ('Algy'), we have already met, and nine daughters, all, of course, Smith Dorriens. Only Thomas Algernon had been interested enough to come to Tresco

to see his uncle Augustus and none of the others plays any significant part in the Tresco story.

Despite Algy's interest, Augustus had felt it unlikely that he would wish to live at Tresco, and so his will stipulated that the lease should be offered to the Duchy, with the proviso that in return it paid £20,000 down and a further £3,000 a year for the remainder of the term. However, the Duchy refused the offer, so the Scilly property became Algy's, as well as Ashlyns. Augustus had stipulated that his heir must take the name Smith, so Algy became Thomas Algernon Smith Dorrien Smith. In practice the first Smith was dropped and he signed his name T.A. Dorrien Smith.

It very soon became evident that the large number of legacies and life annuities that had to be paid out of the estate would eat up most of the money and while Thomas Algernon would have the Isles there would be little money with which to run them. The executors and trustees became convinced that he would never be able to afford to live there and on 12th May 1873, Tresco Abbey and island were advertised in the *Times* to be let either for a term or by the year.

The uncertainty about the future of the property seems to have had little effect on Fanny. Many of the maturing plants were now coming into flower for the first time, presenting tremendous inspiration to a painter. She took up the challenge and set to work. Over the next ten years she created an invaluable record of what were the chief attractions of the garden in Thomas Algernon's first years. There are forty-four paintings in all. The earliest, numbered '10', shows plants flowering in January 1873. It includes: an *Acacia*; *Escallonia macrantha*, a densely leafy, rounded evergreen bush with crimson-red flowers which are rather larger than those of other members of the genus; *Hakea suaveolens*, which was described in the last chapter (page 43); *Pittosporum tobira*, a large Japanese shrub with leaves of a leathery dark lustrous green and fragrant white flowers; *Litsea japonica*, a small evergreen shrub from Japan, also with white flowers and lustrous leaves, downy and strongly veined underneath; and *Westringia rosmarinifolia*, the Victorian rosemary, a shrub from Australia deriving its common name from its pale blue flowers and leaves, which are hoary or silvery-white beneath, its appearance being reminiscent of rosemary.

A month later, at the end of February 1873, Fanny painted another picture, numbered '12', showing an *Acacia*; the striking salmon-pink flower spike of *Aloe succotrina* from Cape Province; *Edwardsia microphylla* (*Sophora microphylla*), a small-leaved species of the kowhai, a large yellow-flowered shrub from New Zealand; *Genista albiflora procumbens* (probably *G.albida*), the white genista from the Middle East; *Hakea denticulata* (*H.glabella*) with pink and white flowers; the morning glory *Ipomoea jasminoides*; *Leptospermum bullatum* (*L.scoparium*), a very bushy and leafy small New Zealand tree about twenty feet high, which has white flowers with a pink

Painting number 10

centre; and a blue-flowered *Salvia*.

As no prospective tenant turned up, and the summer of 1973 began to wane, Colonel Robert Algernon and Mrs. Smith Dorrien, Algy's father and mother, took some of his brothers and sisters to Tresco for a ten-week holiday. Edith Tower joined them in October. For a time a shadow of the old life returned, as the visitors took an interest in the local activities of the inhabitants. Edith herself was not particularly happy; her memories of Augustus and of his regime in the islands were painfully vivid, and she felt rather a fish out of water with the Smith Dorriens, whom she called the 'inter-lopers'. The Smith Dorriens made a good impression on the Scillonians, however, and after their departure the local paper carried a eulogistic account of their visit.

Three others of Fanny's paintings, numbered '6', '1' and '5', may be dated to 1873. Picture '6' shows two species of

Painting number 12

E*scallonia*, E.*organensis*, a beautiful small evergreen shrub of sturdy habit from the Organ Mountains of Brazil, with deep rose-coloured flowers, dark green leaves with a red margin and stems and branches of rich red-brown; and E.*floribunda*, a larger evergreen species from South America with white flowers and the branches covered with a clammy resin. It also includes *Eucalyptus saligna* from Australia, which has already been mentioned (page 53); a *Psoralea* with feathery green leaves and purple and white pea-like flowers; *Pittosporum undulatum*, a handsome white-flowered shrub from Australia with laurel-like leaves and creamy-white flowers, and the bright orange *Arctotis grandiflora* (A.*acaulis*), a virtually stemless plant with a thick woody rootstock and large composite flowerheads.

Painting number '1', executed in October 1873, contains the showy F*uchsia splendens* from Mexico, whose drooping scarlet flowers are tipped with pale green; the yellow-flowered C*innamomum camphora*, the small Japanese tree from which camphor is obtained; the long, musky, grey-green leaves, silvery-felted beneath, of the tall *Olearia argyrophylla*, the muskwood; the green leaves, bronzed underneath, on spiny branches, of E*laeagnus spinosa* (E.*angustifolia*); *Pittosporum undulatum*, mentioned above; and *Malvastrum capense*, a shrubby herb with purple flowers from South Africa. The third painting, number '5', shows, for October and November 1873, the long-tubed, funnel-shaped pale red flowers, striped with yellow of the small evergreen shrub *Cantua buxifolia* from the Peruvian Andes; *Cassia corymbosa*, a shrub from tropical America with flowers of a rich yellow; the curious, very spiny, almost leafless, shrub *Colletia cruciata* also from South America; E*scallonia floribunda*; E*ugenia ugni* (M*yrtus ugni*), which has already been described

(page 53); a *Lithospermum; Schizostylis coccinea*, described in the last chapter (page 48); a *Sedum; Solanum pseudo-capsicum*, a small shrub from Madeira whose scarlet fruits have earned it the name of 'Jerusalem cherry': and *Sparmannia africana*, the African hemp, which was also described in the last chapter.

Relations between Kew and Tresco were revived in 1873, and Kew records show that on 16th July of that year, 120 stove plants were despatched from Kew to Tresco. As on previous occasions, no record was retained of the species included in the consignment.

The only dated painting that can be referred to 1874 is that showing *Furcraea longaeva*, which was described in the last chapter (page 44). The picture shows little plants forming on the branches of the old.

While Fanny was busy painting, Thomas Algernon had other things than flowers on his mind. Serving with his regiment in Ireland, he had been thinking very seriously about his situation and the matter of his inheritance. Now twenty-six years of age, he realized that his uncle had taken special pains to show him round the islands and explain their problems and had been preparing him to take over responsibility for them some day. It would be deplorable if, through want of a guiding hand, the Isles were to fall back into their former poverty-stricken state. His character was much like that of his uncle. He was not deterred by apparent obstacles if he thought a job worth doing, and he had no particular lust for money. The more he thought about it, the more he set his heart on taking up the challenge. He ignored his trustees' advice that he would be poor if he accepted the inheritance, and signified that he would take it. When they found that he could not be moved from his decision, the trustees helped all they could and his mother handed over some capital. He sent in his papers early in 1874 and arrived on Tresco as the new Lord Proprietor in August of that year.

His presence there may account in part for Edith Tower's great interest in the garden. On 10th August 1874 she was writing to her mother that 'the crassulas and mesems are all over' and that the 'geraniums are not in good bloom, the weather has been much against them, with rain and storms'. Two days later, on 21st August, she added 'I have been over every plant and shrub in the garden, the dracaenas are growing capitally and have much increased'.

Painting number 6

However, Edith's interests soon extended beyond the plants. She and Algy fell in love with one another, and were married on 7th April 1875. There were great celebrations in the Isles when they arrived after a fortnight's honeymoon in Paris, but Edith was still aware enough of what was going on in the garden to write to her mother on 25th April that 'the escallonias are beautiful and the mesems are beginning to come out and there are some of the white narcissus still left'. Her brother wrote at greater length saying that 'the garden

is just now less showy in colour than I ever saw it, so many things having been cut back by the winds and frost, even the Gorse does not bloom as it ought and the *Escallonia* hedges are the only things that show any bright effect and they are far from perfection yet, the dead Aloe stalks are also not ornamental: there are some pretty bushes like large ox-eye daisies, a few camellias and azaleas and some double-headed wallflowers.'

Painting number 1

Several of Fanny's paintings are dated to 1875. The first is painting number '18', dated March-April, which includes two species of *Correa*, *C.alba*, the 'Botany Bay tea tree', an Australian shrub of stiff growth with white or pink flowers, and *C.virens*, with red flowers having yellow stamens, from New South Wales and Tasmania; a *Fritillaria* with small chocolate-coloured flowers; *Escallonia macrantha* again; and an *Acacia*.

Other paintings that Fanny produced during April 1875 were numbered '19', '20' and '21'. They include: another *Acacia*; two species of aloe (*Agave*); an *Erodium* with small purple-blue flowers; two species of *Hakea*, *H.oleifolia*, with leaves reminiscent of the olive, and white flowers, and *H.microcarpa* from Australia, which has very thin leaves and small fruit; *Melicytus ramiflorus*, a tree with yellowish-green tufts of flowers on a slender green stem, with light green leaves and round violet-blue berries; *Scilla peruviana*, the so-called Cuban lily from the Mediterranean region, with a very densely-packed inflorescence comprising up to a hundred or more lilac flowers; *Olearia forsteri*, a small tree from New Zealand with thick leathery leaves having wavy margins, grey underneath, and stalks of very small greenish-white flowers; *Lonicera involucrata*,

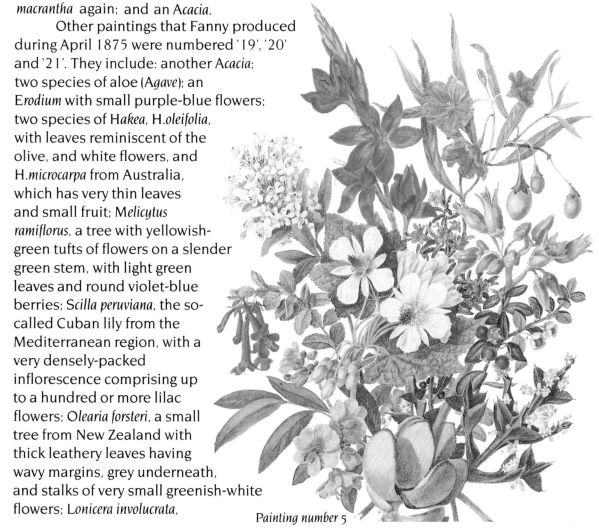

Painting number 5

57

a small erect honeysuckle from California, with red-tinged yellow flowers; *Sparaxis grandiflora* from South Africa with large showy white, red, yellow or purple flowers; and *Viburnum sandankwa* (*V.suspensum*), a Japanese shrub with rather knotty dark brown stems, stout and leathery leaves, and largish panicles of fragrant white flowers slightly suffused with pink. A specimen of *V.sandankwa* was featured in *Curtis's Botanical Magazine* in 1875 (Volume 101, Tab.6172).

Algy and Edith had hardly settled into their home when the realities of Scilly were brought home to them dramatically. On 8th May, two weeks after they had returned from their honeymoon, there was a terrible wreck. The *Schiller*, a German trans-Atlantic steamer carrying 355 passengers and crew lost its way in fog, could not see the Bishop Rock light, and ran on to the Retarrier Ledges near the lighthouse. Her guns were heard by the islanders on St. Agnes but in the dark the sea was too high for even those tough men. When the day broke they did venture out, and finally found the wreck; but by then it was too late to save many. Twenty-seven of the rescuers and survivors made their way to Grimsby harbour on Tresco, and Thomas Algernon took command and succoured them. Bodies were washed up from the wreck and buried in the old churchyard for days afterwards. Thomas Algernon and Edith had received a ghastly baptism in their new role as the Lord Proprietor and his lady.

In writing to her mother on 9th May, about the wreck, Edith included a comment about the garden:

'... the garden does not improve rapidly: the abutilons mauve and white are in full bloom now, but the wind takes off the flowers most ruthlessly and many of the pretty blossoms are strewn on the ground: the *Beschorneria yuccoides* makes a grand show of curious red stalks all along the end of the top terrace, but the mesems get on slowly.'

In June and July Fanny was working on painting number '2'. This is of considerable interest because it shows a spray of the flower of *Furcraea longaeva* said then to have been flowering for the first time in the garden. Edith reported to her mother on 24th June:

'Algy and I had a good turn round the garden yesterday morning, it is getting very bright with geraniums and other things now; fancy, forty-eight aloes (agaves) flowering this year, will it not be a sight! But there will hardly be a decent-sized one left in the gardens afterwards: the *Fourcroya longaevas* are splendid and in perfection now, one nearly twenty feet high ...'

The news about the flowering of the *Furcraea* plants reached the *Gardener's Chronicle*, which reported on 15th January 1876, that:

'Out of the three plants of *Fourcroya longaeva* in the garden two flowered during the past season, the heights of which were 17 and 20 feet respectively.'

In the volume of paintings which contains number '2' there is a photograph of the *Furcraea* in flower showing it with a plant of *Dracaena draco*, the dragon tree of the Canary Islands. The photograph also shows James Jenkins who was head gardener at Tresco for many years. Here, however, he is a boy about twelve years of age in a wide-brimmed hat.

On 29th July Edith reported that:

'the *Crassula* dell is lovely and the Aloes have got on wonderfully but not burst yet.'

A month later, on 31st August, she wrote to her mother:

'The weather is very fine and the garden recovering fast, but all crassulas and mesems are entirely over: the *Fourcroya* has performed a wonderful feat and has thrown out hundreds of little green shoots all over the hanging branches where the flowers were. The gardeners seized on them instantly to strike and no doubt that is how the plant can be propagated, it is much like that fern that has small ones growing on it.'

The *Gardener's Chronicle* of 15th January 1876, had the final word on the mass flowering of the agaves in the garden in the summer of 1875:

'In all forty-eight plants were then blooming, twenty-four of which were in one row, their ages being about sixteen years. Of the forty-eight, forty-four were the common *Agave americana*, and the remaining four of the variegated variety. The height of the plants was about 30 feet and their rate of growth 6 inches in twenty-four hours, the whole growth occupying about 10-12 weeks.'

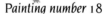

Painting number 18

The *Gardener's Chronicle* of 25th December 1875, had given a list of thirty-nine plants in flower at Tresco in November of that year. Of those names thirteen have been mentioned already. The remainder comprised: *Olearia stellulata*, which might be any one of several New Zealand species of this genus covered by that name; *Dolichos lignosus*, the Australian pea, an evergreen with twining branches and rose-coloured flowers having a purplish keel; *Candollea tetrandra*, a very ornamental evergreen shrub from Western Australia, with bright yellow flowers; two species of *Genista*, *G.canariensis* (*Cytisus monspessulanus*), the Montpellier broom, a much-branched leafy shrub of erect habit and yellow flowers, and *G.racemosa*; *Hakea prostrata*; *Myrsine undulata*, a large climbing, smooth, much-branched shrub from Nepal, with small yellowish-white dotted flowers; and *Cestrum aurantiacum*, a rambling sub-evergreen shrub from Guatemala, with bright orange flowers and oval undulated leaves.

Also included in the list were *Pernettya mucronata*, the prickly heath, a berried shrub with white flowers and smooth thin leathery leaves; *Polygala dalmaisiana* (*P.myrtifolia* 'Grandiflora'), a garden form of a much-branched South African shrub, with large purple or rosy-magenta flowers with a white keel; *Acacia lophantha* (*Albizia lophantha*), which has been previously described (page 39); *Acacia*

newmanii; *Berberis darwinii*, a densely branched spreading evergreen bush with abundant orange flowers from South America; *Statice purpurea* (*Limonium purpurata*); *Spartium odoratissimum* (*S.junceum*), a gaunt shrub from the Mediterranean region, with large shiny yellow pea-like flowers; *Medicago arborea*, the moon trefoil, a herb with yellow flowers from southern Europe; *Pyrethrum grandiflorum* (*Chrysanthemum grandiflorum*) a slender marguerite from the Canary Islands; three species of *Yucca*, which throw up glorious spikes of flowers from dense rosettes of leaves, *Y.gloriosa*, the mound lily, *Y.florida*, and *Y.filamentosa* the silk grass, a virtually stemless species in which the long spike of white flowers, tinged yellowish-green outside, is accompanied by leaves the whitish margins of which are clothed with thread-like filaments; *Boussingaultia baselloides*, a very pretty tuberous-routed plant with very twining stems tinged red, and fragrant clustered white flowers ultimately becoming black; *Psoralea pinnata*, a South African shrub with blue-striped flowers; *Colletia horrida* (*C.infausta*), a shrub with very strong spines from South America; *Teucrium fruticans*, the tree germander, an evergreen shrub from southern Europe with blue flowers; and two hydrangeas which are really one, *Hydrangea japonica* and *H.hortensis*, which are synonyms for *H.macrophylla*, the common hydrangea of our gardens.

By the mid-1870s the comparative prosperity which Scilly had enjoyed for a few years had begun to recede into the past, and hard times had returned. The advent of steam had ruined the St. Mary's shipbuilding trade: modern steamships bypassed the Isles and went straight to Falmouth or Queenstown, so pilots were now rarely required. Fishing was no resource, except for what could be sold locally, as there was no market for it elsewhere; and an attempt to make Scilly a coaling station failed, partly because of the cost of coal. Although farmers were still thriving, their prosperity could not last much longer because there was competition from the cheaper and earlier Mediterranean produce now reaching the London market. Thomas Algernon, soon becoming as familiar a figure as his uncle had been, striding along in his blue serge suit and cheese-cutter cap, was acutely conscious of this. He made several efforts to improve matters, introducing new breeds of cattle and sheep and better strains of vegetables and cereals. He sought and found new markets for fish, and

Painting number 2

60

Fourcroya longaeva

had long fights with the government and the transport companies to persuade them to speed up communications and transport. A new industry, as yet in its early stages, had been started by William Trevellick of St. Mary's, as a result of Augustus Smith's having told him in 1867 that he had received a pound for a small box of cut daffodils sent to Covent Garden as an experiment. Others followed suit and soon built up a trade, digging up the wild bulbs which grew everywhere in Scilly to form a stock. By 1873 they were importing bulbs from Holland to provide new supplies. Thomas Algernon, noting all this, kept his eye on it with a view to taking further action if the new cut-flower industry continued to prosper; but for the moment he held his hand.

By the time Thomas Algernon had taken over, many of the specimens that Augustus had planted were beginning to mature. The winds were, however, still the great problem: as soon as a plant began to grow to any size, it would be damaged or blown down by a storm. This applied to the shelter belts as well as the other plants. There seemed no solution to the problem until one day Thomas Algernon noticed, when sailing up the channel, that one tree was still upright among a number of others that had been blown down. Taking a bearing of it, he found it was a Monterey pine (*Pinus insignis*, now *Pinus radiata*) from California. Following up the hunch that this species might provide a solution to his difficulty, he planted a windbreak of this tree on the South-Western Hill. The hunch proved to be right and more and more use of this tree was made as time went on; beneath the shelter of *Pinus radiata* many plants have grown to a maturity they would never have attained without it. Other subjects used in modern times for wind breaks are *Cupressus macrocarpa*, *Pinus muricata*, *Escallonia macrantha*, *Olearia traversii*, *Griselinia littoralis*, *Olearia macrodonta* 'Major' and *Metrosideros robusta*.

Thomas Algernon Dorrien Smith pictured with his family

Edith's comments in her letters to her mother in 1876 open on a wintry note. She wrote on 16th April telling her that,

'On Friday it blew a strong gale from the north . . . .the garden is much cut and it looks wintry still, there was quite a white frost after the gale with hail storms on Thursday night . . . there are a few bright bits of mauve mesems out and yellow *Genista*, the camellias are coming out but the white ones have been spoilt by the weather.'

On 16th May she noted that . . . 'the *Escallonia* hedges . . . are in full beauty'. A month later, on 18th June, she was able to report:

'You will be glad to know that there has been a clean sweep of the Veronicas on the rocks that you wished away last year, it is an immense improvement, and we have had a lot of mesems, portulacas, geraniums, etc. planted outside, they already look very bright . . . the flowers of the large gum tree in the Long Walk are out beautifully now.' Another month elapsed and on 23rd July she wrote 'the crassulas are in full beauty now also the mesems, the geranium bank by the aloes is a blaze of colour and the *Metrosideros robusta* splendid.'

The year 1876 was, in fact, a notable year for Edith and Thomas Algernon, as their son Arthur was born, the first of a family of seven, two boys and five girls. In the garden there was something else of note, which Edith did not mention, probably because of other preoccupations. The event was recorded by Fanny in painting number '27', which shows part of a flower of *Puya chilensis*, a succulent head of florets with yellow petals and golden stamens. It will be recalled that this was a plant the flowering of which had greatly excited Augustus. A postscript to the mass flowering of the agaves in 1875 appeared in the issue of the *Gardener's Chronicle* dated 7th October 1876, which published a letter from J.H. Vallance, son of the head gardener of Tresco, G.D. Vallance:

'No American Aloes have bloomed this year at Tresco Abbey, Isles of Scilly, but in August last, when there on a visit to my father (the present gardener to Mr Dorrien Smith), the stems of forty or fifty that flowered last year were still standing.'

Edith told her mother on 2nd April 1877 that 'the garden is looking well for the time of year . . . patches of geraniums and mesems about, but the *Escallonia* hedges are the chief beauty at present: there are three more blooms this year on the *Puya*.' On 1st July she repeated that 'the garden is looking very bright with geraniums and mesems, the crassulas are not out yet but' she had to add 'the gale has destroyed the leaves and injured plants,' although 'they are recovering again'. The bad weather, however, continued, and on 2nd September she wrote that 'the garden is washed to rags . . .'

Fanny executed two paintings in 1877, numbers '33' and '36'. Painting number '33' shows the dense red spikes of *Aloe saponaria* and a variety of A.*mitriformis* with short and similarly dense red heads rising from the basal rosette of leaves. *Phormium tenax*, the New Zealand flax, which has been previously mentioned (page 42), is depicted in painting '36'. Plants were again received from Kew during this year: the Kew records show that one hundred temperate plants, together with packets of seeds were despatched to Tresco on 12th October. Again no record of the species has survived.

On 25th May 1878, G.D. Vallance, the head gardener at Tresco, sent a note on *Pittosporum undulatum* to the *Gardener's Chronicle*. This is an Australian shrub with

fragrant white flowers and characteristic laurel-like wavy or undulated leaves:

'There are several large specimens of Pittosporum undulatum growing in these gardens, with racemes of white, sweet-scented flowers, and which seed freely . . . P.tobira also grows freely, and is from 16 to 20 feet high, and in flower nearly the whole year through, and the rich perfume of its flowers has rightly earned for it the name of "mock orange". P.tobira variegatum also grows freely here, and is of more dwarf habit than the type. May not the Pittosporum described by Mr. Saunders . . . be Myrsine tenuifolia. His description answers so well to it. I enclose a piece for you to see. Both this and M.undulatum grow freely in the open garden here. There is a handsome variety of Pittosporum in these gardens—P.crassifolium, with pale crimson flowers, the seed-pods of which manifest the "resinous pulp" from which the name is derived.' **A little later, in the same journal, Vallance wrote:**

Painting number 27

'. . . Mr. Saunders . . . seems to challenge comparisons' (with the Channel Islands) 'and asks, could I . . . show him trees of Eucalyptus globulus, 15 to 20 feet high? I answer Yes, and much larger; there is one here 40 feet high and 48 feet in diameter of branches, and girth of trunk 8 feet at 3 feet from the ground . . . The tree is at present in flower abundantly and very interesting, especially the lid of the calyx, which covers the flower, and drops off just before it expands, and from which the plant derives its name, 'to well cover.' Some years ago the leader of this tree was broken off by a severe gale, and it has since grown out more laterally . . . . There are many varieties of Eucalyptus growing in these gardens, some of them very beautiful, especially the young foliage . . . .Edwardsias grow freely—three varieties, E.grandiflora, E.microphylla and E.macnabiana, all very interesting, especially so when in flower. Camellias grow freely and become quite small trees; there is an old double white one 15 feet high and 54 feet in circumference of branches, up which I have seen a young man climb to cut the pure white flowers; and magnolias . . . M.grandiflora is trained against a wall, but we have M.thompsoni as a standard and in flower. Australian acacias of "fine form and beautiful foliage", one, Acacia brachybotrys, especially so, with its soft golden foliage and, so far as I can learn, the only specimen in England; and A.lophantha and A.newmanii,

Painting number 33

64

literally arching over the walks, and in some parts of the garden growing so rude and rampant that we are forced to use the saw and pruning-hook freely to them. *Phormium tenax*, or New Zealand Flax . . . . Here there are banks of it, and it is planted pretty freely for screens . . . . it flowers freely . . . . We have many ericas growing; most of the Cape Heaths stand out well. Could Mr. Saunders show me a *Pelargonium* stalk 14 inches in girth? We have such here, and only a few weeks ago we cleared away a *Pelargonium* hedge that had stood over thirty years. *Escallonia montevidensis* grows freely, and E.*macrantha* and E.*floribunda alba* are now in full flower. Ixias do well, especially I.*viridiflora*, and all the Cape bulbs and Guernsey Lilies and Belladonnas in abundance, portions of the garden being set apart for their growth. *Calla aethiopica* is quite at home round the margin, and in the lakes, not by hundreds, but by thousands, and no one who has never seen a bank of these beautiful white lilies can conceive the loveliness of such a sight, especially at early morn when bespangled with dew.

Painting number 36

  Vallance invites Saunders to visit Tresco and promises that, if he will come, he will: 'show him sixteen plants of *Agave americana* . . coming into bloom, throwing up large flower-spikes, at the present time 20 inches in girth, and growing at the rate of 4

'Agaves' in full flower

65

to 6 inches a day, and this they will do till they attain a height of from 25 to 30 feet. He would now see the *Metrosideros florida* in full flower, and in a few days' time M.*robusta*, a fine plant, 24 feet high and 55 feet round, covering every green leaf with its brilliant flowers, a sight once seen not soon forgotten. At present he would see avenues of *Dracaena indivisa* in full flower, filling the air with fragrance like some Spice Island. The rockworks are covered with large masses of mesembryanthemums, dazzling to look at when in flower, intermixed with bright *Pelargoniums* that live out the winter through, and cacti and aloes and agaves in variety, and many other choice plants. Here he will see fine specimens of tree ferns growing out, *Dicksonia antarctica* and D.*squarrosa*, and *Chaemerops excelsa* in beautiful flower like large bunches of coral and C.*humilis* and *Seaforthia elegans* with fronds 12 feet long, *Aralia sieboldii*, and large masses 20 feet high of A.*papyrifera* and *Tupidanthus calyptratus* and many other beautiful and rare plants.

... The mere enumeration of the choice plants that grow out of doors here can convey no idea of the tropical and altogether unique appearance of the gardens, so unlike any other gardens they must be seen to be fully realised .... Visitors who have travelled much assure me there is nothing to surpass them in Italy or Algiers in their tropical appearance and general interest.'

The brilliant flowers of M.Robusta

Vallance concludes by observing that, by the liberality of the Lord Proprietor

'. . . the gardens are always open to visitors, and at the entrance lodge is this notice "In case cuttings are desired of any of the peculiar plants growing in the garden, the gardener has orders to supply them".

Of the plants mentioned in this letter, thirteen have not been previously described. These are E*dwardsia grandiflora* (*Sophora grandiflora*) and E.*macnabiana* (*S.macnabiana*), both from Easter Island: M*agnolia grandiflora*, a magnificent evergreen pyramidal tree from the south-eastern United States, with large glossy dark green leaves rusty-felted beneath, and creamy-white cup-shaped fragrant flowers eight to ten inches across; M*agnolia thompsoniana*, a garden hybrid, also with fragrant creamy-white flowers; E*scallonia montevidensis*, an evergreen shrub or small tree with white flowers, from Brazil; I*xia viridiflora*, a South African corm with green flowers having a black centre, borne in spikes; C*alla aethiopica* (*C.palustris*), an aquatic plant with a scarlet berry, widespread along pond margins in the northern hemisphere; M*etrosideros florida*, a vigorous evergreen climber from New Zealand with numerous orange-red flowers in terminal clusters: M.*robusta*, an evergreen tree also from New Zealand with numerous flowers carried in the same way; D*icksonia antarctica*, a large Australian tree fern; D.*squarrosa*, a similar New Zealand tree fern; S*eaforthia elegans* (*Ptychosperma elegans*), an Australian palm; and *Tupidanthus calyptratus* from India, which develops as a small tree at first and then

The tree ferns Dicksonia antarctica

into a tall climber with green flowers.

Edith's comments on the garden in her letters to her mother in 1878 began with a note on 25th July that 'the crassulas are making a blaze of colour now on the rocks and the whole air is laden with the scent'. On 5th September she wrote that 'the Belladonna lilies are coming out fast now and much earlier than usual', and three

days later, on the 8th, 'the aloes are all coming into beautiful bloom'. **Algy had at long last succeeded in having the telegraph brought to the islands; The Scillonians were very grateful, and Edith in her letter of 20th October recorded how they showed their appreciation:** 'Algy was presented with a book of signatures in congratulation for getting the telegraph brought to Scilly'. **Three weeks later there was a climatic freak to report:** 'Such weather on Tuesday!' **wrote Edith on 14th November,** 'A heavy snow storm, the first Algy and I have ever seen here'.

The garden in bloom contrasting with an early portrait of the South Drive by Frances le Marchant

On 27th November 1878, another generous consignment of plants was sent from Kew to Tresco, this time comprising sixty greenhouse plants two to seven feet high, and eighty similar plants of a smaller size; again no lists of the species were retained. In return for this generosity, something was received by Kew from Tresco, on 5th March 1879. A note in the Kew 'Inwards' book records the arrival from Tresco on that day of 'orchids from beyond the Madeira fall on the Amazon river'. Unfortunately it also bears the comment that the plants arrived in 'very bad condition.'

FLOWERS FOR THE MARKET

CHAPTER V

. . . he called the flowers, so blue and golden,
Stars, that in earth's firmament do shine.
Flowers Longfellow

No fewer than eight of Fanny's paintings are dated 1879, paintings numbered '41' and '43' being painted in May of that year. Number '41' is a very attractive picture, showing *Pyrus maulei (Chaemomeles japonica)*, a Japanese dwarf quince with bright red flowers; *Banksia littoralis*, a dense and handsome Australian shrub with a large head of yellow, orange and purple flowers, somewhat hidden among the leaves; *Erica* x *cavendishiana*, a hybrid heath with rich bright yellow tubular flowers; and *Pyrethrum grandiflorum (Chrysanthemum grandiflorum)* already described above (page 60). Painting '43' depicts *Embothrium coccineum*, another very ornamental evergreen tree from the Andes, with long orange-scarlet flowers and dark glossy green leaves; an elegant *Swainsonia*

Painting number 41

from Australia, whose delicate stalk is sprinkled with small, whitish, pea-like flowers; and the Mexican bulbous plant *Bravoa geminiflora*, the twin flower, with large orange-red drooping tubular flowers on the upper part of long stems. Painting number '44' of July 1879, includes *Arthropodium cirrhatum*, a pretty herbaceous perennial from New Zealand, with white flowers and grass-like leaves; and *Dianella tasmanica*, described on page 49. Paintings numbered '4', '7', '8', '37' and '38' are also dated 1879. Number '4' shows *Eucomis punctata* (E.*comosa*), a strong growing South African bulbous plant with green and brown flowers; *Raphiolepis ovata* (R.*umbellata*), a sturdy shrub from Japan, with thick leaves and fragrant white flowers; *Cantua buxifolia*, an elegant shrub with very long pale red

Painting number 43

flowers from the Peruvian Andes; and a species of N*erine*, relative of the showy South African Guernsey lily. The plants appearing in painting number '7' are *Clethra arborea*, a tree from Madeira with sprays of fragrant white flowers resembling those of lily-of-the-valley; an A*loe*; and *Gasteria nigricans*, an aloe-like plant with blotched leaves in two ranks and pinkish flowers, from South Africa. In painting number '8' are A*nigozanthus rufus*, the curious purple-and-white monkey's paw from Australia; *Oxalis crassifolia*; and the cobweb houseleek, *Sempervivum arachnoideum* from the Pyrenees and Central Europe, with small bright rose-red flowers and bright purple stamens, the common name of which is derived from the long soft white hairs which connect the tips of the leaves. Paintings numbered '37' and '38' include a blue A*loe*, A.*prolifera*, and young leaves of the blue gum, E*ucalyptus globulus*.

Edith had a new plant to interest her.

Painting number 44

She told her mother on 14th May 1879, that 'the Himalayan rhododendron planted last year in the Abbey Road is flowering splendidly, the whole plant covered with large blossoms, three flowers to each head . . .'. On 13th June, twenty-two packets of New Zealand seed were sent from Kew to Tresco, but no record of the species from which the seed was derived has been retained. Five weeks later, on 20th July, Edith reported:

'The crassulas are not out yet, there has been no sun enough to blow them; the A*loe* is getting on but not developed enough to send you, the difference at present to the others appears to be that the stalks are more purply green . . . .one of those other purple Arums has blown since you left, it is not like a pig's ear but just like the white ones only deep purple with a purple tongue instead of yellow.'

A correspondent whose letter was published in T*he Garden* on 16th November 1879, added a few more species to the list of plants known to have been grown in Tresco Abbey garden. He writes:

Painting number 4

'I found several agaves 25 feet high in flower, and in the open air such plants as D*olichos lignosus*, *Lapageria rosea*, *Rhynchospermum jasminoides* and, in fact, a whole host of New Holland plants, such as D*icksonia antarctica*, *Alsophila excelsa*, *Cyathea medullaris*, and C.*dealbata*, just now only slightly protected; also E*scallonia montevidensis*, *Pittosporum tobira* (with white scented flowers), acacias full of bud, and the true D*racaena indivisa*, with beautifully striped leaves . . . Banksias, and, indeed, many plants not common elsewhere are luxuriating there; B*rugmansia sanguinea*, *arborea*, *lutea* and *knightii* look well, and of P*hormium tenax* there are quite thickets.'

Painting number 37

Painting number 7

Painting number 38

Painting number 8

Of the species recorded in this note, *Lapageria rosea* from South America is one of the most beautiful of climbing plants, with large rich rosy-crimson pendulous flowers, produced in great abundance, and remaining in full beauty for a long time; *Rhychospermum jasminoides* (*Trachelospermum jasminoides*) is a pretty evergreen climber from the Far East, with very fragrant white flowers; *Dicksonia antarctica* is a tree fern from New Zealand; *Alsophila excelsa* another fine tree fern from Norfolk Island; the two species of *Cyathea*, *C.medullaris* and *C.dealbata* are also tree ferns, both from New Zealand; *Brugmansia sanguinea* (*Datura sanguinea*) is a tree-like shrub with pendulous orange-yellow flowers green at the base, *B.arborea* (*Datura arborea*) is the angel's trumpet, another shrub or small tree, getting its name from its long white flowers; *B.lutea* is a similar shrub and *B.knightii* (*Datura cornigera*) is a Mexican shrub with large drooping funnel-shaped white or cream flowers with a spreading mouth.

Six days later than the note in *The Garden*, on 22nd November 1879, the *Gardener's Chronicle* published a much longer article on Tresco, written by R. Irwin Lynch, the Curator of the Cambridge Botanic Garden, who had recently made a visit there. This again refers to some hitherto unmentioned plants:

The Valhalla and its collection of ship's figureheads

'. . . in front of this '(Valhalla)' is a green and well-kept lawn, bounded on one side by a striking bank of *Mesembryanthemum edule*. From this we enter the "Wilderness", which consists of a grove of alders, Cornish elms and sycamore . . .. First we observe a *Musa ensete*, which has been out all last winter, seeming, however, to require a more open spot . . . *Cyathea dealbata* and *Dicksonia antarctica* are both conspicuous . . . there is nothing to exceed *Lomaria magellanica* in noble appearance

and effect . . . *Phormium tenax* is a grand feature, the spikes frequently reaching 12 feet in height. We . . . reached a nook wholly planted with *Jaborosa integrifolia* . . . the elegant white flowers are produced in profusion. *Grevillea thelemanniana* is in flower . . .. *Pittosporum undulatum* is a fine shrub 20 feet in height, and laden with its pleasantly-scented flowers. There are several other species . . . .Among them is *P.crassifolium* . . . .

Bamboos seem not at all numerous . . . *Arundinaria japonica* we noticed as particularly good . . . *Leptospermum lanigerum*, the Tasmanian tea tree . . . is . . . covered very thickly with pure white flowers. *Hakea suaveolens* is greatly valued as a dark green evergreen shrub for the fragrance of its white deliciously scented flowers. *Abutilon vitifolium* . . . is conspicuous . . . for its large mauve flowers.

. . . We notice some fine trees of *Eucalyptus*, *E.globulus*, about 40 feet; and *E.obliqua*, about 30 feet in height . . . .A few Palms we notice, and among them are *Livistona chinensis* and *Rhapis humilis* '(which)' . . . do not seem to flourish, *Chamaerops humilis*, *Seaforthia elegans* and *Corypha australis*, however, we noticed of fine size . . .. *Araucaria bidwilli* would be a fine tree if it could stand the winds . . . *Arundo donax* grows luxuriantly.

In a sheltered corner we . . . find *Tupidanthus calyptratus* doing well . . . .A number of trees of *Dracaena australis* . . . branching into large trees . . . are . . . one of the finest of the garden features . . . .*Cordyline baueriana* is largely planted, and . . . a hybrid . . . between it and *D.australis* x *D.erythrorachis* . . . We could just imagine the splendour of *Metrosideros robusta* . . . showing its scarlet colour here and there . . . .*Eugenia ugni* here flourishes well . . . ..*Candollea tetrandra* is an interesting plant, conspicuous and pretty . . . . It has much the appearance of *C.cuneiformis*, but the leaves and blossom are fully twice as large . . . It is a native of the Swan River. The seeds are remarkable for the size and orange colour of the aril . . . '.

Some of the plants in this description, which is the first half of a two-part article, have not been previously mentioned. These are *Mesembryanthemum edule*, the Hottentot fig from Cape Province, whose long trailing stems carry large yellow or purple flowers producing edible fruit; *Musa ensete*, the Abyssinian banana, the bright green leaves of which, eighteen feet long and three feet wide when fully developed, have a red midrib; *Lomaria magellanica* (*Blechnum tabulare*), a stout erect fern from the West Indies and the southern hemisphere; *Jaborosa integrifolia*, a creeping plant from South America, with large oval leaves and greenish-white flowers; *Grevillea thelemanniana*, a West Australian shrub with pink and yellow flowers; *Arundinaria japonica*, a Japanese bamboo; *Leptospermum lanigerum* (*L.pubescens*) an erect Australian shrub or small tree with downy twigs and silky leaves, having white flowers; *Eucalyptus obliqua*, a very tall Australian tree with white flowers having yellow stamens, with bark which easily peels off in large slabs, used by the aborigines for a variety of purposes; *Livistonia chinensis*, a small Chinese palm with many broad deeply segmented leaves; *Rhapis humilis*, a ground rattan cane palm from Japan; *Corypha australis* (*Livistona australis*), a tall Australian palm with a dense crown of leaves; *Arundo donax*, a tall reed-grass with a large knotty rootstock and reddish flowers turning white; *Cordyline baueri*, a Norfolk Island tree carrying its dense cluster of leaves and white flowers at the top of its four to ten feet stem; and *Candollea cuneiformis*, a West Australian shrub with clusters of bright yellow flowers.

The second part of Lynch's article appeared a week after the first, on 29th November 1879. It follows on without a break:

'. . . In a series of beds, containing much that is rare and choice, we find a tree of *Acacia brachybotrys* . . . a fit companion for the very silvery *A.cultriformis* . . . The Madeira *Musschia wollastoni* does here remarkably well; near it is *Anopterus glandulosus*, with the beautiful white flowers for which it is famous. The Peruvian Mastic, *Schinus molle* . . . '(is present)' . . . Shrubs we notice of interest, and in fine health . . . are *Cassia corymbosa*: *Magnolia fuscata*: *Coprosma baueriana variegata*: *Olearia* or *Aster argyrophylla*, the Muskwood: *Corokia buddleoides*; *Embothrium coccineum*: *Olearia dentata* and other species (of *Olearia*): species of *Epacris* and Cape *Erica*: and *Banksia grandis* and *B.integrifolia* . . . *Araucaria excelsa* promises to be a grand tree . . . .

Banksia grandis

Of all things we saw, nothing was more striking than the development of the Rice-paper tree, *Aralia papyrifera* . . . .*Dracaena draco* we saw, but it was not vigorous. *Polygala dalmaisiana* makes a rampant shrub and . . . we found a splendid row of *Phormium tenax* in flower . . . .*Beschorneria yuccoides* was most charming: though the flowers are dull, the bright scarlet stalks are most attractive. Near here '(the old priory church)' is a fine camphor tree . . . .*Primula verticillata*, in a corner, was growing to a fine size . . . .We turn to . . . a bulb garden, rich in ixias, babianas and other *Irideae*. On a wall near is a fine *Mandevilla suaveolens* which . . . .had many flowers . . . .On the other side . . . is a whole border occupied with enormous rhizomes of *Hedychium gardnerianum* . . . The fine mass of *Puya chilensis* is one of the most noteworthy points of interest. Originally one plant, there are now several from the branches which have rooted in the ground, not, however, yet separated from the parent.

On the . . . rockwork . . . are planted . . . many species of *Kalosanthes*. There are also *Aloe dichotoma* . . . vigorous plantations of *Richardia aethiopica*, the Arum Lily . . . '(and)' . . . immense shrubs of *Myoporum laetum* . . . with white flowers dotted with lilac.

As a case of rampant growth nothing was more curious than the covering of a summerhouse with *Muehlenbeckia complexa*. It so completely enveloped the building that approach could only be made by creeping through a cavern-like hole.'

Of the twenty-eight species mentioned by name in this second part of the article, thirteen have not been previously described. These are *Acacia brachybotrys*, an Australian shrub with wide yellow flower heads; *Acacia cultriformis*, a bushy shrub from New South Wales, with yellow flowers in globose heads; *Schinus molle*, the pepper tree or, as referred to, the Peruvian mastic tree, an evergreen of rounded shape and graceful pendulous branches with yellowish-white flowers and rosy-red fruit the size of a small pea; *Magnolia fuscata* (*Michelia figo*), a bushy shrub from China, with dark green shining leaves and yellowish-green flowers stained brown-purple; *Coprosma baueri*, a shrub or small tree from New Zealand with male and female flowers borne separately: *Corokia buddleoides*, a New Zealand shrub with leaves silvery white underneath, star-shaped bright yellow flowers and blackish-red fruit; *Banksia grandis*, an Australian tree up to forty feet high, with yellowish flowers in cylindrical spikes: B.*integrifolia*, another Australian shrub or small tree with dark green leaves silvery white beneath: *Primula verticillata*, an attractive species from southern Arabia with long bell-shaped yellow flowers in two to four whorls on the stalk; *Hedychium gardnerianum*, a tall perennial herb from north India with yellow flowers: *Aloe dichotoma*, a flat-topped tree from Cape Province, with lemon-coloured flowers having red stamens; *Myoporum laetum*, the ngaio, a round-headed tree from New Zealand with white purple-spotted flowers and reddish-purple juicy fruit; and *Muehlenbeckia complexa*, a deciduous climber from New Zealand with stems making a tangled mass and greenish-white flowers.

Edith mentioned the garden only twice in her letters in 1880, commenting first very briefly on 27th June that 'the garden is looking very gay with its masses of mesems, geraniums, etc. and the *Metrosideros* bushes in full bloom', and noting on 1st August that 'the *Cantua dependens* flowered a little while ago which it has not done for eight years. I recognised it immediately from your drawing.'

On 6th January 1881, J.G. Mitchinson of Penzance visited Tresco and recorded his impressions in an article which appeared in the *Gardener's Chronicle* on 15th January:

'... I noticed the annexed list of plants with an abundance of flowers ... The A*loe socotrina* is magnificent, with scores of beautiful spikes, and the *Acacia lophantha* tremendous-sized plants with a profusion of flower. The *Lasiandra macrantha*, which is on a wall, looks splendid. I could have very much enlarged the list, but it is sufficient to say that all the plants named are in full vigour and full of flowers.'

There are eighty-four items in Mitchinson's list, but only thirty-five of these have not been mentioned already. The added species are *Aloe ciliaris* from Cape Province which has a long slender scrambling stem having dark green leaves with white teeth along the edge and red flowers: the silky-leaved *Acacia brachybotrya* from Australia; *Antholyza aethiopica* (*Chasmanthe aethiopica*), a large-cormed South African plant carrying its reddish-yellow flowers in a many-flowered spike; *Anopterus glandulosus*, an evergreen shrub, occasionally a tree, from Tasmania, with leaves crowded at the ends of the twigs and white bell-shaped flowers; A*ponogeton distachyus*, the Cape pondweed or water hawthorn, an aquatic plant, the second

common name being derived from its hawthorn scented white flowers with purplish-brown stamens; *Correa carnea*; *Callistemon linearis* from New South Wales, called the bottle brush because of the shape of its crowded inflorescence, the individual purple-pink flowers of which have beautiful crimson stamens; *Cineraria maritima* (*Senecio cineraria*) a sub-shrub with a woody base from southern Europe, the whole shrub being densely white woolly, and the flowers yellow: *Daphne indica rubro-variegata*, which is probably D.*odora*, an evergreen shrub from China and Japan, with reddish-purple flowers; and two species of E*pacris*, E.*alba* and E.*rubella*, heath-like plants from Australia and New Zealand.

Also added are E*rica melanthera*, a small compact shrub with red flowers having black stamens, E.x *willmorei*, a small hybrid shrub of unknown parentage, with deep pink white-tipped flowers; *Echeveria metallica* (E.*gibbiflora* 'Metallica'), a shrubby plant from Mexico with waxy leaves and scarlet flowers; *Fuchsia cordifolia*, a bush, also from Mexico, with long scarlet and deep red flowers: *Fuchsia thymifolia*, another bush from Mexico, with red flowers; *Genista filipes*; *Genista fragrans* (*Cytisus x racemosus*) a hybrid evergreen bushy shrub with bright yellow flowers; H*abrothamnus elegans* (*Cestrum purpureum*), a graceful evergreen climber from Mexico, with tightly packed clusters of reddish-purple flowers; H.*fasciculatus* (*Cestrum fasciculatum*), a slender-branched Mexican evergreen shrub with deep rosy-carmine flowers; *Leptospermum bracteatum*; *Lachenalia tricolor* (L.*aloides*), a South African bulbous plant with bright green, red and yellow flowers, and dark green leaves having dark purple spots; *Lithospermum fruticosum*, an erect sub-shrub from southern Europe, with deep blue faintly striped reddish-violet flowers in terminal leafy spikes; *Lasiandra macrantha* (*Tibouchina semidecandra*), a vigorous shrub from southern Brazil, with large rich purple flowers; P*uya tectora*; and *Passiflora caerulea*, one of the passion flowers from South America, with whity-pinkish blue and purple flowers, and orange fruit; *Richardia aethiopica* (*Zantedeschia aethiopica*), the arum lily from South Africa, with arrow-shaped leaves and dead-white spathe; *Senecio petasites*, an evergreen bushy shrub from Mexico, with bright yellow flower heads; *Sedum arboreum* (*S.moranense* Arboreum), an erect much-branched bush only three to four inches high with crowded triangular leaves and white flowers tinged red at the back; *Sedum albicans* (*S.telephium*), orpine, a plant with a stout rootstock, scattered leaves on a twelve-to-eighteen inch stem, and red-purple flowers; *Sedum aureum* (*S.acre* 'aureum') a variety of the mat-forming stonecrop with the leaves and tips of stems a bright golden-yellow in spring; *Saxifraga latifolia*; *Tetranthera californica* (*Umbellularia californica*), a strongly aromatic evergreen tree from the western United States with yellowish-green flowers and green fruit becoming purplish; and *Westringia grandiflora*.

Edith wrote on 11th March 1881 that 'the camellia shrubs are covered with flowers' but spread herself much more on 3rd July when she reported that:

'The garden has picked up a good bit in the last month I am glad to say, all the geraniums are shooting again well from the roots even the *lobatum*, there are more than twenty aloes flowering, several on the rockery and some of the larger ones in the garden. Ten can be seen out of the day nursery window and two on the Malekoff, one in the Duckery and the last aloe of the hedges at the end of the garden, four just below

the Biscornias, three where the mass of pink geraniums used to be and there are five Fourcroyas in full flower, the light pink mesem on the rocks is out like in your sketch.'

In July, on the 31st, she noted that 'what crassulas there are are ... bright now, but the geraniums are a great loss for colour this year.' When autumn came, she was able to say, on 2nd October that 'the garden looks fairly well, but has been much spoilt by the wind.'

Thomas Algernon's interest in the developing flower industry had not flagged and by 1880 prospects were so promising that he began to study its potentialities in earnest. In 1881 he visited Holland, Belgium and the Channel Islands, calling on the principal growers, studying their methods and investing in new varieties for himself and his tenants. One fact stood out: Scilly could produce cut flowers in full bloom for the London market a month before anyone else. There was money to be made by all in the Isles prepared to work to develop their production and get the flowers to the buyers. Thomas Algernon did not hesitate. He spent considerable sums buying bulbs from Holland and took great pains to establish which varieties best suited the cut-flower market, passing on his knowledge to the other growers. The industry gathered momentum year by year in a great rush of expansion, in which his own holding led the way.

November 28th 1881 saw the distribution to several gardens of plants of F*urcraea bedinghamii* from Mexico, raised by Tresco. The distribution was done through Kew. The 'Inwards' record of Kew shows the receipt from Tresco on 24th November, four days before the distribution, of 'one large plant of F.*bedinghamii*, five smaller plants, and a large number of small plants.'

Edith's comments on the garden begin very early in the year in 1882. She wrote on 25th January that 'the *Narcissus* are coming out in profusion now but the *Camellias* are very backward.' Five days later, on 30th January, she reveals that she, too, is interested in the new economic developments, saying 'the *Narcissus* are fetching a fairly good price' but she had also sent her mother other flowers as she asks 'What do you think of the Arum from out of doors in January?' On 16th February she reverted to the trade interest, recording that 'three hundred dozen of *Narcissus* went from the garden by Tuesday's boat, they have flowered abundantly this year.'

Four of Fanny's paintings are dated to 1882, numbers '11', '14' and '25' to January of that year, and number '31' to February. Painting number '11' is one of the most charming. It includes an *Oxalis* with a large white flower; *Callistemon linearis*, already described above (page 76); *Eugenia apiculata* (*Myrtus luma*), a Chilean shrub with large white flowers and black sweet fruit; an *Epacris*, a genus of small shrubs from the southern hemisphere; and a tall sprig of *Escallonia pterocladon*, an evergreen bushy shrub from Patagonia, with small white fragrant flowers. Painting number '14' shows a *Mesembryanthemum*, *Melaleuca hypericifolia*, a shrub or small tree from New South Wales with dense spikes of salmon-pink flowers; and *Senecio mikanioides*, the German Ivy from South Africa, a much-branched vigorous shrub with long yellow fragrant flower heads. Painting number '25' is another charming picture, depicting *Habrothamnus elegans* (*Cestrum purpureum*), already described above (page 76); a beautiful white garden variety of *Abutilon globosum* called 'Boule de Neige'; *Correa pulchella* (*C.speciosa*), which again has been previously

described (page 56); and *Pittosporum crassifolium*, showing both its chocolate flowers and a seed-box containing tiny black seeds. Painting number '31' is also a delightful picture, made up of *Escallonia rubra*, an evergreen shrub from Chile, which has delicate red flowers and leaves with resinous dots underneath; *Anopterus glandulosus*, with large succulent darkish-green serrated leaves and loose clusters of small whitish flowers; a *Statice* (*Limonium*) with attractive heads of small blue-purple flowers with yellowish centres; a fine branch of *Acacia lophantha* (*Albizia lophantha*), with sulphur-coloured brushes of flowers; and *Crowea saligna*, an erect evergreen Australian shrub with willow-like leaves and rich rosy-red flowers. Two of Fanny's paintings, numbers '18a' and '13a' respectively, are dated September and October 1883. Number '18a' shows a large brownish head of flower of *Agave filifera*, notable for the edges of its leaves splitting into irregular, spreading, grey wiry threads. Number '13a' depicts the dome-shaped thistle-head of *Banksia serratifolia*. A few days after this picture was completed, on 3rd November, tubers of *Convulvulus chrysorhizus* (*Ipomoea chryseides*), a slightly woody evergreen

Painting number 11

twining plant with small yellow flowers, were despatched from Kew to Tresco; these were followed on 28th of the same month by forty packets of seeds of Australian trees from the Melbourne Botanic Garden, of which no list has been kept at Kew, and, on 7th December, seeds of *Nannorhops ritchieana*, a dwarf prostrate palm from the Punjab.

In its issue of 18th October 1884, the journal *The Garden* carried a long article by C.A.M. Carmichael on Tresco Abbey garden; this gives an excellent, detailed description of the garden as he saw it, and mentions many plants, of which forty-five have not been included in any previous account. These are *Picea nobilis* (*Abies nobilis*), a large conifer from the western United States; nine species of *Rhododendron*, *R.arboreum*, an evergreen tree with blood-red flowers darkly blotched at the base,

Painting number 14

Painting number 31

Painting number 25

R.*argenteum* (R.*grande*), another evergreen tree with long silvery-white leaves, tawny beneath, and ivory-white flowers blotched purple at the base, R.*edgworthii*, a straggling evergreen shrub, tawny-felted, with fragrant waxy-white flowers tinged pink, R.*thomsonii*, an evergreen shrub with roundish oval leaves and blood-red flowers, R.*ciliatum*, an evergreen shrub with bristly stalks and pink flowers turning white, R.*hodgsonii*, an evergreen shrub or small tree with large very leathery leaves, brown-woolly beneath, and magenta-lilac flowers, R.*jasminiflorum*, an evergreen shrub with white slender tubular flowers from Malacca, R.*maddenii*, an evergreen shrub with papery bark and very fragrant white flowers often flushed with rose, and R.*nuttallii*, an evergreen shrub or tree of thin erect habit but very stout branchlets, with fragrant, ivory-white flowers suffused with yellow.

Painting number 18a

Also mentioned in the article were *Sempervivum tabulaeforme* (Aeonium tabulaeforme) from the Canary Isles, which has pale yellow flowers rising from a flat rosette of many leaves; *Aloe spicata*, a species from Africa and Australia; *Apicra deltoidea*, a small succulent plant from Cape Province, with clustered stems only a few inches high and yellow-green flowers; *Rochea perfoliata* (*Crassula perfoliata*), a short-stemmed succulent from Cape Province, with white or red flowers; *Cotyledon velutina*, a shrubby succulent from Cape Province, with yellow and red flowers; *Araucaria imbricata*, the well-known monkey-puzzle: *Alsophila australis*, an Australian fern with a short trunk and massive head of arching fronds; *Bambusa variegata* (B.*fortunei*), one of the many species of bamboo; *Griselinia lucida*, a New Zealand shrub with leaves that have one side much narrower than the other; *Coprosma* 'variegata' (C.*baueri* 'Variegata'), a variegated form of C.*baueri* previously described (page 75); *Gasteria glabra*, an aloe-like plant *Pachyphytum bracteosum*, a succulent with thick stems and leaves and bright red flowers; *Senecio fosteri* (*Brachyglottis repanda*), a New Zealand evergreen shrub or tree with dark shining green leaves, tinged purple and white-felted beneath, and greenish-white flowers; *Solanum concedatum*; and *Dodonaea viscosa*, a large shrub with resinous dots on the leaves, and greenish flowers.

Painting number 13a

The article concluded with reference to eight species of *Fuchsia*, four of which have been classed as varieties of *F.magellanica*, a Peruvian shrub with scarlet and blue flowers. These were *F.riccartonii*, *F.thompsoni* (*F.gracilis*), *F.globosa* and *F.conica*. The others were *F.corymbiflora*, a small weak-stemmed Peruvian shrub with deep red flowers; *F.corymbosa*; *F.splendens*, which has already been described (page 55); and *F.coccinea*, a bushy shrub with slender downy branches and scarlet and violet flowers. It also mentioned *Solanum jasminoides*, the potato vine, a deciduous twining plant with many stems and bluish flowers, from South America; *Abutilon vexillarium* (*A.megapotamicum*), an evergreen shrub from Brazil of lax, graceful habit with striking red and yellow flowers; *Clianthus puniceus*, the parrot's bill, a New Zealand evergreen shrub with strikingly-shaped brilliant red flowers; *Areca sapida* (*Rhopalostylus sapida*) the nikau palm from New Zealand; *Phoenix dactylifera*, the date palm, too well-known to require description; *Aralia dactylifera*; *Banksia serrata*, a small Australian tree with wide leathery toothed leaves and red flowers carried in spikes; *Ozothamnus rosmarinifolius* (*Helichrysum rosmarinifolium*), snow in summer, an Australian shrub with snow-white flower heads; *Brachysema acuminatum*, a free-flowering West Australian climber with deep carmine flowers; *Mitraria coccinea*, an evergreen shrub from Chile, with glossy leathery leaves and bright scarlet flowers; *Taxodium sinense* (*T.distichum*) the deciduous cypress, a large conifer of which this may be the variety *heterophyllum*, and *Agapanthus africanus*, a South African plant with deep blue-violet flowers rising from a rosette of evergreen leaves.

The *Gardener's Chronicle* of 14th March 1885, carried an interesting article by W. Trevithick, the pioneer Scilly bulb-grower; he set out the early history of the growing of narcissi on St. Mary's and listed the varieties that had recently been imported:

'... of all the *Narcissus* varieties now in bloom (nearly forty) on St. Mary's Island, Soleil d'Or takes the lead here in cultivation, followed by two kinds of native, White and Grand Monarque. All these kinds are supposed to have been on the island 200 or 300 years, and not very long since, before the rage set in for collecting these bulbs, could be found all over the island in hedges and ditches from the sea level to 150 feet above it. The soil is light and sandy; manure I never use. Seaweed is used by many growers principally on the higher ground. In addition to the very high value set on our early naturalised sorts for market purposes in bloom, we anticipate a higher commercial value for our native bulbs, as no kind yet imported, including the *pallidus praecox*, blooms so early by more than a month. I may add that the market trade for the 'natives' commenced before Christmas and the weekly supply to Covent Garden gradually increased to about 35,000 bunches of twelve blooms, which represent about half the island's export, showing a total export of nearly one million blooms.'

Much the same story could have been told of Tresco. The list of newly imported varieties totalled more than forty.

A fortnight later, in the issue of the *Gardener's Chronicle* dated 28th March 1885, another article appeared. This suggested that the 'Easter Lily', said to be 'only a form of *Lilium longiflorum*', might be worth trying as a marketable cut flower on Tresco.

This provoked a reply, printed later in the same issue, from C.A.M. Carmichael, author of the article in the *Garden* quoted above on page 78.

'...the suggestion made to Mr. Dorrien Smith that he should devote a portion of his insular domain to Lily culture, has already been taken up by him to some degree. Although, at present, his main object is *Narcissus* growing, large patches of ground are planted with *Amaryllis belladonna*, the Guernsey Lily, and *Lilium candidum* .... *Calla aethiopica* again may ... be described as growing wild in the marshy portion of the Tresco Abbey grounds; and in Mr. Trevithick's garden on St. Mary's Isle it increases in a wonderful manner. This grower last year lifted and sent away to England hundreds of roots in the beginning of September at an extremely low price. Mr. Dorrien Smith could well be pardoned if his affections were alone centred on daffodils, but it is a great pleasure to be able to report that he is cultivating ixias, irises and lilies.'

The Kew records show that on 7th April, 1885, seeds of *Lilium* species were sent to Tresco, but whether or not this had anything to do with the suggestion in the *Gardener's Chronicle* is not known. The species from which the seeds were taken were not identified by name. At the same time as these seeds were sent, a plant of *Rhododendron falconeri*, an evergreen tree from the Himalayas, with leaves rusty woolly underneath and wrinkled deep-set veins above, and flowers creamy-white to pale yellow, purple-blotched at the base, was sent from Kew to Tresco.

An article in the *Gardener's Chronicle* on 2nd January 1886, praised the beauty of various species in the garden but did not add anything to knowledge of what was growing there. On 31st March 1886, large quantities of glass were destroyed on Tresco by a severe hailstorm. There was, however, one consolation: had the storm arrived a day earlier, it would have disrupted Tresco's participation in an important event that was taking place on St. Mary's, reported by the *Gardener's Chronicle* in its issue of 10th April.

'... The first flower show on the Scilly Islands was held on Tuesday, March 30th, in the infant school, St. Mary's, Scilly, under the auspices of the Scilly Islands Bulb and Flower Association, of which the President is T. Algernon Dorrien Smith, Esq.: the Secretary, Mr. Clement W. Mumford: and the Treasurer, Mr. William R. Mumford. The exhibition to these islanders was one of unusual interest, the exhibits consisting mainly of well grown daffodils, of which the three groups were well represented ...

One end of the room was occupied by Mr. T.A. Dorrien Smith's exhibits, consisting of upwards of 160 varieties of daffodils tastefully arranged, on a groundwork of green moss and as the exhibitors generally may adopt this mode of staging their flowers in 1887, it is not unreasonable to expect that even our metropolitan daffodil shows will be put in the shade, as enterprise is one of the characteristics of the natives of Scilly, and it is likely that some of the growers from these islands will come up to the April daffodil shows to take notes, so that under these circumstances the London exhibitors will do well to make preparations for 1887, so as to maintain their position. The prize of the day was £5, offered by the Earl of Mount-Edgecumbe for the best exhibit of marketable flowers; this was carried off by Mr. W.P. Mumford, with an assortment of fifty varieties of daffodils. The same prize will be offered in 1887, and possibly others, as many who visit these islands and enjoy the hospitality of Mr. T.A. Dorrien Smith may desire to follow the spirited example of the Earl of Mount-Edgecumbe.

In August there will be an exhibition of dry narcissus bulbs, grown in the Scilly Islands, of the most marketable sorts: prizes by T. Algernon Dorrien Smith, Esq. £10; and, again, 1887, prize £25.'

The *Gardener's Chronicle* of 30th October 1886, carried another long article on Tresco, of interest because it presents a word picture which brings out well the attraction of the Abbey Garden at that time:

'Tresco is not so rich in native flora as the two larger islands, St. Mary's and St. Martin's, but it contains naturalised plants, e.g. *Mesembryanthemum edule*, in greater numbers. Among the common wild flowers are the horned poppy, sea holly, tree mallow, *Euphorbia paralis; Lavatera sylvestris* and *Acanthus mollis* have also been found. Curiously enough, the Nile lily might perhaps be put down as a garden escape. *Agave americana* and the New Zealand Veronicas are to be seen in most of the cottagers' gardens. The cultivated fields are divided from each other by hedges of tamarisk, 'vastly pretty' in its flowering stages, and *Escallonia macrantha; Myoporum laetum* has been employed as a hedge plant with great success . . . .In a former number I mentioned the somewhat curious fact of the ling and gorse being about the same height in a very windswept part. The blaze of colour when both are in flower together, as they are throughout August, is equal to that of any mainland ribbon border.

In the Abbey gardens there is always something fresh to interest, no matter how often one may tread its beloved alleys and cul-de-sacs. An *Agave americana*, the flower-scape of which was only beginning to burst from durance vilest (at least mortals would call 20 years captivity so) on Whit Sunday, is now 27 feet high, and will probably grow another 3 feet. The horizontal flower-stalks number over 40. As Whit Sunday was 13th June, and we measured the scape on 11th September, it must have been growing at the rate of 2 feet per week. *Dasylirion acrotrichum* has not flowered here as yet, though this desirable result cannot be far off if the size of the plants be any index. *Puya chilensis* and *Fourcroya longaeva* can be seen in flower every year.

Flowering plants are scattered about in a charmingly ingenuous manner. Mr. Vallance must be a 'pawky chiel' to have at his command so many surprises. His taste in bedding out is technic enough when he chooses, however, e.g. the *Dracaena* flower garden and his bed of *Portulaca* with a *Erythrina crista-galli* in the centre thereof. What is called the Hop-circle could be copied in other gardens to their gain. It consists of concentric circles of bay, hop and fuchsias, one of each in the order named. The hops are trained in festoons along iron and wire-work. The fuchsia hedge is about 3 feet high, very dense and covered with bloom. A path divides the circles into semi-circles. On the one side the vacant spaces are filled with dahlias, which in Scilly are left in through the year; on the other are diverse flowering plants and a fine *Aralia papyrifera*, which a tall *Dahlia imperialis* huddles up close to much to the satisfaction of both, apparently. Only those who know the hop as a trailing plant, and the beauty of the old-time species of fuchsia could cordially realise any word painting that would adequately limn this fair garden within a garden. The rockwork on which the Abbey stands, is brightest when the crassulas and pelargoniums are in their heyday. Still, there is always something in bloom every month. The most attractive bloom now perhaps (September) is *Arctotis grandiflora* . . . An unusual form of vegetation is to be seen growing among the rocks in the form of the *Equisetum*-like foliage of a rather tall

Casuarina. Close by this *Casuarina* is a *Dracaena draco*, decidedly dwarf for his years. The eucalypti grow well enough in Scilly, but when they get above protection immediately become wind-scorched. A large tree has been unfortunately almost killed by exposing it to the winds . . . The same fate that fell upon the Great Eucalypt, which Baddeley's "Thorough Guide" mendaciously states to be the 2nd tallest in Europe, also awaited an ambitious *Araucaria bidwilli*: the headless tree is now enclosed in a rough casing of tubular form, over which *Muehlenbeckia complexa* has spread in a rampant fashion. This climber is the most luxuriant of all the alien weeds that have obtained a footing in these gardens . . .'

Eight of the plants dealt with in this article have not been previously mentioned. These are *Dasylirion acrotrichum*, a large herb from Mexico with a tall densely-packed flower spike of white flowers arising from a similarly dense rosette of long leaves; *Erythrina crista-galli*, the common coral-tree from Brazil, with oval leathery leaves, prickly stalk and bright deep-scarlet flowers in large clusters; *Euphorbia paralis*; *Dahlia imperialis*, a large Mexican herb with nodding white flower heads with a tinge of red; *Acanthus mollis*, a stately ornamental plant from Italy, with large heart-shaped leaves and white or rose flowers; *Casuarina*, a genus of evergreen trees and shrubs from the southern hemisphere, with slender wiry branches resembling the horsetail; *Lavatera sylvestris* (*L.cretica*), an erect annual herb from southern Europe, with deep purple flowers; and *Portulaca*, a genus of widespread perennial herbs, with purple, yellow or pink flowers which open only in sunshine.

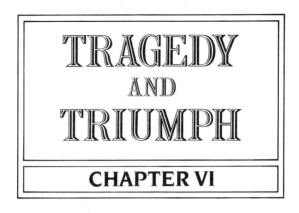

TRAGEDY AND TRIUMPH

CHAPTER VI

For some we loved, the loveliest and the best
That from his Vintage rolling Time hath Prest.
Rubáiyát of Omar Khayyám Translated by Edward FitzGerald

Thomas Algernon and Edith saw their family completed in 1887 with the birth of the last of their five daughters, Charlotte. The increase in the number of their children would in itself have necessitated an extension of the house, but there was also another factor causing pressure on space. The square tower which was added, which looks so splendid from the sea, was built to cope not only with the need for more rooms for the family, but also to house the many visitors who came to stay.

An article in the *Gardener's Chronicle* of 2nd April 1887, is of interest because it carries some details of the current year's flower show in the Isles of Scilly:

'We have before us as we write the prize list of the Scilly Islands Bulb and Flower Association, which held its annual Narcissus Show on Tuesday, 22nd March. To show what progress had been made, we may say that the exhibits of narcissi alone occupied 400 feet of staging, and that the number of entries was 540 as compared to 360 last year. Mr. Dorrien Smith himself contributed for exhibition no fewer than 162 varieties, all grown out-of-doors . . . .The Prize List contains some sixty-eight classes in the great majority of which all three prizes were competed for and won in each class. In addition to the varieties of *Narcissus*, there were classes for *Chionodoxa*, *Anemone*, *Allium neapolitanum*, hyacinths, marguerites and freesias'.

In the next year, on 7th August 1888, Kew records show that the Tresco collections were augmented by another plant sent from Kew, *Richea pandanifolia*, an evergreen tree from Tasmania, with long tapering leaves and inconspicuous flowers.

One of the unnumbered plates in the Abbey collection is dated 1889. It shows *Brachysema acuminatum*, previously described (page 81), with fat pointed chocolate buds and dark green leaves, grey underneath, the purple-flowered *Anigozanthus tyrianthus*, and a *Swainsonia*, an Australian plant with rose-purple heads of pea-like flowers. Another, a painting given the name of *Iris robinsonii*, dated August 1891, has had added to it *Iris tuberosa*, dated March 1902.
Fanny did not date a proportion of her paintings. Among the plants represented in these undated paintings are *Myrsine tenuifolia*, a slender evergreen Australian shrub, the red stems and crinkly light green leaves of which are shown in painting

number '3' together with *Polygonum complexum* (*Muehlenbeckia complexa*), which has already been described (page 75) and *Acacia diversifolia* (*Leucaena diversifolia*), an evergreen tree from America and the Pacific islands. *Acacia brachybotrya* and *Myoporum laetum*, which have also already been mentioned (pages 74 and 75), and a *Calothamnus*, an Australian evergreen shrub, probably C.*longissimus*, are all three seen in painting '9.' Painting '13' includes the large-cupped flowers of A*butilon vitifolium* from Chile, *Babiana* and *Ixia* from South Africa, the scarlet and green flowers of *Fuchsia cordifolia*, and *Callistemon*, the Australian bottle brush. The yellow flowers of *Candollea cuneiformis* and the red lobster-claws of *Clianthus puniceus*, both previously described, together with *Lachenalia versicolor*, a South African bulbous plant, the light pink of *Diosma speciosa* (*Adenandra umbellata*), a small South African evergreen shrub with pink flowers stained red, and densely set glandular dotted leaves, the purple tubes of *Paulownia imperialis* (*P.tomentosa*), a sizeable Chinese tree with thick shoots and soft broad leaves, woolly-grey underneath, and blue-purple foxglove-shaped flowers, and three large mesembryanthemum flowers, purple, orange and a darker orange, all appear in painting '15.'

Painting number 3

Painting number 9

Painting number 15

Ceanothus Dentata

Leptospermum
Laurigerum
or
Grandiflora

Cordifolia
1 Fuschia Splendens

2. Abutilon Vitifolium Alba

3 Pabiana's

4 Ixia Viridiflora
Calistemus Viridiflora
Melaleuca Ericifolia

6 Abutilon Vitifolium
7 Calistymen Pinaifolia

8 Ixia Longiflora

Painting number 13

One of the finest of the paintings is number '16', which includes a spray of a *Eucalyptus*, said to be *E.coccifera*, a small Australian tree, showing two different kinds of leaf and whitish rosettes of flowers; *Psoralea pinnata*, with blue flowers and very narrow leaves, the bright red brushes of a *Callistemon*, mentioned above, the small daisy-like flowers of one of the many species of *Sedum*, the smooth shiny evergreen leaves of *Griselinia lucida* from New Zealand, one of the species of *Babiana*, bulbous plants from South Africa, and a light purple *Ixia*, also from South Africa. Painting '17' shows the large yellowish-green leaves and rather ragged-looking reddish flowers of the nutmeg tree, *Myristica fragrans*, the yellowish-white flowers of the sacred Japanese *Illicium religiosum* (*I.anisatum*), and *Vitex littoralis*, a hard-wooded New Zealand tree with pink flowers and large leaves.

Painting number 16

Another very attractive and skilfully-arranged painting, number '22', includes the white *Crassula decussata* (*C.tetragona*), *Convolvulus mauritanicus*, a prostrate twining perennial from North Africa with delicate blue-purple flowers having a white throat and stamens, and *Funkia lancifolia* (*Hosta lancifolia*), a perennial from the Far East with narrow leaves and pale lilac flowers on a tall slender stem. The similarly attractive painting '23' contains the red flowers of *Metrosideros robusta*, with long leaves, yellowish-green above and greyish below, *Diosma hirta* (*Agathosma villosa*) showing the fine leaves and tufts of purple flowers of this hairy heath-like plant from south-western Africa, the long spike of reddish-yellow slender tubular flowers of the South African *Antholyza praealta* (*Chasmanthe floribunda*); *Olearia dentata* (*O.tomentosa*), a bushy Australian shrub with reddish-brown felted shoots and leaves with forked hairs underneath, the flowers of which, pale rose with a yellow centre, are strongly reminiscent of Michaelmas daisies,

Painting number 17

Painting number 23

Painting number 22

and *Drimys aromatica*, Winter's bark, which has already been described (page 53).

Painting '26' shows the slender green stalk of a plant with clusters of greenish-white flowers, given the name of *Kennedya alba*; the tiny chocolate flowers and dark green leaves, grey below, of *Pittosporum crassifolium*, previously described (page 64), the long leaves of the Australian *Eucalyptus globulus*: and *Edwardsia grandiflora* (*Sophora grandiflora*), also previously mentioned (page 67). Another *Acacia* is featured in painting '28', this one with a very thin stalk and leaves, and sparse yellow balls of flower. The same painting also contains a peacock iris of a very beautiful delicate blue, *Mesembryanthemum tricolor* (*M.mutabile*), whose reddish flowers have pale yellow centres; *Melaleuca taxifolia*, with white brushes of small flowers; a bright orange *Moraea*, possibly M.*pavonia*; *Citharexylum cyanocarpum* (*Rhaphithamnus cyanocarpus*), an evergreen much-branched spiny Chilean shrub with small pale-blue tubular flowers and bright blue fruit; and *Pomaderris lanigera*, a small

Painting number 26

Australian shrub with clusters of small yellow starry flowers, and long leathery yellowish-green leaves with whitish rusty-coloured wool underneath.

Painting '29' contains the dark purple flower of the common spider-wort (*Tradescantia virginiana*) from the eastern United States, the orange flowers of the Kaffir lily, *Clivia gardenii*, the fat red stalks and reddish flowers of *Beschorneria yuccoides*, previously described (page 44); and the contrasting clusters of purple flowers of a *Brodiaea* species, one of a genus of slender American herbs. The thin stalks and tiny white flowers of one of Tresco's own hybrids, *Dracaena scilloniensis*, together with a *Callistemon*, are shown in painting '30', and in painting '32' *Pittosporum crassifolium*, *Myrsine tenuifolium*, and *Teucrium fruticans*, (also previously described, page 60) together with *Buddleia globosa*, a semi-evergreen shrub from South America with bright yellow fragrant flowers

Painting number 28

Painting number 32

Painting number 35

Painting number 29

Painting number 30

densely packed in long-stalked globose heads. Painting '35' shows the flowers of an unnamed rhododendron.

Painting '39' features *Ornithogalum arabicum*, a bulbous plant from the Mediterranean area with white aromatic flowers having a black centre, *Aponogeton distachyus* again previously described (page 75), and a species of *Jaborosa*, a genus of American perennials with white or yellowish bell-shaped or tubular flowers. The light red flowers, also tubular, hanging from a succulent slender brown stalk of the Cape figwort, *Phygelius capensis*, are associated in painting '40' with a knobbly branch of *Illicium religiosum* (*I.anisatum*), the star anise, a shrub or small tree with greenish-yellow flowers which, although the wood and leaves are strongly aromatic, are not

Painting number 39

themselves fragrant. The bright blue flowers of *Dianella caerulea*, previously mentioned (page 49), also appear in painting '40.'
Gasteria carinata, a South African succulent plant with red flowers, is shown in painting '42.' Two unnumbered and undated paintings show an *Iris* and tulips respectively, and a third a spray of *Abutilon vexillarium* (*A.megapotamicum*).

On 16th April 1890, Thomas Algernon read an interesting paper to the Royal Horticultural Society on 'The Progress of the Narcissus Culture in the Isles of Scilly.' The paper is too long to include in full, but the following paragraphs add something to our knowledge:

'Twenty-five years ago some eight varieties of the narcissi were growing in the Isles of Scilly, besides those in the Abbey gardens, some almost wild, some in the hedges, and some in the gardens attached to the little farms.

These varieties were: *Telamonius plenus, odorus major* (Campernelli), *Tazetta ochroleucus* (Scilly White), *Tazetta aureus* (Grand Soleil d'Or), *Tazetta Grand Monarque* (two vars.), *biflorus poeticus fl.pl.* and *poeticus recurvus*.

Painting number 40

The date of the introduction of these is extremely obscure, except Campernelli, of which two bulbs were presented to Mrs. Gluyas fifty years ago by the captain of a French vessel . . . . The others were introduced probably by the Governors . . . or . . . they may have been introduced by the monks . . . .

We formed a bulb and flower association in 1885 to promote the culture, and

Painting number 42

held annual shows under its auspices, and the flower show is now quite the event of the year in the island . . . .The contrast between the first show and the one held this year was most remarkable. There were over 700 exhibits this year, and they were so good that, on the advice of a friend, I ventured to send the prize flowers and others to her Majesty the Queen, who was graciously pleased to accept them . . . .

The narcissus fly (*Merodon equestris*), or rather the grub of the same, has given us a taste of its powers, though I think, if it were likely to become thoroughly acclimatised, we should have had a severer example of its voracity than this. It seems to have the most extraordinary proclivity for selecting the most valuable bulbs. I first obtained it in Sulphur Kroon from Holland; it has since attacked Sir Watkin, *Barrii conspicuus*, C.J.Backhouse, and Nelsoni major, but very little else . . .'

In 1884 the Duchy had granted Thomas Algernon a thirty-one year extension of his lease. In 1890 one of his long-cherished plans came to fruition. The Council of the Local Government Board issued an Order setting up a County Council for Scilly, the Council to be made up of four aldermen and twenty councillors under the chairmanship of Thomas Algernon. The Council had power to deal with every aspect of the islands' administration, and the Isles thereafter were no longer an outpost of mainland local government but themselves an administrative entity with powers equal to those of mainland County Councils.

At this time, also, Thomas Algernon was concerned with the extension, at a personal cost of £14,000, of the pier, to cope with the ever increasing flower traffic. Parliament authorized him to levy quay dues to recoup his capital outlay but these caused a good deal of grumbling among the ungrateful users.

The Kew record books show that *Puya chilensis* plants, together with plants of *Eurybia purpurea* (*Olearia purpurea*), both previously described (on pages 43 and 53), were received by Kew from Tresco on 9th September 1890, and, four days later, on 13th September, bulbs of *Amaryllis belladonna*. On 14th October 1890, Kew responded by sending Tresco seventeen large agaves, followed by a single agave plant on 23rd October and, on 5th February 1891, cuttings of *Psoralea pinnata*. The summer of 1891 saw another substantial contribution from Kew. On 14th May thirty-one stove plants, one greenhouse plant and two packets of seeds were sent from Kew to Tresco; and, four months later, seventy-nine species and varieties of the genus *Haworthia*, small succulents from South Africa, were also sent from Kew to Tresco.

From time to time the high winds experienced by Scilly brought tragedy to one or more of the treasures of Tresco. On 19th December 1891, Thomas Algernon reported one such incident in the *Gardener's Chronicle*:

'I send you a photograph of the *Eucalyptus globulus*, a victim of the late gales, which may be of interest to your readers. It was planted in these gardens about forty years ago and was probably the oldest gumtree in England, if not in Europe. The stem, 3 feet from the ground, is 9 feet in circumference. Its height, a very little over 40 feet, the top having constantly been blown off by the wind, which gave it a bushy appearance, in contrast to the usual erect habit of the tree. It was blown down on the morning of November 11th, in a severe north-west squall. A well-known gardener advised me to clear some of the undergrowth from around it, so as to show the trunk.

This I did, with the result that the draught was let in, and half the tree killed: hence the crevice seen in the illustration. I have been told by some Australians that if you grow a gumtree in the bush, and cut the bush away, it invariably kills it, and this was the result with one half of my tree; the other half was apparently improving till blown down, then only one side of the undergrowth was cut away in the case of my tree. Of course, I do not mean that you cannot grow *Eucalyptus* in the open.

We only registered frost 2 nights last winter, and did not lose much—pelargoniums cut down. I had 500 young *Metrosideros* ready to go out; these were pretty well destroyed: they will not stand frost in their younger stages, but stand the wind better than anything else I know, and grow in rock—anywhere, in fact, where there is ever so little soil. The palm shown in the illustration near the *Eucalyptus*, *Areca baueri*, was also considerably damaged by the fall of its neighbour.

The happy life of Thomas Algernon and Edith and their children came to a sudden end little more than a matter of days after Thomas Algernon had penned this account. An epidemic of influenza swept through the Isles in January 1892, striking almost everybody down. Twenty of the twenty-three inmates of the Abbey were affected. Edith, saddled with responsibility for them all, and with no doctor at hand, the physician on St. Mary's being himself too ill to come, rose from her bed to nurse the others when she was really unfit to do so, and collapsed. The Penzance doctor was sent for, but when he arrived she was dying. With her death a light went out of Tresco life. She had loved the garden so much that perhaps, for some, her spirit may seem to haunt it still.

On 10th June 1893, another tribute to Tresco featured in the *Gardener's Chronicle*. H. Tonkin, who lived on the neighbouring island of St. Mary's, wrote:

'Never have the famous sub-tropical gardens at Tresco Abbey presented such a remarkable appearance as at the present time, nor has its equal been seen in any other part of the United Kingdom—perhaps not in Europe. For some years past, great attention was paid to the cultivation of Dracaenas, especially D.*indivisa* and D.*australis*, and with great success. Thousands of them have been planted all about the gardens, and on the other islands as well. Year by year these plants have bloomed, and ripened seed which has been carefully preserved; but the present year eclipses all previous years in the matter of flowering, hundreds being now in full bloom, their noddy plumes meet the eye at every turn, and the air is redolent of their fragrance. In some cases the foliage is almost hidden by the mass of flowers, and it is impossible to give an adequate idea of their appearance.'

Tresco received a very substantial consignment of plants from Kew on 12th April 1894. They came in two cases, and included agaves, aloes, *Cotyledon*, *Crassula*, *Mesembryanthemum*, *Furcraea* and *Gasteria*, the whole totalling 170 plants in all. Nine days later, in its issue of 21st April, the *Gardener's Chronicle* carried another note about the flower trade, showing the tremendous growth of this industry and Thomas Algernon's own part in it:

'On a single day last week, says the *Western Mercury*, 3760 cases, weighing 16 tons, were despatched from the Scilly Isles to Penzance; and another day the total was 1900 cases, weighing 9 tons 6 cwts., all containing lilies and narcissus. Mr. T.A. Dorrien Smith, the Lord of the Isles, is one of the largest growers, and by one steamer alone he sent across to the mainland no less than 32,000 bunches of blooms.

Mr. Dorrien Smith is ever on the alert to promote this industry so important to Scillonians.'

There was another addition to the Tresco garden on 26th April 1894: *Calceolaria fuchsiaefolia*, a fine shrubby species of considerable ornamental value, was sent from Kew to the island on that day. Nine months later Tresco received a further contribution from Kew. On 20th January 1895, tubers of *Oxalis crenata* (*O.tuberosa*), a Colombian species with yellow flowers, were sent from Kew to Tresco.

A long article in the *Gardener's Chronicle* of 30th March 1895, describes the Isles very well. It includes the following paragraphs about Tresco:

'While standing on the quay at St. Mary's, one sees across the Sound, about 2 miles distant, a richly-wooded island, in the midst of which stands a stately house. This is Tresco Abbey, the home of the Lord Proprietor . . . Here is one of the most beautiful gardens in Europe, and at the back of it, sheltered from "all the airts", is the "Home of The Lilies". Acres upon acres, in several hundred varieties, are grown here, with nothing to protect them but reed or lath fences, or the *Escallonia* hedges . . . .

The flowers vary greatly in shape, size and colour from the noble Sir Watkin, Emperor and Empress, 5 to 6 inches across, to the tiny Angel's Tears, barely half an inch. The colour, too, varies, through all the golden tones from deep orange with crimson-margined corolla, to the purest snow-white. Codlins-and-cream, butter-and-eggs, and the ordinary daffodil of the cottage garden, are all here, down to the chaste elegant wilding of the English meadows . . . .

The narcissus tribe, however, are not the only flowers grown; hyacinths, tulips, freesias, ixias, *Gladiolus*, and anemones, are also grown. The last-named, A.*fulgens*, is a very early bloomer, and of the most brilliant scarlet. Then there are acres of wallflowers and stocks, which arrive at Covent Garden market some weeks in advance of those grown at home.

By the 'Lily gardens' are ten spacious glass structures in which are grown the earliest flowers. The latter are followed by enormous crops of tomatoes, which also find a ready market in London and the great provincial towns.'

According to another article in the *Gardener's Chronicle* of 4th May 1895, the *Western Morning News* of 30th April 1895, had carried the following note about the flower trade which shows that it had its setbacks like any other business:

'The flower season at the Isles of Scilly is now about finished. Although the prices at the beginning of the season ruled high, the returns to the islands will fall considerably below the average. The early narcissus crop, the Soleil d'Or, was a failure throughout the islands and the total quantity sent for the year will be about 100 tons short of last year.

To redress the balance on the exchange of plants, Thomas Algernon sent 200 bulbs of *Amaryllis belladonna* to Kew on 16th August 1895.

The first Spring Flower Show at Truro in Cornwall took place on Wednesday, 17th March 1897. Thomas Algernon was honoured by being asked to serve as Vice-President under the Presidency of Mr. J. Williams of Caerhays. On 15th May two plants of *Puya chilensis* arrived at Kew from Tresco, followed on 18th August by cuttings of five species of *Mesembryanthemum*. Signs of trouble in the flower trade were again evident in 1897. The *Gardener's Chronicle* of 18th December

carried the following report:

'It is said that the flower crops in the Scilly Islands are not so forward as they were last year, which was a record one, and the general opinion among the farmers is that the early blooms will not be so prolific as last season. Various reasons are given for this, one being that the bulbs are somewhat exhausted after the exceptionally heavy crops they produced last year. It is to be hoped that good prices will compensate for any deficiency in quantity . . .'

In 1898 the Truro Show took place on 15th March, and to this Thomas Algernon sent a collection of Narcissus and several tropical and sub-tropical plants. Three consignments were sent from Tresco to Kew during this year. The first, which arrived at Kew on 20th September, comprised eighteen bulbs of Iris tingitana, a lilac-purple early-flowering species from Morocco. Twelve of these bulbs had been imported, the other six being home-grown. The home-grown bulbs, it was noted, were twice the size of the imported ones. On 4th October fifty more bulbs were sent to Kew from Tresco. Two days later, on 6th October, Tresco sent cuttings of Hedycarya arborea and plants of a hybrid Dracaena, named D.trescoensis, bred from D.australis and D.banksii. On 13th October Kew sent Tresco two bulbs of Amaryllis belladonna presumably for some special reason in view of the number previously sent from Tresco to Kew. On 31st October Kew also sent Tresco a large collection of other plants.

The selection, which totalled seventy plants, included some hybrids and species not fully named. Species included which are still to be found in the garden or are otherwise identifible were (in the order of the list): Pedilanthus padifolius; Agave dasyliriodes from Guatemala; A.filifera (previously mentioned page 78); A.kewensis from Mexico; A.attenuata, a Mexican plant whose large rosettes of leaves stand up on three feet stems when old; A.vivipara (Furcraea agavephylla F.cubensis), a tropical American plant with bright green leaves, having hooked brown prickles on the edges; and A.rigida sisalana from Mexico; Aloe hildebrandtii from tropical Africa, and A. gasterioides also from Africa; Gasteria radulosa; Dyckia altissima, a South American stemless perennial, with bright yellow flowers rising from a dense rosette; Furcraea gigantea (F.foetida), a South American plant with a rosette of leaves on a short stem and a very tall flower spike of milk-white flowers greenish on the outside, F.selloa, a Guatemalan plant with a long flower-spike of white flowers rising from a stemless rosette of spiny leaves, and F.macrophylla; Dasylirion acrotrichum (previously mentioned page 84); Kalanchoe marmorata, an East African succulent with brown markings on the leaves and large white flowers; Cotyledon pulverenta (Echeveria) a Californian herb with reddish-yellow flowers rising from a rosette of mealy-covered leaves, C.coruscans from Africa, and C.barbeyi, a tall shrubby north-east African herb with green and red flowers.

Also in the list were Beaucarnia longifolia (Nolina longifolia), a tall woody-stemmed herb with long thin narrow pendent dark green leaves having a beautiful vase-like centre; Lilium lowii (L.bakerianum) from West China and upper Burma, which has creamy-white pendulous bell-shaped fragrant flowers red spotted within; Dombeya schimperiana from tropical Africa; Hypericum lanceolatum (Vismia glabra), a Peruvian shrub with yellow flowers; Quercus incana, an evergreen oak from Nepal, with branches which are hoary and velvety when young; Leptosyne gigantea

(*Coreopsis gigantea*), a large Californian yellow daisy; *Callitris muelleri* from Australia; *Callicoma serratifolia*, a tall Australian shrub with woolly shoots, coarsely-toothed leaves and yellow flowers in globose heads; *Olearia stellulata*, a daisy bush from New South Wales; *Agonis marginata*, an Australian evergreen shrub with white-margined flowers reddish-purple in the centre; *Convulvulus scoparius*, a broom-like shrub from Tenerife with white flowers hairy outside; *Eucalyptus cornuta*, a tall West Australian shrub or small tree with ball-like masses of horn-shaped beaked rich red flowers with a dense crown of yellow stamens; *Hovea lanceolata* (*H.longifolia*) an erect evergreen Australian shrub with reddish leaves downy underneath, and pale blue flowers having a yellow base; *Dermatobotrys saundersii*, a small South African shrub with fleshy leaves and pale red flowers, yellow within; *Rhodoleia championii*, a small tree from Hong Kong, with bright green leaves and flowers with rose-coloured clawed petals within many-coloured sepals; *Olearia solandri*, a tall New Zealand daisy bush with yellowish flowers; *Prostanthera nivea*, the Australian evergreen mint bush, with snow-white flowers sometimes tinged with pale blue; and *Callistemon pithyoides*, an Australian shrub with yellow-stamened flowers.

The list concludes with *Ficus australis* (*F.rubiginosa*), a small tree with spreading numerous branches, from New South Wales, having handsome elliptical leaves covered when young with a ferrugineous down, especially on the underside; *Celastrus australis*, an Australian climber with white flowers and orange-yellow fruit; *Olearia moschata*, another New Zealand daisy bush; *Romneya coulteri*, a medium-sized Californian herb with white showy flowers terminating the branches; *Sphaeralcea abutiloides*, a shrub from the Bahamas, with rose-coloured flowers; *Spathodea campanulata*, an evergreen tree from tropical Africa, with long orange flowers; *Kunzea pomifera*, a prostrate evergreen Australian shrub, found on sandy shores, with dense white stalkless flower heads; *Protea cynaroides*, a bushy South African shrub with white to delicate pink silky-downy flower heads; *Notelaea longifolia*, a tall Australian shrub with small white flowers and dark-bluish berries; *Chrysanthemum nipponicum*, a Japanese herb resembling a shrubby ox-eye daisy; *Caesalpinia mexicana*; *Moraea robinsoniana*, a showy plant from Lord Howe Island, with a habit like that of New Zealand flax, and pure white flowers; *Haemanthus magnificus*, a South African bulb, with bright green leaves and bright scarlet flowers in a dense globose head; and *Pseudopanax ferox*, a slender New Zealand evergreen tree with spiny-toothed leaves. A collection of seeds was sent from Kew to Tresco, on 3rd December 1898.

The issue of the magazine *The Garden*, dated 10th December 1898, carried a long and informative article entitled 'An August Visit to Tresco Abbey Gardens'. Plants included in this article, which have not been mentioned before and can be clearly identified, are: *Kalosanthes* (*Rochea*), shrubby South African succulents; *Crinum moorei*, a large bulb from Natal, with greenish-red clusters of flowers and long spreading leaves; *Commelina coelestis*, a Mexican perennial herb with blue flowers; *Nymphaea flava*, a water-lily from the southern United States with yellow flowers; *Francoa ramosa*, a Chilean perennial herb with white flowers in clusters; *Fuchsia fulgens*, a small Mexican shrub with long scarlet drooping flowers in terminal clusters; *Lilium auratum*, the golden-rayed lily of Japan, having ivory-white flowers with a bright yellow band and numerous deep purple spots; *L.speciosum*,

with pure white flowers more or less suffused with claret-red; and L.*tigrinum*, the tiger lily, with deep bright orange-red flowers with many purplish-black spots; *Canna*, stout unbranched herbs from tropical America and Asia; *Tritonia*, South African corms with a few narrow leaves and loose spikes of yellow, orange and red flowers; and *Kniphofia*, tufted African herbs with very long narrow leaves and long, many-flowered inflorescences.

Also included were *Tecoma radicans* (*Campsis radicans*), a north American climber with clusters of large trumpet-shaped yellow to deep scarlet flowers; *Leonotis leonurus*, a small South African shrub with square shoots and bright orange-scarlet flowers; *Lithospermum prostrata* (*L.diffusum*), an evergreen prostrate sub-shrub from southern Europe, with deep blue faintly striped reddish-violet flowers; *Iris stylosa alba* (*I.unguicularis*), a white form of a small winter-flowering iris from Algeria and the eastern Mediterranean; *Desfontainea spinosa*, an evergreen shrub from Chile and Peru, with holly-like leaves and crimson-scarlet and yellow flowers; *Eriostemon buxifolium*, a small Australian shrub with pink or rose flowers; *Olea fragrans* (*Osmanthus fragrans*), an evergreen shrub or tree from the Far East with leathery leaves and white flowers; *Callistemon speciosus*, a tall West Australian bush with long narrow leaves and deep scarlet bottle-brush flower heads; *Dryobalanops aromatica*, a large evergreen tree from Sumatra, with leathery shiny leaves and yellow flowers; *Echium calythyrsum*, a robust woody bristling herb with pale red to bluish-violet flowers; *Eurya latifolia* (*E.japonica*), an evergreen shrub or tree from the Far East, with glossy dark green leathery leaves and white flowers; *Libonia floribunda* (*Jacobinea pauciflora*) , a showy South American sub-shrub with drooping scarlet flowers tipped yellow; *Metrosideros floribunda* (*Angophora intermedia*), an Australian evergreen tree with clusters of yellow-stamened flowers; *Pimelea decussata* (*P.ferruginea*), an erect much-branched Australian shrub with rose-coloured flower heads; *Casuarina quadrivalvis* (*C.stricta*), the sheoke, a tree or large dense shrub with dark green branchlets from Australia and Tasmania; and *Arundinaria simoni*, a tall Japanese bamboo.

The article concludes with references to *Phyllostachys aurea*, an evergreen bamboo from the Far East, with tufted yellowish stiffly erect stems having a swollen band beneath each joint; *P.virido-glaucescens*, a Chinese bamboo of graceful spreading habit with very hollow stems; *Thamnocalamus falconeri* (*Arundinaria falconeri*), a tall Himalayan bamboo with olive green stems purplish near joints, and rather pale green leaves; *Phoenix canariensis*, a slender-stemmed graceful palm from the Canary Islands; *Rhodostachys littoralis* (*Fascicularia littoralis*), a stemless Chilean plant with blue flowers centred in a rosette of narrow spiny leaves; *Gunnera scabra* (*G.chilensis*), a Chilean herbaceous perennial with very large toothed leaves, stout prickly stalks and reddish flowers; and *G.manicata*, a very large plant also with large toothed leaves, prickly stalks and reddish flowers.

The third Spring Flower Show took place at Truro on 21st March 1899. At this show Thomas Algernon was awarded a Royal Horticultural Society Gold Medal for the best display of narcissi. He also exhibited cut sprays of *Grevillea rosmarinifolia*, *Ribes speciosa*, *Ilex dipyrena*, *Leptospermum bullatum*, *Genista filipes*, *Edwardsia grandiflora* (*Sophora grandiflora*), *Acacia dealbata*, *A.melanoxylon*, *A.grandis*, *A.armata*, *Andromeda japonica*, *Viburnum rugosum*, *Pittosporum tobira* and *Solanum crispum*.

Kew sent him four consignments in 1899. The first, despatched on 24th February, comprised seeds from Sikkim-Himalaya which were not listed. This parcel was followed on 23rd March by corms of *Acidanthera aequinoctialis*, and, on 14th and 18th October respectively, by seeds of *Lithraea (Rhus) molleoides* and *'Hesperaloe Engelmann' x Yucca recurvifolia*. In the years 1900-01, Kew sent two other consignments. The first, sent in October 1900, comprised a collection of Australian seeds and seedling *Mammillaria;* and the other, stolons of *Gloxinia maculata*, sent on 14th February, 1901. In 1902, three consignments were sent from Kew to Tresco. On 21st February seeds of *Callitris arborea* were despatched; on 9th April, twenty-three packets of seeds which had been received from H.J. Elwes in Buenos Aires; and, on 24th September, seeds of *Statice imbricata* and two *Statice* hybrids. Nothing was sent from Tresco to Kew during the years 1899-1902, which were the years of the Boer War, in which, as an army family, the Dorrien Smiths were heavily involved. During his service in South Africa, however, Thomas Algernon's son, Captain (later Major) Arthur Algernon Dorrien Smith, already showed those qualities as a plantsman which were to bring him to the forefront in later years. As he rode over the South African veldt he kept his eyes open, and whenever he saw a likely plant, had it packed up and sent home.

THE UTTERMOST PARTS

CHAPTER VII

The hills look over on the South
And southward dreams the sea . . .
Daisy Francis Thompson

The England of Queen Victoria was a land of enterprise and change, not least in the extension of British power into new and hitherto unexplored lands. Tresco, with its interest in exotic vegetation, its eager absorption of plants from the uttermost parts of the earth, was thoroughly in tune with the prevailing mood, to which the death of the old Queen in 1901 made no difference. It was indeed, to the uttermost parts of the earth to which energy was chiefly to be directed in the ensuing years, since it was apparent that Tresco's climate and situation was more adapted to foster the outdoor growth of plants from the Antipodes than any other part of the British Isles except some similar islands and the west of Ireland.

The periodical *The Garden* continued to be interested in Tresco and on 5th April 1902, followed up its article on Tresco in August, 1898 with another of similar length, entitled 'Early March in Tresco Abbey Gardens'. It describes the spring scene very well but includes in its account no plants that have not already been mentioned. A new painter now began to work in the garden, Arthur's young sister Gwendoline, born in 1883, started in 1902 to make pictures of it. Although Fanny had painted a number of scenes, particularly around the Abbey, Fanny's plant pictures were mainly of individual specimens without background. Gwendoline adopted a different approach, giving prime attention to scenes showing plants as they grew among their fellows in the garden. Some of her paintings are very colourful and attractive, capturing the beauty of the garden in the sunshine in all its brilliance. The pictures are bound in two volumes. Among those well worth looking at in the first volume are a purple *Veronica*, a blue *Iris*, a dark blue *Echium*, a border of *Gazania* and *Abutilon vitifolium*. In the second volume there are fine pictures of *Metrosideros*, an aloe, belladonna lilies and flowering sempervivums. There are two other volumes containing paintings of specimens of mesembryanthemums and pelargoniums, some by Gwen and some by her sister Cicely, who also painted some seascapes.

The exchange of plants with Kew continued in 1902-03, but no plants or seeds passed either way between Kew and Tresco in 1904. According to the *Gardener's Chronicle* of 28th January 1905, the winter of 1904-05 was very mild:

'The winter at Scilly has been the best on record. The thermometer at Tresco Abbey has only on one night fallen below 40° Fahrenheit. There has been little wind. The flowering of the pelargoniums is the best ever experienced in winter.'

In 1906 plants from Tresco began to be featured from time to time in Curtis's *Botanical Magazine*, a publication which has appeared continuously since founded by William Curtis in 1787, is edited from the Royal Botanic Gardens, Kew, and whose name has recently been changed to *The Kew Magazine*. The first plant from Tresco to appear was *Rhodostachys pitcairniifolia* (*Fascicularia pitcairniifolia*), which was published as Tab.8087 in Volume No. 132. The primary purpose of this magazine is to present '... coloured figures with descriptions and observations on the botany, history and culture of choice plants.' Appearance in it is a kind of accolade for the plant concerned.

Exchange of plants between Kew and Tresco continued in 1907 and in November of that year a new source of supply was tapped. New Zealand scientists mounted an expedition in that month to the Auckland and Campbell Islands in which Captain Arthur Dorrien Smith took part. They landed first on Stewart Island on 14th November, and could progress only with difficulty. Captain Arthur in his report, said that:

'The island is very rugged and covered with dense bush comprised of *Metrosideros lucida*, which is dominant and exceedingly gnarled and straggling. *Podocarpus hallii, Dacrydium cupressinum* and *D.intermedium* are very prominent, whilst *Panax simplex, Leptospermum scoparium, Veronica buxifolia, Dracophyllum longifolium* and *D.pearsoni*, form the lower scrub. But the chief feature of the island plant-life is the wonderful moss cushions, the carpet of the forest appearing as if the whole was covered in boulders clad with moss, but in reality these heaps are solid moss and liverworts, whilst *Sphagnum* abounds in the bogs. The Tree Ferns, *Hemitelia smithii*, are plentiful as well as Polypodiums, Aspidiums and other ferns.'

On the morning of the 15th November they landed on the Snares Islands. These islands Captain Arthur described as:

'...composed of basalt, rising some 500 feet, with precipitous cliffs ... covered with dense semi-prostrate scrub, composed of *Olearia lyallii* and *Senecio muelleri*: the former with its silvery foliage is easily distinguished from the vivid glossy green of the latter. On the edge of this scrub, and along the cliff, grow the long coarse grasses *Poa littorosa* and *P.foliosa*, and mixed with them is *Veronica elliptica*, and a plant which resembles in foliage a vegetable marrow, but in reality is *Stilbocarpa*, the flower of which, although green and black, forms a fine head ....'

Moving some distance further south to the Auckland Islands on 16th November they found exploration when they landed even more impeded:

'... The hills rise abruptly to 2,000 feet. The Rata (*Metrosideros lucida*) dominates the lower zone to 600 feet. Then comes the long Tussock grass, *Danthonia bromoides*, mixed with *Suttonia divaricata*, stunted Rata and *Coprosma*, to about 800 to 1000 feet .... The *Danthonia* forming large tussocks grows in its own peat, and where it is absent the bushes have grown in the shelter of the pits thus formed, and have had the effect of making the surface rough and exceedingly difficult to traverse. It resembles a succession of peat hags, and a fall off a *Danthonia* tussock means complete

disappearance and much annoyance. But if this form of country is bad, perhaps the *Suttonia* scrub is worse, for matted together by the necessity of protection from the violent gales, it is about waist deep. There are three methods adopted for progressing: you must either walk on the top, roll over the top, or crawl underneath. The two former methods were generally adopted . . . .it took four of us two and a half hours to drop down a hill from 700 feet to sea level, the distance scarcely a mile.'

They carried on their explorations in these appalling conditions for ten days, visiting among other places, Ewing Island, occupied by a 'forest of *Olearia lyallii*, which covered the low island from one end to the other.' Where clear places did occur they found *Poa littorosa* growing in large tussocks. Next day they landed on Disappointment Island, which had not hitherto been explored botanically. Here they:

'saw up the hill a *Poa littorosa* (tussock), and a magnificent meadow of *Ligusticum latifolium* . . . whilst in addition *Pleurophyllum speciosum*, *Stilbocarpa polaris*, *Veronica benthami* and *Bulbinella rossii* formed the chief vegetation of the island.

Seeds and plants collected for Tresco by Captain Arthur were in due course made available to Kew and details of the various consignments may be found in Kew records. Many plants did not of course survive at either Tresco or Kew and a proportion only of the seeds germinated. The Appendix lists all the plants growing on Tresco in 1982, some of which may be traced back to these introductions.

Captain Arthur embarked on another expedition in 1909, this time to Western Australia. Starting on the 1st October for Cape Naturaliste, he began to see interesting plants from the train:

'One of the large species of *Conospermum* was very conspicuous: the local name is Smoke Bush . . . .Then would appear in masses of bright blue a species of *Leschenaultia* . . . .*Anigozanthus manglesii* also abounded in the moister places . . . .the forest trees are . . . composed of several kinds of *Eucalyptus*, chiefly *E.marginata* (Jarrah) and *E.patens* (Blackbutt) . . . .we ran through a forest of magnificent great trees of *E.gomphocephalus* which, with their great white trunks towering up to between 120ft. and 150ft. in height, were very striking.'

On the way to Yallingup Cave House they found the neighbourhood:

'. . .especially prolific in leguminous and myrtaceous plants, especially scrub acacias, melaleucas and *Agonis*; these formed a veritable jungle, through which it was very difficult and prickly to push, the acacias being largely represented by the sub-genera *Pungentes* and *Bipinnatae* . . . .*Agonis flexuosa* showed to great advantage, with its thick, short butt, large-headed, much-branched top, and its beautiful weeping habit; it was covered with a mass of small white flowers . . . .'

After passing through a large swampy flat:

'. . .covered with low-growing *Melaleuca*, *Hypocalymma robusta*, *caladenias* (terrestrial orchids) and droseras (sundews). . . .I noticed a large patch of *Boronia* (pink) growing in a swampy place, and every minute we passed fresh flowering plants, including a large variety of most lovely pimelias, the white *Pimelia spectabilis*, and all shades of pink to the bright little *P.ferruginea*; the brilliant blue dampieras; the yellow hibbertias and *Conostylis*; and both mauve and yellow patersonias (fringe lilies) . . . .'

The next morning they went down the ravine to the seashore, finding stunted *Melaleuca* and the sea-grass *Spinifex longifolius*, a shrub about three to four feet tall like *Correa virens*, but with a pendulous orange and red flower, which Captain Arthur thought was *Diplolaena dampieri*, and some magnificent *Xanthorrhoea* (black boys).

All round the Cave House and south towards the Margaret River Captain Arthur found, 'an excellent place for collecting', the species being very numerous. They were all in flower and presented a gorgeous sight

'. . .*Banksia grandis* is especially fine, and so is *B.attenuata*; then there was a fine holly-leaved *Dryandra*, which was very striking, and several species of *Boronia*, and species of *Tetratheca* with both pink and white flowers. Ferns are only very poorly represented in Western Australia; their place is taken by species of *Macrozamia*, *Xanthorrhoea* and *Kingia*, the first two being very abundant.'

A visit to the lighthouse at Cape Naturaliste revealed more floral riches:

'. . . Every yard almost disclosed more flowering plants; the leguminous plants are very lovely, especially the chorizemas and kennedyas. We found a large patch of *Acacia saligna* . . . and here and there were patches of the blue *Leschenaultia*, a creeping *Dryandra*, a *Calythrix* and the little Iris-like *Sisyrinchium* . . . we . . . were much struck by finding masses of *Templetonia retusa* in flower; it is a fine thing . . . .'

Captain Arthur concluded his account by saying 'thus ended our first insight into the flora of South-Western Australia, over which I was greatly dazzled and much confused; but its magnificence has left a very deep impression.'

The next base was at Bridgetown. Striking east from there, the first day's collecting was very wet. They got, however 'a good many specimens of plants—hibbertias, hakeas, dryandras, leucopogons and the brilliant blue dampieras, and very many bright-flowering leguminous plants'. Later they saw the 'gorgeous red *Leschenaultia*' on the way to Kojonup and the white gum, *Eucalyptus redunca* and a Kangaroo Paw (*Anigozanthus*), new to them. This variety was of a terracotta colour. On the way to Cranbrook they encountered: 'yellow *Verticordia*; a small smoke-bush (*Conospermum*), a heath-like shrub, with a mass of small white cottony flowers, *Beaufortia* (scarlet after the manner of *Callistemon*); a *Billardiera*, a bell-flowered creeper . . . gastrolobiums, with their bright pea-flowers; *Kunzea*, *Calythrix*, *Andersonia*, bright blue dampieras and *Leschenaultia* . . . many white-flowered epacrids, and *Chamaescilla corymbosa*, with its crinkly foliage, varying from green at the base to bright red at the tips, with a beautiful bright-blue flower head, some four or five inches high . . .'

They also saw the 'orange-flowered *Bossiaea*' . . . Orchids and droseras,' commented Captain Arthur, 'seem to grow anywhere and everywhere, in swamps, on sand-heaps, or mountain-tops alike; but the species seem to be ever-changing, and their flowers are very lovely, especially the latter, which were white, red, coral, mauve and yellow.'

At Cranbrook itself they found many new plants on the sand-plain, 'especially banksias, dryandras, scrub hakeas, melaleucas, lambertias and flame-flowered *Eremaea*.' Driving along the north side of the Stirling Range they saw 'large numbers of hakeas, banksias, leucopogons, dryandras and beaufortias, and . . . the beautiful blue *Dampiera eriocephala* . . . .'. Further on, at Warrungup Hill, they found the 'mountain bell' they had been told about:

'very near the base of the hill, . . . it proved to be a *Darwinia*, with its beautiful pink bell-like flowers; it grew in the shade of the lovely white Epacrid *Lysinema*, and close by were glorious bushes, eight feet tall, of the striking Protead *Isopogon latifolius*, with cones of pink flowers. We found also *Dryandra formosa*, a mass of golden-yellow flowers; and a species of *Beaufortia*, as well as a yellow *Melaleuca*, *Dampiera eriocephala*, a climbing *Stylidium*, with a flower-head like a pink phlox, and many other Myrtaceous and Epacridaceous plants, and perhaps least, but yet none the less glorious sight on the top of the mountain, a species of *Utricularia*, and a beautiful crimson orchid, an inch high. I should also mention a mauve pea-flowered shrub, called *Burtonia*; a fern, *Asplenium flabellifolium*, to say nothing of the various gastrolobiums, with their many-coloured pea-flowers.'

On the other side of the hill they 'saw masses of a heath-like blue-flowering shrub, which . . . turned out to be a *Conospermum* . . . .Not very far away we obtained our first sight of *Banksia coccinea*, a truly beautiful little *Banksia* with brilliant scarlet cones of flowers.' **Moving their camp nine miles further on they found** 'a large bushy *Pimelea*, *Xanthosia rotundifolia* (the Southern Grass-flower), both white and very pretty, as well as many Leucopogons and a very brilliant *Chorizema*, and also the lovely blue *Platytheca galioides*, a heath-like plant about eighteen inches high . . . .We found here fine specimens of the silvery-foliaged *Kingia*, which is by far the most graceful of the "Black-boy" tribe.' **Not far away they encountered** '*Banksia brownii*, remarkable for its pinnate leaves and the great size of its flower,' **another *Banksia*, which they could not identify, a *Bossiaea*, and *Aotus gracillima*. There was** 'scrub gum at a height of over 3,000 feet' and a veritable jungle of a species of *Thomasia*, an *Acacia*' **which he could not identify,** 'a variety of *Acacia longifolia* out of flower; also a *Mirbelia*, a mauve pea-flowered prickly bush.'

In December 1909 Captain Arthur transferred his collecting activities to Chatham Island which lies some distance off the east coast of New Zealand. The island is a little over 30 miles long and has an area of about 350 square miles. On the day of his arrival he visited the swamp on the shore of Lake Huro:

' . . . In the wettest part I found . . . various forms of swamp plants such as *Leptocarpus simplex* and *Carex appressa* vr.*sectoides*, with here and there *Phormium tenax*; but as soon as the swamp became the least bit drier one came upon the lowland forest, first *Copromosa propinqua*, then *Suttonia coxii*, with more flax, and *Arundo conspicua*, while further in one found plenty of *Olearia traversii*, *Pseudopanax chatamicum*, *Coprosma chatamica* and *Suttonia chatamica*; *Dracophyllum arboreum* also occurs, and a very fine *Astelia* . . . (probably) A.*nervosa* . . . On the edge of this swamp I saw *Senecio huntii* . . . .'

The next day he turned his attention to the forest:

' . . .On the island the trees grow to no great height(20 to 25 feet) and the tops are kept well in order by the wind and form a compact mass. I saw some fine trees of *Veronica gigantea*, 20 feet high, in full flower and *Senacio huntii* just coming into flower. The commonest trees were *Corynocarpus laevigata* (the Karaka), *Coprosma chatamica*, *Hymenanthera chatamica*, *Olearia traversii*, *Corokia macrocarpa*, *Pseudopanax chatamicum* and *Suttonia chatamica*. The native pepper, *Piper excelsum*, was fairly common and the whole was entwined with endless Supple Jacks(*Rhipogonum scandens*), while I saw at least five varieties of tree ferns, *Cyathea dealbata*, *C.medullaris*, *C.cunninghamii*, *Dicksonia antarctica* and *D.squarrosa*, and a few *Rhopalostylis sapida* dotted about . . . .filmy and other ferns

abound . . . sphagnum patches were colonised by several plants, chiefly *Gleichenia dicarpa* and some *Pteris esculenta* . . . and the lovely little *Pratia arenaria* . . .'.

Captain Arthur next visited the southern part of the island. On the way there he found the country covered with *Pteris esculenta*, some *Phormium tenax*, *Dracophyllum arboreum* and *Styphelia robusta* in the drier parts, while *Dracophyllum paludosum* occupied the more swampy ground. After some time, he says, 'we came across *Olearia semidentata* in full flower; it is a beautiful sight, covered with its purple daisy flowers like a glorified Michaelmas Daisy; the ray florets a light mauve and the centre is a dark purple.' A 'peculiar kind of rush-like grass, *Lepyrodia traversii*, seems to grow in association with it.' He went to some trouble to collect *Aciphylla dieffenbachii*:

'. . . growing on the precipitous slopes of the cliffs, which are here 600 feet high, one flowering plant only being accessible . . . .The edge of the cliff was covered with *Phormium tenax*, long grass, some *Astelia nervosa*, *Veronica chathamica*, more erect than the type, and the lovely little pink or white flowered *Geranium traversii*, while on the ledge of a cliff below I noticed . . . a mass of *Myosotidium nobile* (the Chatham Island Lily) and the giant nettle *Urtica australis*. I also found *Olearia chathamica* in abundance growing on the cliff a little further along; also *Senecio lautus* and *S.radiolatus*.'

In the country between the Great Lagoon (Te Whanga) and Lake Huro there were more plants:

'Growing on the low limestone cliffs bordering the lagoon I found *Styphelia richei* . . . .*S.robusta*, *Sophora tetraptera* (Koi), *Phormium tenax*, *Linum monogynum*, *Geranium traversii*, *Veronica dieffenbachii* and *Samolus repens* . . . a lovely little creeper.'

Although many of the most striking plants found by Captain Arthur in the course of his expeditions are mentioned and illustrated in articles which he wrote about them for the *Journal of the Royal Horticultural Society* and elsewhere, comprehensive lists of all plants found by him seem to have survived in respect of his Western Australian journeys only. Three lists exist at Kew of these plants as named by a contemporary botanist, Dr. Domin. These contain 270, 84 and 133 plants respectively, totalling 487 in all.

Volume 135 of the *Botanical Magazine*, published in 1909, contained Tab.8291, which was a plate of another Tresco-grown plant, *Euryops virgineus*, which is a native of South Africa. The next year, 1910, three plants were figured in Volume 136 of the *Magazine*, Tab. 8301, *Agonis marginata* from Western Australia, Tab. 8305, *Pittosporum colensoi* from New Zealand and Tab. 8331, *Psoralea affinis*, from

Olearia semidentata as discovered in an upland bog on Chatham Island, New Zealand

South Africa. This year the Scilly flower industry began to run into difficulty. The tremendous prosperity which it had experienced for many years was threatened by decay from within. Slackness in feeding the land and varying the crops ended in 1912 in catastrophe, thousands of bulbs failing to flower, or rotting where they stood. When war broke out, in 1914, the industry collapsed.

For a year or so after 1910, however, matters continued as usual. Plants from Tresco appeared once again in the *Botanical Magazine* in 1911 and 1912. Volume 137, for the former year, contains Tab. 8379, portraying *Prostanthera pulchella*, and Tab. 8407, showing *Aciphylla latifolia* (*Anisotome latifolia*). Volume 138, for 1912, shows in Tab. 8419 *Leptospermum scoparium var. nichollsii* and in Tab. 8420, *Olearia chathamica*. All these were introduced by Captain Arthur.

Although nothing was sent from Tresco to Kew in the ten years between 1914 and 1923, material was sent from time to time from Kew to Tresco and plants from Tresco continued to be featured in the *Botanical Magazine*. The quiescence of Tresco was doubtless due in the first part of the period to the prolonged illness of Thomas Algernon, who died in August 1918, and in the latter part to the absence of Captain (now Major) Arthur on war service. The plants which appeared in the *Botanical Magazine* were *Senecio kirkii* from New Zealand, which appeared in Tab. 8524 of Volume 139, issued in 1913; *Olearia semidentata* from Chatham Island, which had flowered at Scilly in 1913 and was shown in Tab. 8550 of Volume 140 of 1914; and *Metrosideros diffusa* from North Island, New Zealand, which had flowered at Tresco in 1914 and was figured in Volume 141, of 1915. After a blank year in 1916, *Senecio hectori* appeared in 1917 in Volume 143. This is also a New Zealand plant.

Nothing further appeared in the *Botanical Magazine* until 1920, when *Metrosideros collina*, which had flowered for the first time at Tresco in June 1918, was featured in Tab. 8846 in Volume 146, issued in 1920. In the aftermath of the war there were urgent problems which had to be faced and Major Arthur devoted considerable effort to resuscitating the flower, potato and farming industry of the Isles. The cost of restoring various buildings on Scilly which had become very dilapidated, and of other restorative measures, was however far beyond his personal means. The days when an 'Emperor' could shoulder everything had long since gone. Major Arthur relinquished responsibility for all but Tresco and the uninhabited islands to the Duchy of Cornwall in 1922, although as Chairman of the Council he continued to exercise much influence over the rest. The popularity of the Isles as a holiday resort increased year by year and the income of the islanders was correspondingly augmented. On 2nd August 1919, a note in the *Gardener's Chronicle* showed the way things were going:

'*Trade with the Scilly Isles*: The question of the development of these islands for the purpose of securing a permanent steamboat service between the islands and the mainland has engaged the attention of the landed proprietor, the islanders and the Chamber of Horticulture for some time. Certain steps have been taken, and it has been mutually decided that the Secretary of the Chamber shall prepare an independent report on the present condition and future possibilities of the isles, for use among the various interests concerned.'

A year after this article appeared, Sir Arthur Hill, Director of the Royal Botanic Gardens, Kew, published in *Kew Bulletin* No.5, of 1920, an article coupling the Tresco garden with the famous garden of Sir Thomas Hanbury at La Mortola in Italy; both contained magnificent plant collections of inestimable value to any botanist and horticulturist who cared to visit them. Sir Arthur's article is of interest because it presents a picture of the Tresco garden as it had developed and as it was seen by an authoritative outsider at a time when many of the exotic trees and shrubs were coming to maturity. It divides the garden into three: the granite rocks and cliffs near the house, with their colourful covering of mesembryanthemums and similar plants that enjoy the hot and dry situation, the higher ground above with numerous sheltered spots harbouring exotic trees and shrubs such as the Cape silver tree (*Leucadendron argenteum*), and the northern slope of the central hill which is ideal for shrubs such as rhododendrons which like cooler and moister conditions.

On 23rd September 1922, the *Gardener's Chronicle* carried an article which recorded the formation, under the Chairmanship of Major Arthur, of the Tresco Bulb-Growers Association, to foster cooperation within the industry. On 3rd and 17th February 1923, it carried the two parts of an article by Sidney P. Wells, who was at that time general manager of the Tresco estates. This article set out in considerable detail the situation as it was in the early 1920s and, although too long to be included here, is of value as a portrayal of the conditions of its time.

Another plant from Tresco was featured in Volume 149 of the *Botanical Magazine*, issued in 1923. Tab. 8998 shows the silvery foliage and compact racemes of bright yellow flowers of *Callistachys ovata*, which Major Arthur had raised from seed sent from Sydney in 1911. The next year, 1924, another Australian plant, *Kunzea ambigua*, appeared as Tab. 9032 in Volume 150. In its issue of 25th April, 1925, the *Gardener's Chronicle* published a letter from Major Arthur on a new subject, the growing of freesias in hanging baskets:

'References have been made in your paper to the cultivation of freesias in hanging baskets. I therefore enclose a photograph ... showing two baskets of freesia in our conservatory, as the illustration may interest many of your readers. These freesias are grown ... with great success, in wire baskets. The baskets are lined with moss, and sandy soil is then used, and the freesia corms are "built" in about 2½ inches from the wire frame, all round. The growths take the shortest route to the light, consequently flowers appear all round the basket. There is no great art in producing a fine effect, providing the corms have been thoroughly well dried off before planting is done and the usual attention paid to watering and cleanliness.'

The issues of the *Gardener's Chronicle* of 1st and 8th August 1925, carried letters from E.Brown of Hillside, Doddington, Kent, on yet another subject, *Echium* species grown at Tresco and their hybrids, mentioning the native species, *Echium vulgare*, the shrubby *E.callithyrsum*, the biennial *E.pininana* and *E.wildpretii*. Although Tresco continued to increase in popularity, the *Gardener's Chronicle* does not mention it again for ten years.

In December 1929 Tresco suffered one of the worst storms ever known there. The Major was away at the time. On the Wednesday the gale reached

ninety-three miles an hour from the south-east; on the Friday it reached 110 miles an hour, now blowing from the south-west; and on the Sunday, still as severe as ninety-one miles an hour, it had veered to the north-west. Six hundred trees were blown down and the garden was so strewn with branches and debris that it was hardly recognizable. Recovery was rapid, however, once the mess had been cleared away.

Five years later, in 1934, Tresco experienced very abnormal weather of another kind which had an effect on the flowering of plants there. Major Arthur wrote a letter about this which was published in the *Gardener's Chronicle* of 2nd February 1935:

'Very little rain fell at Tresco between mid-April and July 20th, 1934, but between the latter date and August 6, 3.24 inches were recorded, after which there was practically no rain until one and a quarter inches fell in mid-November, followed by over eight inches in December. The effect of the drought on the autumn-flowering and winter-flowering plants was peculiar. The first plants to flower after all the summer subjects had passed their best were the pineapple-scented *Salvia rutilans, Luculia pinceana* and the great bush groundsel, *Senecio grandifolius,* fifteen feet high by eighteen feet in diameter. These were certainly a month late, and were not at their best until quite the end of November. The curtain then seems to have dropped on tardiness and we found plants flowering at the latter end of December which normally do not flower until the end of March. To name some, *Buddleia paniculata* and B.*madagascariensis, Kennedya nigricana* and K.*prostrata, Sophora tetraptera, Erica melanthera* and E.*arborea, Rhododendron grande (argenteum)* and *Acacia decurrens var.normalis* were full out, while *Hardenbergia monophylla* and *Clianthus puniceus,* and the many *Cytisus* species, like C.*stenopetalus,* C.*hildebrandtii* and C.*proliferus* are close on their heels.'

The *Gardener's Chronicle* of 10th August 1935, contained a long letter from E.Brown of Cranleigh, Surrey, which gives an excellent description of what he saw on a visit to Tresco in June and shows that the garden had already recovered from any ill-effects it had suffered from the aberrations of the weather experienced a few months before. A beginning was made in 1935 of the compilation of an official list of species and varieties cultivated at that time in the garden, a preliminary count of which showed that the total reached about 3,500.

Volume 160 of the *Botanical Magazine* issued in 1937, portrayed in Tab. 9493 *Melaleuca linariifolia,* a plant supplied from Tresco. From this time onward, however, the shadow of the forthcoming 1939-45 war seems to have fallen over activities and caused a slackening off. Not until 1947 was Tresco again in the limelight. The *Gardener's Chronicle* of 25th January of that year carried a long article by J.W. Hunkin, the Bishop of Truro, describing the many flowers in bloom in the Tresco garden on New Year's Day. He divided them broadly into two classes, those which, although normally flowering at other times of the year, were showing some flowers on New Year's Day and those that normally flower in the winter. The tally was very impressive. The day before the article appeared, however, the show had been greatly damaged: a cold spell had begun which was more severe than any for over forty years, and very closely paralleled a similar spell in 1895, which had begun two days later but ended on the same day, 10th March. An article by Major Arthur in the *Gardener's Chronicle* of 24th May 1947, set

out in detail the effect of this severe weather on the vegetation at Tresco. Those who are impressed by coincidence will be struck by the fact that Bishop Hunkin's article drawing attention to the winter flowers on Tresco appeared at the precise moment they were destroyed!

Bishop Hunkin wrote two other articles on Tresco, which appeared in the issues of the *Journal of the Royal Horticultural Society* for May and June, 1947. These interesting contributions summarized the foundation and history of the garden on Tresco and gave an informative description of the plants it contained at the time he wrote. He followed these with another published in the *Gardener's Chronicle* for 4th October 1947 describing the state of the garden, which had made a remarkable recovery from the hard frosts of the previous winter and was displaying its accustomed mid-September show.

The lists of plants in flower at various times were augmented by a further list compiled at Tresco on Christmas Day, 1948, and published in the *Gardener's Chronicle* of 22nd January 1949. The list is surprisingly large, totalling more than 200 species and varieties in all, including nineteen pelargoniums, more associated with the summer than the winter. The *Gardener's Chronicle* for 5th March 1949, carried an article about the cut-flower industry:

'Heavy shipment of flowers from Scilly Isles: R.M.S. *Scillonian*, the steamer plying between the Scilly Isles and the Cornish coast on Tuesday, 15th February, carried a load of twenty-two tons of flowers, the largest of the season. With a continuance of mild weather and good conditions, cargoes will probably become larger as the season advances.'

The journal followed this on 31st December 1949, with another article forecasting a good season for 1950.

Major Arthur, who had for so long held the reins that it was difficult to imagine Tresco without him, died in 1955, and was succeeded as the leaseholder by the only one of his sons to survive World War II, Commander Thomas Mervyn Dorrien Smith.

An interesting development took place in the cut-flower industry in 1956; it was recorded by the *Gardener's Chronicle* in its issue of 7th January 1956:

'Flowers from the Isles of Scilly. The decision of the British European Airways to run a freight flower service from the Isles of Scilly to Cornwall is causing considerable discussion among the islands' daffodil growers. The new communally-owned steamer *Scillonian*, which comes into service in the spring, should in the opinion of many growers be given full support. Other growers feel that the air service which proved an excellent stand-by last year, when the boat was held up owing to bad weather, should not be neglected, for the flowers arrive in better condition after 20 minutes in the air, than they do after 3½ hours by sea.'

Another long article about Tresco written by Moira Savonius, and giving an excellent account of the garden as she found it, was published in the *Gardener's Chronicle* on 12th November, 1960. She prefaced her account by commenting that the garden now contained 4,000 species, a large proportion of which came from the southern hemisphere; she found it 'difficult to believe that only 125 years ago Tresco was a bleak island without a single tree and with no shrub larger than a dwarf gorse bush!'.

Another informative article about Tresco, from the pen of W.Sykes, appeared in the *Gardener's Chronicle* of 7th October 1961. Three years later, on 3rd October 1964, D.A.J.Little used the columns of that journal to give an account of the plants there which were originally all classed as *Mesembryanthemum* but are now split into a number of separate genera. These flourish at Tresco, cascading in profusion over the rocks and cliffs (even outside the garden) in all colours from white to pink, yellow, copper and red to purple and providing a large part of the colour of the garden. Could he see it, the sight would delight Augustus Smith, who had so greatly enjoyed the 'mesmerisms', as he called them.

In 1973 Commander Thomas Mervyn died and the lease passed to the present holder, his son Robert Arthur Dorrien Smith, who continues, in a greatly changed and more difficult world for estate owners, to maintain the garden in the great tradition of his predecessors.

Silvery Kingias discovered on the 1910 expedition in New Zealand

INCREASE AND MULTIPLY

CHAPTER VIII

*Where'er you tread, the blushing flow'rs shall rise
And all things flourish where you turn your eyes.*
Pastorals: *Summer* Alexander Pope

Although in the foregoing chapters we have been dealing with sub-tropical plants, nowhere has the term 'sub-tropical' yet been defined. Perhaps the best way to describe them is to say that they are plants that do not like extremes. They die if frosted and do not care for temperatures not far above freezing point if exposure is prolonged. Many of them, however, short of jungle or desert conditions, will stand a good deal of heat, drought, or wet, and virtually all like plenty of light. A great many will thrive in an English summer but go under in the damp cold of an English winter. Beyond that it is not possible to say much more. Sub-tropical bedding was, indeed, a feature of Victorian parks and gardens and may still be seen in municipal gardens. Tresco gets over the winter problem quite simply. Frosts are rare, the climate is equable most of the time, and high temperatures and prolonged drought are equally uncommon. There are, however, borderline plants which struggle even at Tresco: plants whose names appear in one list of introductions but are absent when the tally is next taken; plants which are reintroduced only to vanish again. But most of these are rare enough to be notoriously difficult.

If you set out to grow sub-tropical plants in a garden on the mainland of the British Isles you have to resign yourself to tackling that winter problem first. It is no good buying plants or raising them if you cannot keep them. Of course, there are many sheltered gardens, particularly near the west coast under the influence of the Gulf Stream where what is said applies only in part, but for the average British garden a greenhouse or frame which will keep out frost is essential. It is true that mature plants which have developed a woody stem will often be found to be hardier than they were when young, and will get through quite a cold winter outdoors if in a sheltered place, and protected by a covering, but this stage comes later. The first piece of advice for the would-be grower of sub-tropical plants must therefore be to think hard as to how plants can be nursed through the winter, with the idea always in mind that they will soon get too large to keep under shelter. That's your main problem. Solve that one, and you are well on your way!

The next problem to be faced is the stocking of your new garden. Plants are multiplied by various methods of propagation. In a single chapter it is not possible to do more than deal very superficially with this subject. Whole books are available which specialize in various aspects of it, and those who want more precise and detailed information must look elsewhere. As in everything else, science has stepped in with sophisticated methods which the amateur cannot achieve unless he has considerable means at his command. The large nurseries which supply garden centres which themselves supply the few plants in the high street shop nowadays begin their operations in the laboratory test-tube, methods of the multiplication of plants by what is called micro-propagation now being used which are far removed from the rule-of-thumb practices of our forefathers. But that does not mean that rule-of-thumb practices do not work any more and it is these that will produce pleasing results for amateurs.

There are a number of ways in which your collection may start. You may be given a plant by a friend who has grown it himself. If that happens, pump him to see what he did to produce it. You may buy or be given one as a house plant and then wonder what to do with it when it stops flowering, and how you can get it to flower again. You can't pump the shopkeeper, who is likely to know very little about the plants he sells, but if you bought it from a nursery you may get some useful practical advice from them. The nurseryman is likely to be helpful because it doesn't pay him to sell plants which die very quickly, as customers won't return. Most people begin in this way, often when they are quite young, but it is not really the best way to start, nor the best way to get the most enjoyment and satisfaction from your sub-tropical gardening. That comes when you have raised a plant from seed, tended it perhaps over a period of years and then, the first flower appears on it. This brings us to getting the seeds to germinate.

Seeds are usually sown in pots or pans, which must be clean. If you use an old pot, see that it is thoroughly scrubbed and dried before use. This is to get rid of any harmful microscopic organisms that might attack the seedlings. Soil through which water cannot pass freely will become sour, so you must put some clean crocks, bits of old pots or stones in the bottom to ensure adequate drainage. The earth will, however, wash through these if there is not some barrier to prevent it doing so and it is usual to put in some coarse dead leaves on top of the crocks. These, while effectively retaining the soil, allow the water to pass through. Then comes the potting soil itself or, if you prefer a more accurate description, the seed germination medium. Prepared potting material may be bought but, if you prefer to do so, you may mix your own or, as some gardeners do, use the bought material as a base and add to it or alter it as their experience has taught them.

Whatever you do, the result should be light in texture. A standard mixture which achieves this result may be made up from one part sand, one part compost and two parts well-aerated soil. The last constituent, the soil, must be sterilized before use. This can be achieved by putting it in a metal container and heating this over a fire or stove, stirring it so that all is adequately heated, or mixing it with a certain amount of water and bringing it to the boil. In the latter case it will have to be dried before use.

Burnt earth is also suitable. Fill up your pot or pan with this potting soil to within about an inch of the top. It is advisable to sift the top part so that the surface is a layer of fine particles. The soil must then be pressed down with a block of wood, and it is ready for the sowing of the seed.

Large seeds may be placed individually, but whatever their size, all but the smallest seeds must be covered with a layer of fine sifted soil about equal to the thickness of the seeds. Smaller seeds may be mixed with sand before being shaken on to the surface in order to ensure an even distribution. The very smallest seed should not be covered. When the surface has again been pressed down with the block of wood, pots containing larger seed may be watered from a can through a fine rose, but those containing the smaller seeds should be placed in water until it has soaked up through the soil and the surface is moist. Never on any account water directly from a can without a rose, or you will wash your valuable seeds away.

If you have a propagator, and small plastic versions for the amateur have been available for some time, you may place your pot in it and await germination. Otherwise, your pot may be covered with a piece of glass, leaving a small space for ventilation, and put in a sheltered place. Now we come to the trickiest part. Seeds that are germinating need to be kept just moist, but not too wet. If they are allowed to become too dry, they will receive a check and possibly die. If they become too wet, and this is the more common fault, air will be excluded from around them and 'damping off' fungi seize their chance to attack and kill them. All experienced gardeners will probably agree that there is no more doleful sight than a pot of healthy seedlings to which this has happened. Upright and vigorous yesterday, today they lie about wilting and dying in sad disarray.

As soon as the seeds germinate, and under-soil heating is often used to encourage this, they may be brought into the light, but not directly into full sun, or where they will be battered by rain. When they are big enough to handle they may be transferred into more permanent quarters. If they are to be used as pot plants and are sturdy enough this may be the pots in which they are to flower, although some smaller and weaker species and varieties may, while they are gathering strength, need an interim spell in a smaller pot. Again, potting soil specially prepared for the purpose may be bought, or your own mixture made up from sterilized soil or burnt earth mixed with compost in the proportion of three to one. The bottom of the pots must, of course, be covered with drainage crocks as described earlier.

Some plants which propagate themselves by seed also have other ways of increasing. The most familiar of these are the spring flowers, daffodils, tulips, crocus, etc. that are grown from bulbs or corms. After flowering the old bulb makes small ones around it which may be detached and grown on until they are large enough to flower. Gardeners do not, however, usually attempt to grow their own replacements, but buy in new stock every year from the specialist growing areas of which, of course, the Scilly Isles is one. Some plants make tubers, runners or suckers which may be used to produce new plants. Other plants make bulbils or even miniature versions of themselves along the stem or leaves or

elsewhere which drop off and root to make new plants. Others merely grow into clumps which divide or may be divided as the years go on, the older parts eventually dying away. Not satisfied with these natural methods, man has invented for himself other ways of increasing plants vegetatively, i.e. without the intervention of the seed-making process or the formation of parts which separate naturally from the parent.

One artificial method of increasing plants is the growing of new ones from portions cut off from an existing plant. These pieces, known as cuttings, are taken in such a way that it is known that with a little encouragement they can be induced to form a separate plant. The pieces may be part of the stems, leaves or roots, the first being most commonly used. Cuttings may come from the hardwood or the softwood. Hardwood branches are mature enough to have replaced the original soft green skin of the young shoot with a thin layer of brown bark. Cuttings taken from hardwood are usually between six and fifteen inches long. They should be cut off cleanly with a sharp knife at both ends, the lower cut being made just below a bud. Many hardwood cuttings will root outdoors in a bed of sand or sandy soil, which should not contain too much organic matter because this may encourage harmful fungi. The leaves should be removed from the lower third of the cutting, a hole made with a blunt-ended dibber, and the bared part of the cutting inserted into the hole. It is important then that the soil should be firmed around it all the way up from the bottom of the hole. Failure to do this, leaving large air spaces around the cutting at its lower end, may deter it from rooting properly.

Cuttings may also be rooted in pots and, if this method is used, should be placed in the sand or sandy soil near the edge of the pot. With either method the cutting should be sheltered from strong sunlight and the soil kept moist. An indication of the process of root formation may be obtained from the growth of the leaf buds. These will begin to shoot before roots are developed and, if these are forming, will grow with increasing vigour as they begin to take up nourishment. Prepare for disappointment, therefore, if the leaves begin to grow but gradually fail. When the cuttings are obviously in good heart, take them from the pot with the greatest care to avoid injury to the new roots, half-fill a new pot with soil prepared as for potting seedlings, place your plant in the pot and fill with soil gently pressed down. Vigorous hardy rooted cuttings may, if preferred, be planted straight into the open ground.

Softwood cuttings come from the green ends of branches and, being immature, must retain their leaves, which produce their food supply, so that they lose water readily. They must always, therefore, be protected from sun and drying winds. Otherwise they are treated in the same way as hardwood cuttings, put in a pot and, when rooted and well established, given similar treatment. Cuttings may also be made from pieces of stem with a leaf-bud and from pieces with a bud without a leaf taken from dormant ripened wood. They may be made too from leaves and from pieces of root. Guidance on these more specialized cases may be found in books devoted to plant culture.

Both hardwood and softwood cuttings, and other types which are known to be slow-rooting, may benefit from being dealt with in a closed frame in which

the moisture level may be maintained at a high level. The humidity may be kept high by fine water sprays, a method called mist propagation, but this is for the professional or the advanced amateur rather than the average gardener. A sophisticated treatment that is available to the least pretentious gardener is, however, the use of plant hormones to stimulate rooting. These proprietary preparations contain growth promoting substances. They may be bought freely and should be used in accordance with the instructions provided. Their introduction has greatly increased the success rate of both professional and amateur gardeners with cuttings of difficult subjects.

Another often easy method of increasing plants is known as layering. This is a process which occurs naturally in many plants. Stems lying on the soil are stimulated by the conditions to put out roots and in time grow into separate plants. The process may be seen operating with large trees in parks and public gardens. Beeches and horse-chestnuts often make low branches which, rubbing on the ground as the tree is moved by the wind, receive injuries to the bark from which roots develop, forming in time a new tree which grows as large as its parent. As the old tree ages and dies, the process continues, the group of trees forming around it eventually spreading, if unchecked, into a copse. Plants which cannot be raised from seed, such as hybrid rhododendrons, and which are also difficult subjects for cuttings may often be successfully layered. The process used with shrubs generally is simple in the extreme and designed to follow the natural process as closely as possible. The branch to be layered is twisted or bent and the leaves removed from the injured part so that it may be pegged down under about an inch of soil. The damage to the bark and the splitting of the tissue by the artificial injury simulates the natural occurrence, the flow of sap is checked, healing tissue is formed on the wound and, being under the soil, roots are encouraged to emerge. As well as pegging down the branch, it is usual to tether its tip to a small stake to avoid accidental disturbance. In a few weeks time, gentle and careful inspection will establish whether or not new roots have been formed.

It is essential that during this period the layer should be well watered, as drying out will hinder or stop growth. When it is clear that the layer has taken hold and is growing well, the link with the parent may be severed, but the new plant should be allowed a period to adjust itself to its new separate role before being lifted to be planted elsewhere. The eventual move may, of course, be facilitated if the layer is induced to root itself not directly in the ground, but in a box of soil. Layering of plants other than shrubs follows the same general lines but the part to be layered is not bent or twisted but actually cut to expose the tissue. The cut is made with a sharp knife about halfway through the stem and then upwards through its centre for about an inch so that a tongue is formed. The tongued portion is then placed in the soil with the wound held open so that the soil is in contact with every part of the wound surface.

The habit of growth of some plants is not favourable to layering in the ground, or the process is found to be difficult. To overcome such problems the layering may be transferred into the air. While avoiding some difficulties this, however, introduces another: drying is far more rapid in the air than in the soil.

Air layering in the past was therefore a more chancy business than it is now, since the invention of modern waterproof plastics, and was confined almost entirely to greenhouse plants which could more easily be kept constantly moist.

As in ground layering, a cut is made with a sharp knife to the centre of the chosen stalk just below a leaf or joint and the knife is then turned upwards to make a further cut up the centre of the stalk for about an inch and a half. A small wedge or twist of sphagnum moss or other moisture-retaining material is inserted to keep the cut open. A loose tube of transparent plastic is then slid over the section of branch with the cut and firmly secured with adhesive tape several inches below the cut so that it forms a bag with the branch inside. This bag is then packed with wet sphagnum moss and the top is closed and secured to the branch with adhesive tape above the cut, thus surrounding it with a covering which will remain permanently moist. The plastic tube should be long enough to allow the wet moss to extend several inches above and below the cut and the moss itself should be firmly packed into the cut. As the success of air layering depends upon the sap flowing freely, it is best done in April. The branch chosen should preferably be mature one-year-old wood which is, of course, in its prime.

As with cuttings, all the cut exposed surfaces of layered branches, whether in the soil or in the air, from which roots are expected to grow should be treated with a proprietary hormone preparation, used in accordance with the manufacturer's instructions. This will again greatly increase the chances of success. The layered branch will need support from a cane or another branch. When it is certain that roots have been formed, which can be ascertained by inspection of the moss through the plastic, the branch may be severed below the cut and the new plant gently transferred, doing as little damage as possible to the delicate new roots, to a pot, in which it may remain until it is firmly established.

Two slightly more delicate and difficult operations are also used to propagate desirable plants. These are called budding and grafting. Although they have different names and the techniques differ, these are basically the same process, the bringing of the tissues of two different plants together so that they will unite and grow as one unit. In each case one plant supplies the rooted part, which is called the stock and the other the bud or graft, which is called the scion. The two must be compatible with one another, which usually means that they must be within the same genus. Desirable varieties of plants developed in cultivation which will not come true from seed often lack vigour when asked to form their own roots. Propagation by cuttings or layering does nothing to solve this problem, and the only way they can be got to grow vigorously is to utilize the services of another plant which has a stronger root system, often the wild species, or one allied to it, from which the garden variety was developed. Budding and grafting are the means by which this is done.

Budding is extensively used in the propagation of bush roses, which are produced in many thousands on a commercial scale, but it is also used for fruit trees and ornamental trees. A good flow of sap is essential for successful budding and if the season is dry the subjects to be used should be copiously watered for some time before the operation is carried out. A trial cut of the root stock will show whether the supply of sap is enough. If it is, the bark will separate

easily from the wood and the sap will be obvious. The bud is obtained from the current year's growth of the scion, the most vigorous buds being found near the base of the stalk. Buds are in the axils of the leaves, which are not needed and should be cut off. The bud, together with its adjacent leaf-base, is detached from the stem with a sharp knife. The knife is inserted about half an inch below the bud and drawn up behind it, taking in a certain amount of wood, and brought out again about an inch above the bud, so that when the bud comes away it is on a narrow shield-shaped section of bark. The small amount of wood attached to the back of it is removed. A T-shaped cut is now made in the bark of the stock, just sufficiently deep to cut through it and no more, but enough to enable it to be gently lifted. The thin sliver of bark on which the bud is growing is slid into this cut so that its inner surface is pressed against the sappy tissue of the stock. Any small excess protruding above the cross-bar of the T is cut off so that the insertion may fit snugly. The whole is then bound with raffia, tightly enough to hold it together but not tight enough to cause strangulation. When it is obvious that a union has been made and the buds are swelling, the raffia may be cut to allow for expansion. A watch should be kept at all times to see that the stock does not become dry. When the bud is growing well and the sap obviously running, the stock above the bud may be cut off.

There are a number of methods of grafting, which have different names, based on the way the living tissue or cambium of the scion and stock are brought together. Although used but rarely, the simplest is splice grafting, where the pieces of scion and the stock are of the same thickness. Each is cut off with a sharp knife to form the joining surface, one with a downward and the other with an upward sweep at a narrow angle so that a long thin tongue is formed on each to fit the other. Care must be taken that the growing or cambium layers of each are together and the joint is then tied with raffia, which should be moistened and sealed with grafting wax.

The great problem with this method is that the sappy surfaces of the scion and stock slide easily against one another and it is very difficult to maintain them in the right position. Another method was therefore developed, known as whip and tongue grafting, which is basically the same but provides a means of preventing slipping. In this method downwards and upwards cuts of scion and stock are made as before but a second cut is also used. This is made from the other side to the first and slightly above or below it as required so that the cuts do not meet but when the excess is removed a short tongue and notch is formed across the centre of the stem. The process is carried out in opposite ways on scion and stock so that the results will fit together, the notch preventing any sliding. The joint is tied with moist raffia and sealed with grafting wax as before.

These methods are of use only when scion and stock are of the same diameter. When small scions have to be grafted on to stocks of a larger diameter different methods are used, but all are based on the same principle. The stock is split between bark and wood so that the long tongue made by shallow-angled cuts of the base of a scion may be introduced into the split which is thus held firmly and the growing layers are brought together. This is called cleft grafting. Several scion grafts may be put round the edge of a larger stock in this way. This is

called crown or mid grafting. There are also various other ways of grafting, stub grafting, side grafting, slit grafting and inverted L bark grafting, but these are specialist methods used in the rejuvenation or frameworking of old fruit trees, and those interested may consult specialist manuals. In all these cases the graft is kept firmly in place by tying with raffia and the wound covered completely with grafting wax until union is effected and the graft established.

It has, of course, been possible in this chapter to do no more than indicate broadly the methods by which the stock of plants in any garden, including the sub-tropical subjects which flourish so well at Tresco, may be increased and it should perhaps be said that each gardener works out for himself many variations and special treatments which he finds are effective in his case but are not in the manuals. The chapter would not be complete, however, without one word of warning. Many of the shrubs and trees bought by the gardening public have already been budded or grafted before purchase. In the case of bush roses the budding can hardly be discerned since it is below soil level. In other cases it may be more visible, but there are many people who buy such plants without being aware that they are not growing on their own roots. Nor are they aware that, given half a chance, the strong growing stock will throw up the sponge so far as fostering the weaker-growing scion is concerned and turn its energy to making shoots of its own. Beware, therefore, when that plant which looked so good in flower in the illustration in the nurseryman's catalogue, and seemed so healthy and vigorous when you bought it, starts throwing out a strong shoot from the base which looks different from the others. Given an inch it will take an ell and rob your cherished scion of its vigour.

Let us not dwell on this sour note. In everything one does with plants there are traps and enemies which the gardener learns by experience to avoid, and you will have to buy your own experience like everyone else! A more attractive subject concerns the sub-tropical plants you could try to grow to enhance the attractiveness of your garden. It is obviously impossible, in a group of islands like the British Isles, with many variations of climate from the notorious Rickmansworth frost pocket to the mildness of Torbay, to make suggestions for planting that will be applicable to all gardens. If you live outside the British Isles, then you must work out your own possibilities by trial and error.

The chances are, however, that you already grow some sub-tropical herbaceous plants. Nearly everyone has a geranium or two (correct name Pelargonium), either as part of a bedding scheme, as a clump in the herbaceous border or dotted among the shrubs. The roots have to be lifted before the winter and stored in a frost-free place if you want to keep them from year to year. Dahlias, too, are a popular favourite, but you must remember to lift and store the tubers or they will rot in frosty weather. Other half-hardy plants grown outdoors in the summer are abutilons, *Alternanthera* (much used in carpet bedding), begonias, calceolarias, cinerarias, cannas, *Coleus*, echeverias, fuchsias, gladiolus, lobelia, mesembryanthemums, petunias, *Plumbago*, salvias, *Santolina* and *Solanum*. There are others which may be found in nurserymen's catalogues.

If your ambition rises above herbaceous plants and you have the room, there are many trees and shrubs you may try. Some twenty-six species and

varieties of A*cacia* grow at Tresco and are one of the sights of the garden. A*cacia longifolia* and A.*melanoxylon* are two species that could be tried. A.*longifolia*, the long-leaved Sydney golden wattle, forms a large bush fifteen to thirty feet high with long yellowish-green leaves, and carries its flowers in long cylindrical spikes growing from the leaf-axils. At Tresco the sunny yellow of the flowers of this species makes one of the most striking shows of the winter months.

Among the hardiest acacias is the evergreen A.*melanoxylon*, the blackwood, which makes an upright dark green tree with yellowish-white fragrant flowers. Among other possibilities is A.*dealbata*, the silver wattle, which has grown at Tresco since 1853.

A*lbizia lophantha*, an Australian evergreen shrub similar to the acacias with pink or white flowers and fine fern-like leaves has survived outdoors at Tresco since 1855 and is therefore another possibility. A*nopterus glandulosus*, with white bell flowers is another. It, too, survives outdoors at Tresco. Two relatives of the hardy monkey-puzzle (A*raucaria araucana*), which are themselves less hardy, the Norfolk Island pine (A.*excelsa*) and the bunya-bunya pine (A.*bidwillii*) were established at Tresco in 1851 and 1857 respectively. The Tasmanian conifer A*throtaxis cupressoides* has been there nearly as long.

Four of the thirteen B*anksia* species in the garden have been growing at Tresco since 1890 and will have experienced many vicissitudes of weather in that time, which suggests that they might succeed elsewhere in conditions which were not too dissimilar. The species in question are B.*grandis*, B.*integrifolia*, B.*littoralis* and B.*aemula*. The bright scarlet flowers of B*eaufortia sparsa*, a West Australian shrub, may be seen on the Top Terrace at Tresco and B*omarea caldasii*, a twining plant from the Peruvian Andes with orange-yellow flowers spotted crimson decorates the Well Garden. The small rose-coloured flowers of B*oronia alata*, also from Australia, are found on the Agave Bank. B*ossiaea linophylla*, another elegant Australian shrub, with orange and purple flowers, also inhabits the Top Terrace.

One of the most attractive and useful large evergreen shrubs is B*rachyglottis repanda*, the rangiora from the North Island of New Zealand. Growing about twenty feet in height and the same width across, it has large leathery leaves which are white beneath, and very large terminal heads of small whitish flowers. On Tresco it is a very useful plant, being used to form broad hedges and thus provide shelter for other plants.

Two species of B*rachychiton* (*sterculia*), B.*acerifolia* which in its native Australia carries its bright red flowers amid its long-stalked deeply-lobed leaves to a height of 100 feet, and B.*diversifolia* from the same country, which is much smaller, have been in Tresco since 1904 and 1914 respectively. Their generic name is derived from their covering of hairs and scales, from the Greek *brachys*, short, and *chiton*, a coat of mail. Several of the nine species and hybrids of B*uddleia* grown at Tresco, for example B.*auriculata*, B.*madagascariensis* and B.*officinalis* are normally regarded as needing protection, but could be tried outdoors in suitable conditions. The Australian bottle- brushes, *Callistemon* species, so called because the flower-spike resembles a bottle-brush in shape, of which eight species are grown at Tresco, all grow well outdoors there and are well worth trying. A plant of

Callistemon citrinus var. 'Splendens' has grown by the front porch of my house at Weybridge for many years and, although cut back to ground level by severe frost in the late 1970s, recovered to some extent and still year by year encourages me by producing its lovely flowers. Since they are so prominent by the front door, the flowers often produce comment from visitors and a quite spurious reputation as a grower of exotic plants. This plant throws long arching branches in front of the bay window of my dining-room which, although they sometimes produce weird and ghostly scratching noises on the lattice window panes on winter evenings, make up for it in the summer by waving their glorious red spikes between the diners and the intrusive evening sun.

Callitris rhomboides (*C.cupressiformis*), the Oyster Bay pine from Australia seems from its locality of origin as if it fed on luscious seafood but, in fact, is rather a starved looking conifer, having long, very slender-jointed branches with minute scale-like leaves. It has, however, survived at Tresco since 1894, but would not be my first choice for an ornamental tree. On the other hand, *Calodendron capense*, the Cape chestnut, which was planted at Tresco in 1907 and is a most handsome evergreen tree (the name means beautiful tree, from *kalos*, beautiful, and *dendron*, a tree) with flesh-coloured flowers, is regarded as one of the finest trees from the Cape of Good Hope.

The yellow-flowered *Candollea tetrandra*, another very ornamental evergreen shrub from Australia, is an old Tresco inhabitant, having been there since 1890. One of the attractive features of the shrub *Carmichaelia cunninghamii* (named after the famous botanical collector Alan Cunningham) which has been at Tresco since 1914, is the long period during which it bears its lilac flowers, which seems to last all summer. The name *Cassia* is of some importance: it is the name used for the spice allied to cinnamon, for which the bark is used as a substitute, and is thus applied to plants having considerable economic value. There are more than two hundred species, mostly yellow-flowered. *Cassia corymbosa*, of South American origin, was the first species used as an ornamental plant, and has been grown at Tresco since 1856. The casuarinas take their name from a fancied resemblance of their long weeping leafless branches to the drooping feathers of the cassowary, an ostrich-like bird from Australia and Papua. Two species, *Casuarina equisetifolia* and *C.stricta*, the sheoke, have been at Tresco since 1914. Male and female flowers of *Casuarina* are borne separately.

One South American cactus is a long-standing inhabitant of Tresco: *Cereus peruvianus* var. 'Monstrosus', introduced into Tresco in 1854, may still be found on the Cactus Bank. The whitish-yellow flowers of *Cestrum parqui*, an evergreen shrub with long leaves, tapered at the ends, have scented the air of Tresco at night for the last fifty years, having been introduced from Chile in 1933. This fragrance is, however, a labour in vain, since the night-flying insects the plant hopes to attract in its native country are not here to be drawn. These plants are exotic enough, but asked what tree they thought was most characteristic of a sub-tropical garden, and by its appearance gave any garden an exotic air, the thoughts of most people would turn immediately to a palm-tree. If they had travelled in the Mediterranean area, they would probably think of the ubiquitous European fan palm, *Chamaerops humilis*. This has displayed its characteristic graceful and (to the

northern European) unfamiliar fan-shaped leaves in the Hop Circle at Tresco since 1856. Decorative to the highest degree, it is well worth growing, establishing itself easily from suckers.

Chrysocoma coma-aurea, called goldilocks from its mop of yellow flowers, a dwarf-growing South African evergreen, has been known in Britain since 1731, but was not established on the Top Terrace at Tresco until 1914. A specimen of *Cinnamomum camphora*, the white-flowered Japanese tree which is the source of camphor, has long been growing at Tresco, having been planted in the Long Walk in 1890. For more than a century, since 1863, the Australian kangaroo vine, *Cissus antarctica*, has thrown up its long climbing stems in the Well Garden. *Cistus albidus*, too, the rock rose with pale rosy-lilac flowers, has been there a long time. Together with its relatives, *C.monspeliensis*, with white flowers, and *C.salvifolius*, with white and yellow flowers, it has been in Tresco since 1914. The natural hybrid *C. x florentinus*, also white and yellow-flowered, has been there even longer, having been introduced in 1894.

Coleonema album, a small fragrant heath-like South African shrub with white flowers, which has grown on the Top Terrace since 1894, was joined in 1950 on that Terrace by its rather larger and more flamboyant relative, *C.pulchrum*, which has large red flowers. Also grown on the Terrace since 1914, the spines of *Colletia cruciata* from Uruguay are so formidable that it is sometimes planted below a window as a deterrent to burglars.

The palm-like genus *Cordyline*, named from the Greek *kordyle*, a club, because some species have large fleshy roots, is often seen in gardens under the name *Dracaena*. One of the most well-known species, *Cordyline australis*, the New Zealand cabbage tree, has been in Tresco since 1856, spreading its leaves in the Long Walk. Two of the varieties of this species in which the green of the leaves has been replaced by other colours, named 'Atropurpurea' and 'Aureo-striata' respectively, joined it in 1914, being planted in that year in the Hop Circle and by the ruins of the Old Abbey. The ribbon-like leaves of another species *C.banksii*, which was planted in the same year, may be seen on the Middle Terrace. When these were planted, however, two other species had already become well established in Tresco. *C.indivisa* from New Zealand, with narrow green leaves, to be found on the Long Walk, is a real veteran, having been planted in 1853. *C.baueri* from Norfolk Island, which grows on the Podalyria Bank, arrived in 1890. By the Old Abbey there also grows a hybrid bred at Tresco, *C. x scilloniensis*, raised from a cross between *C.australis* and *C.banksii* made in 1882.

One species of *Corokia*, a shrub with yellow flowers from New Zealand, grows well at Tresco outdoors, *C.buddleioides* having been in the Abbey Drive since 1856. The scent of *Coronilla glauca*, a small shrub from southern Europe whose beautiful yellow flowers are scented only in the daytime, has charmed visitors to the Middle Terrace since 1894. The attractive genus *Correa* from Australia is very free-flowering and a number of species and varieties are grown at Tresco. The first introduced were the white or pink-flowered *Correa alba* and the scarlet *C.pulchella* (*C.speciosa*) which arrived in 1850, closely followed in 1851 by the greenish-yellow *C.lawrenciana*. Since then *C.backhousiana* has been added, together with some varieties of *Corynocarpus laevigata*. The karaka from New Zealand is

another of the older inhabitants of Tresco, having been planted in 1856. The Chilean shrub *Crinodendron (Tricuspidaria) patagua* may be found in the Fernery, where it has grown since 1914. Four species of the tree fern *Cyathea* from New Zealand grow at Tresco. The graceful arching fronds of *C.dealbata*, the ponga, and *C.medullaris*, the mamaku, together with those of *C.smithii* (*Hemitelia smithii*), have been a familiar sight at Tresco since 1865, 1891 and 1894 respectively. The tree tomato, *Cyphomandra betacea* from Brazil, has lived in the Pear Tree Garden since 1914. Another plant from the early days of the garden is the scented *Cytisus fragrans* from southern Europe which was introduced in 1865 and which, together with the variety 'Magnifoliosus' of *C.maderensis* from Madeira, introduced in 1914, grows on the West Rockery. One other tender species of *Cytisus*, the white *C.proliferus* from the Canary Islands, introduced in the same year, may be found on the Long Walk.

The rimu, *Dacrydium cupressinum*, a large ornamental evergreen tree from New Zealand, has grown since 1914 near the tree ferns in the Abbey Drive. The striking creamy-white trumpets of *Datura cornigera*, known as the horn of plenty, have decorated the Lighthouse Walk South in the summer since 1914. Its relative, with orange-yellow flowers, *D.sanguinea* from Peru, is a more recent addition, having been planted in 1959 by the entrance gate. Three species of the tree-fern genus *Dicksonia* grow at Tresco. *D.antarctica* from Australia known as the tall tree fern because of its long trunk, has been in the Fernery since 1863. *D.squarrosa*, the wheki, has grown near it since the same year, but the third species, *D.fibrosa*, the wheki-ponga, was not introduced until 1914. *Dolichos lignosus*, the Australian pea, a twining plant with rosy-purplish flowers, has lived near the Old Abbey since 1890. The fine evergreen tree, *Drimys winteri*, from South America, which decorates the Long Walk, was planted in 1914.

Dryandra formosa from Australia, a member of a genus very like *Banksia* and as well worth growing for its beauty as members of that genus, has occupied a place along the Top Terrace since 1914. A noteworthy New Zealand tree-like evergreen shrub is the white-flowered *Entelea arborescens*, which has been in the Old Nursery Garden since 1914. The scarlet-flowered shrubby coral tree, *Erythrina crista-galli* from Brazil, is a fine sight during the flowering season from May to July and is a long-standing attraction at Tresco, having been planted in the Middle Terrace in 1853. Most of the fourteen escallonias growing at Tresco are cultivated varieties, but by far the longest established, with the exception of the variety *Escallonia paniculata* 'Floribunda' (*E.montevidensis*), which has been growing on the Podalyria Bank since 1850, are the three species, *E.laevis* (*Vigiera laevis*) from the United States, planted in 1856, *E.rosea* from Chile, planted in the same year, and *E.revoluta* also from Chile, planted in 1894.

Some twenty species of the Australian genus *Eucalyptus* grow at Tresco, all planted in this century with the exception of the Tasmanian blue gum, *E.globulus*, which has grown in the Long Walk since 1848 and the stringy-bark, *E.obliqua*, which was planted in the part of the garden called Higher Australia in 1894. The latter has the peculiar property of releasing its bark in large slabs, a quality rendering it of great use to the aborigines for building and canoe-making.

Eugenia paniculata, a myrtle-like shrub from Puerto Rico planted in 1959

also grows in the part of the garden called Higher Australia, and its relative *E.smithii* which grows into a small tree with very numerous small white flowers, may be found in the Long Walk Centre where it was planted in the same year. *Fatsia japonica*, the fig leaf palm, familiar to many as a house plant, and its variegated variety, both grow outdoors at Tresco, the former having been planted in the Long Walk in 1856 and the latter in Higher Australia in 1890. The Brazilian tree *Feijoa sellowiana*, introduced to Tresco in 1908, bears its white and red-centred flowers in autumn in the garden area called Old Abbey South. The genus *Ficus*, the fig-trees, contains many species. One notable species grown at Tresco is the Moreton Bay Fig or Australian banyan, *Ficus macrophylla*, planted in 1894 in the area called Lapageria Corner. The tall-growing evergreen climber *Freycinetia banksii*, planted in the Fernery in 1935, bears large edible fruit of a rich brown colour in its native New Zealand.

One of the most noteworthy collections in Tresco is that of the species and varieties of the genus *Fuchsia*. The varieties total in all more than 120, and with them are fourteen species. Some of the latter arrived at Tresco very early and were planted against Augustus Smith's Wall. Of these the first was the scarlet *Fuchsia corymbiflora* from Peru, planted in 1851. Three more were planted in 1856, *F.fulgens*, also scarlet, the deep red *F.microphylla* (this was planted in the garden area called Jam Tart), and the very showy scarlet and green *F.splendens*, all from Mexico. *F.cordifolia*, also scarlet and green and also from Mexico, was planted in the Well Garden in 1865. Three more species were added in 1894, the rose-coloured *F.arborescens* from Mexico in the Pebble Garden, *F.excorticata* from New Zealand on the Middle Terrace, and *F.procumbens* from New Zealand, which bears large magenta-crimson berries, in Jam Tart. Of the remaining five species, *F.colensoi* from New Zealand was planted in the Lily Garden in 1914, and the red *F.thymifolia* from Mexico in the same year at Augustus Smith's Wall. The rich crimson *F.boliviana* from Bolivia, *F.perscandens* from New Zealand, and *F.regia* (*Quelusia regia*) have all been planted more recently, the first in the Well Garden in 1950, the second near the Stone Table in 1977, and the third in the Long Walk in 1959.

Goodia lotifolia, an Australian shrub whose yellow flowers resemble those of the familiar laburnum, was planted near the Old Abbey in 1856. The showy white flowers of the Chinese *Gordonia axillaris*, planted in 1932, are an attractive sight in summer among the evergreen leaves of this superb shrub, which grows in the Long Walk. One of the most beautiful of genera characteristic of Australia is *Grevillea*, of which there are many species. Six of these, together with a hybrid and a variety, are grown in the Tresco garden. The red and yellow *Grevillea alpina*, planted in 1905, grows in the area called South Africa Flat. The earliest planted, however, was the pale yellow and green *G.juniperina* 'Sulphurea' (*G.sulphurea*), also planted in the South Africa Flat, but as long ago as 1854. The planting of two other species followed shortly after, the golden-yellow *G.robusta*, an exceptionally fine ornamental plant, being located on the Top Terrace West in 1856 and the red rosemary-leaved *G.rosmarinifolia* sited in the same year on the Top Terrace itself. The other species and the hybrid are modern additions.

The white-flowered evergreen shrubs of the Australian genus *Hakea* have

long been represented in Tresco by H.*oleifolia* and the fragrant H.*suaveolens*, the former having been planted in the Long Walk West in 1873 and the latter in the East Rockery on the Top Terrace in the same year. These were joined on the Top Terrace North by H.*lissocarpa* in 1914, and by H.*elliptica* and H.*crassifolium* on the Top Terrace South and the Top Terrace Quarry respectively in 1959 and 1973. The reddish large drooping flowers of the African Honeysuckle,. H*alleria lucida*, have been seen since 1890 on the Long Walk East.

The earliest representative of the numerous species and varieties of the genus H*ebe* (*Veronica*) to be planted at Tresco was a variety called H*ebe* x *andersonii* 'Variegata' which was placed on the Lighthouse Walk in 1854. Two species, H.*elliptica* from the Falkland Islands and H.*salicifolia* from New Zealand followed in 1856, the former finding a place in the West Orchard and the latter in the Hop Circle. It was not until 1914 that four more species were added, H.*chathamica* and H.*gigantea* from the Chatham Islands and H.*colensoi* and H.*pimeleoides* from New Zealand, the first two being planted in the Long Walk South and the Grassy Walk, and the others in the Old Abbey area and the Nerine Bank respectively. H*ebe brachysiphon* was planted in the Grassy Walk South in 1959 and the remaining species and a variety added in 1978. These were H.*armstrongii*, located on the Conifer Lawn, the variety H.*edinense* in Higher Australia, H.*glaucophylla* in Higher Australia East, and H.*rakaensis* on the Nerine Bank. All these came from New Zealand.

The white-flowered New Zealand shrub H*oheria populnea* has grown in the Well Garden since 1914. The flowers of the poplar-leaved Australian shrub H*omalanthus populifolius* are pale green and yellow. This is a more recent addition, being planted in the Old Nursery Garden in 1959. The star anise, I*llicium anisatum*, a Japanese shrub, dispenses the fragrance of its flowers in the summer from the Top Terrace, where it has grown since 1881. The blue flowers of the shrub I*ochroma cyaneum* (H*abrothamnus cyaneum*) from tropical America have been seen since 1944 against the Mulberry Wall and two allied species from Peru, the orange-scarlet fuchsia-like I.*fuchsioides* and the rich purple large-flowered I.*grandiflora* have since 1959 grown in the Pebble Garden and the Long Walk respectively. The very handsome I*soplexis canariensis* from the Canary Islands displays its orange-yellow flowers in the Old Nursery Garden, where it has been established since 1914. A more recent acquisition is I.*sceptrum*, whose yellowish-brown flowers have decorated the Well Garden since 1973. In the same garden, where it was planted in 1970, is the hybrid between the two species, I. x *scilloniensis*, which was bred at Tresco.

In the Pebble Garden East may be seen a specimen of the large Chilean honey palm, J*ubaea spectabilis*, a species whose acquaintance I first made in the Temperate House at the Royal Botanic Gardens, Kew, where there is a very large specimen more than sixty feet high grown from seed collected in South America by Thomas Bridges in 1843. This is a very good illustration of the remark sometimes made that the Tresco garden is the Temperate House at Kew with the lid off. The Tresco tree is smaller, having been planted much later, in 1914.

One of the trees of above average interest in Tresco is the New Zealand rewa, K*nightia excelsa*, which was planted near the tree ferns in the Abbey Drive in 1914, the habit of growth of which resembles that of the Lombardy poplar. It has

flesh-coloured flowers, and the wood of the tree when cut is found to be mottled with red and brown; this decorative colouring is useful in making furniture. The tree *Lagunaria patersonii*, which bears large, solitary, pale rosy-pink flowers and leaves with whitish scales beneath, and comes from Norfolk Island, also dates from 1914, as it was planted in the Long Walk in that year. The climber *Lapageria rosea* from Chile, whose rosy-crimson waxy tubular flowers, produced each year in great abundance for several months, are among the most beautiful in nature, was planted in the Pebble Garden at Tresco in 1854. The scarlet-flowered *Leonotis leonurus*, the lion's tail from South Africa, has grown near the Stone Table since 1890.

There are eight species of the genus *Leptospermum* at Tresco and seventeen varieties. The first species introduced was *L.scoparium* from New Zealand, the leaves of which are reputed to have been used to make a kind of tea. This species was planted in the Lighthouse Walk in 1890. In 1904 it was joined in Monument Walk by the Australian *L.lanigerum* (*L.pubescens*). Two more species, *L.ericoides* from New Zealand and *L.flavescens* from Australia were added in 1914, both being planted in Gardeners' Walk. *L.liversidgei* from Australia and *L.rodwayanum* from Tasmania arrived in 1959, the former being found a place in Gardeners' Walk and the latter in the area known as Miss Innis's Garden. *L.sericeum* (*L.erubescens*) from New Zealand was brought into the Gardeners' Walk in 1973.

The handsome silver tree of South Africa, *Leucadendron argenteum*, was for a long time the only representative of its genus in Tresco, having been planted on the South Africa Flat in 1914. In 1959, however, other members of the genus, all from South Africa, began to be introduced. *L.discolor* (*L.buekianum*) was planted in that year on the Top Terrace, and in 1973 nine other species were brought into the garden. *L.comosum*, *L.salicifolium* (*Euryspermum salicifolium*) and *L.sessile* were planted on the South Africa Rockery, *L.eucalyptifolium*, *L.gandogeri* (*L.decorum*), *L.laureolum* (*Protea laureola*), *L.uliginosum* and *L.tinctum* on the Top Terrace and *L.xanthoconus* (*Protea xanthoconus*) on the South Africa Flat. Another South African genus, *Leucospermum*, is represented by five species from that country, all introduced at different times, ranging from *L.conocarpodendron* (*L.conocarpum*), which was planted on the Cypress Rockery in 1914, through *L.reflexum*, planted in 1954 on the Top Terrace East, *L.cordifolium* (*Leucadendron cordifolium*) planted on the Cannon Rockery in 1959, to *L.ellipticum* and *L.tottum*, both planted in 1973, the former on the Top Terrace and the latter on the Podalyria Bank. *Limoniastrum articulatum* is a small pink-flowered Mediterranean shrub of long standing in the garden, having been introduced in 1865. The white-flowered Japanese shrub *Litsea japonica* has occupied a place on the Long Walk since 1914.

Another palm may be found in the Pebble Garden, increasing the exotic profile of that area. *Livistona australis*, from Australia, called the fountain palm, has spread its ornamental dark green nearly circular much-divided leaves in a crowded head above that garden since 1860. Among the most elegant of shrubs grown for the beauty of their foliage are those of the genus *Lomatia*, three species of which may be found in Tresco. The very dark green leaves of *L.ferruginea* from Chile, which has rosy-red and yellow flowers, have ornamented the Lighthouse Walk since 1857. The much smaller *L.tinctoria* from Australia has occupied a place

in the Pear Tree Garden since 1912. To these was added in 1974 in the Lighthouse Walk the erect-growing L.*ilicifolia* from Australia, which has prickly holly-like leaves, and sometimes reaches the stature of a small tree.

In the Long Walk an evergreen shrub, *Luculia gratissima* from the Himalayas, whose rose-coloured somewhat fleshy flowers exude the most delicious fragrance, has been growing since 1863. In 1934 a second species, L.*pinceana*, from Assam, was planted in the Pear Tree Garden. It has larger flowers than L.*gratissima* which are even more highly scented. Although *Macrozamia communis* from Australia, which was planted in the area of the garden known as Lower Australia in 1980, is called the Swan River or giant fern palm, it is not in fact a palm but belongs to the Cycadaceae, allied to but earlier than the conifers in the scale of evolution. It is grown for the ornamental effect of its very graceful green feather-shaped fronds.

Mandevilla suaveolens, sometimes called the Chile jasmine, a climbing shrub native to Argentina, has scented the ruins of the Old Abbey with the fragrance of its large white flowers since 1854. A dozen species of the Australian genus *Melaleuca* have been established at Tresco, the earliest to arrive being M.*linariifolia*, whose white flowers have been seen in the Long Walk since 1856. The rich red of the cylindrical spikes of M.*hypericifolia* have provided a brilliant splash of colour in Monument Walk since it was planted in 1865. The section of the garden called Arcadia received the white-flowered M.*armillaris* in 1890 and M.*preissiana* was planted in the West Rockery in 1896. The handsome erect yellowish-white M.*squarrosa* and the white M.*styphelioides* were planted in 1914, the former in the Gardeners' Walk and the latter on the Grassy Walk. Not until 1943, when M.*squamea* was added to the West Rockery did another species arrive.

M.*nesophila* and M. *rhaphiophylla* were planted by the Monument Walk in 1950 and the Toy Greenhouse Path in 1952 respectively. The remaining three species, the greenish-yellow M.*diosmifolia*,M.*pubescens*(M.*preissiana*) and M.*violacea*, were added in 1973, the first to the Gardeners' Walk, the second to the area below the Toy Greenhouse Path and the last to the Middle Terrace.

The deeply divided leaves of *Melianthus major*, a South African shrub that has grown since 1890 in the Old Nursery Garden, are highly ornamental, which has led to considerable use of the shrub for sub-tropical bedding. The small greenish-white flowers of the New Zealand shrub *Melicope ternata*, which was planted in the Long Walk in 1959, are not particularly striking, but this species, which has gland-dotted leaves and grows from twelve to twenty-five feet high, is not unattractive as a whole. The genus *Mertya* derives its name from the Greek *merys*, to roll up, referring to the male flowers forming something like a rolled-up ball. M. *sinclairii* from New Zealand has been located in the Long Walk since 1914. Only the female flowers are of any size. Some of the species of *Metrosideros* are among the most noteworthy sights in the garden, which contains examples of seven of them, as well as of two varieties. M.*excelsa*, the pohutukawa of New Zealand, was the first species introduced. This was planted in the garden below the area called Mexico in 1851-M.*robusta*, the northern rata with its showy red flowers, followed in 1856 and occupies a prominent position in the Long Walk. All the other five species are much more recent plantings. Three of them were established in 1914, M.*diffusa* in the Lapageria Corner, M.*umbellata* (M.*lucida*), the

southern rata, on Lighthouse Walk and M.*villosa* by the Neptune Steps. The next planting was the variety of M.*excelsa* called 'Hallii', which was placed on the Grassy Walk in 1950. M.*carminea* (M*elaleuca diffusa*), the climbing rata, was located in 1959 on the Middle Terrace. All these species and varieties originate in New Zealand. M.*kermadecensis* (M.*villosa*), however, planted near the Limpet Midden in 1965, and its variety 'Variegata', placed on the East Rockery in 1977, come from the Kermadec Islands.

Michelia figo from China, a member of a genus closely allied to the magnolias, has occupied its place in the Well Garden since 1851. For more than a hundred years it was the sole representative of its genus in Tresco. Then, in 1953, its relative M.*doltsopa* from the Himalayas was also planted in the Well Garden. The scarlet blossoms of the mitre flower, M*itraria coccinea*, an evergreen shrub from Chile, so called because of the resemblance of its seed-pod to the shape of a bishop's mitre, has displayed its brilliance every summer since 1856 in the part of the garden called Mexico. The small Australian evergreen tree *Monotoca elliptica* has borne its white flowers since 1959 on the South Africa Flat. *Myoporum laetum*, the ngaio, a New Zealand shrub with transparent spots on the leaves has grown in the Duckery since 1890. The candleberry myrtles, members of the genus M*yrica*, are represented in Tresco by one species only, M.*faya* from the Canary Islands, which was also planted in 1890. M*yrsine africana* was another shrub planted in that year, finding a place in the Long Walk.

The common myrtle of southern Europe, M*yrtus communis*, white-flowered and strongly scented, has long been a favourite and from it have been developed a number of varieties, some four of which have been planted in various parts of Tresco to supplement M.*communis* itself, which has had a home in the Long Walk since 1894. Some other species of M*yrtus* and varieties developed from them are also grown in the garden. The earliest to arrive was the Chilean guava, M*yrtus ugni*, whose white flowers are followed by glossy red or black berries of agreeable aroma and pleasant taste. It was planted in the Aloe Walk in 1854. M.*apiculata* (B*lepharocaly* x *apiculatus*), also from Chile, was established in the Long Walk in 1856 and M.*bullata* from New Zealand, whose white flowers precede dark red berries, was placed in the Grassy Walk in 1857. The last species added was M.*lechleriana*, again from Chile, located in the Pebble Garden in 1953. N*andina domestica*, the heavenly bamboo, a houseplant which ornaments almost every domestic interior in China, has grown in the Pear Tree Garden since 1914.

The southern beeches, N*othofagus*, natives of the southern hemisphere that resemble the beech trees of the north, are represented outdoors in Tresco by several species. N.*cunninghamii* from Tasmania was planted among the tree ferns in 1856, and N.*menziesii* and N.*solandri*, both from New Zealand, followed it in the same area in 1912 and 1914. N.*dombeyi* from Chile was also planted among the tree ferns in 1973. All these grow into large trees. O*dontospermum sericeum*, found on the Middle Terrace, is in considerable contrast, being a rather handsome but dwarf shrub from the Canary Islands, reaching barely four feet in height. *Olea europaea*, the wild olive from southern Europe, is somewhat larger, maturing into a small tree. A specimen of this ubiquitous inhabitant of the Mediterranean coasts has occupied a position on the Top Terrace since 1890. In 1974 an allied species,

O.lanceolata from New Zealand, was planted in the Long Walk.

One of the specialities of Tresco is the genus *Olearia*, the daisy bushes, natives of New Zealand and Australia, of which no less than thirty-four species grow in the garden, together with thirteen varieties, too many to enumerate each individually. Only four species were planted in the nineteenth century, *O.argyrophylla* from Australia, which was planted in the Well Court in 1853, *O.macrodonta* from New Zealand, placed by the Stone Table in 1873, *O.rotundifolia* from Australia, located in the East Orchard in the same year, and *O.stellulata* also from Australia, established in 1873 in Lighthouse Walk. The only variety planted before the turn of the century was O. x *haastii*, planted near the Stone Table in 1890. *O.paniculata (O.forsteri)* was planted in the same year on the Top Terrace. Sixteen more species were introduced in 1914, the remainder having all been planted since 1949.

Three species of the South African genus *Osteospermum* and five varieties developed from them have all been introduced to Tresco comparatively recently. The three species, *O.barberiae (Dimorphotheca barberiae)*, *O.ecklonis (Dimorphotheca ecklonis)* and *O.hyloserioides (Tripteris clandestinia)* were all planted on the Middle Terrace in 1973, and three of the varieties, including one called 'Tresco Peggy' were also planted in that year on the South Africa Rockery. The other two varieties were planted in 1976 and 1977 on the Middle Terrace and Podalyria Bank respectively.

A handsome variety of the small yellow-flowered shrub *Oxylobium ellipticum* with narrower leaves than the species, was established in 1959 on the Lighthouse Walk and a smaller allied species *O.lineare*, with yellow or dull red flowers was planted on the Grassy Walk in 1973, both species being natives of Tasmania. Two species of *Ozothamnus*, *O.diosmifolius* and *O.thyrsoides (Helichrysum diosmifolium)* both now classified as attractive Australian shrubs with small white flower-heads, have occupied positions on the Lighthouse Walk since 1950 and 1959 respectively. *Passiflora caerulea*, the passion flower from Peru, has climbed since 1894 over the Mexico Pergola and a hybrid of this species, planted in 1973, may be found on Augustus Smith's Wall. Another *Passiflora* hybrid has been growing on the Middle Terrace since 1894.

More than thirty Pelargonium species are grown at Tresco, and upwards of fifty varieties, the basic stock of each being held in the Peach House. The earliest introduction was a variety called 'Scarlet Unique' which was planted in 1856. Two more varieties were added in 1865, 'Prince of Orange' and 'Smith's Supreme'. The first species to be introduced was *P.quercifolium*, planted in 1890 and in that year the hybrid *P.x fragrans* was also added, together with a variety called 'Rollinson's Unique'. Another hybrid *P.x ardens* was planted in 1894. Twenty years later, in 1914, nine more species were brought in, *P.betulinum*, *P.capitatum*, *P.crispum*, *P.cucullatum*, *P.echinatum*, *P.gibbosum*, *P.glutinosum*, *P.odoratissimum* and *P.tomentosum*. Nine varieties were also added in that year. Apart from the planting of *P.inquinans* in 1929, nothing further was introduced until *P.filicifolium* and *P.radula* arrived in 1953. Other plantings of both species and varieties have been made from time to time since then.

The large seed of the avocado pear, *Persea americana (P.gratissima)*, a fruit

familiar in Europe but a native of the warmer parts of America, germinates very easily and is often grown by those who have eaten the pears until the tree gets too large to be kept in the house. At Tresco it grows outdoors below the Toy Greenhouse, having been planted there in 1973. A Chinese relative, *P.ichangensis* (*Machilus ichangensis*), was also planted in the Grassy Walk in the same year. A curious plant of unusual origin is the bigeneric hybrid *Philageria veitchii*, a scrambling shrub raised by Veitch and Son, the nurserymen, by crossing *Lapageria rosea* and *Philesia magellanica*. With this parentage of attractive-flowered plants, it might be expected that the hybrid would be worth growing. Unfortunately it is shy of flowering and therefore of little use as an ornamental plant. A specimen has inhabited the Well Garden at Tresco since 1959. The very showy flowers of the Jerusalem Sage, *Phlomis fruticosa*, from Greece, which have graced the Middle Terrace since 1894 contrast so much with the pale lilac blossoms of its Kashmir relative *P.cashmeriana* which was planted on the Middle Terrace in 1973, that anyone seeing both for the first time might be excused for doubting the relationship between them.

A specimen of the date palm of North Africa, *Phoenix dactylifera* has grown near the Old Abbey West since 1856 and helps to create the exotic profile of that part of the garden. Its somewhat smaller relative from the Canary Islands, *P.canariensis*, which was planted in 1894, produces a similar effect in the Lighthouse Walk. Another relative, *P.reclinata*, from south-eastern Africa, of more spreading habit, was planted in the Pear Tree Garden in 1914 and plays a similar exotic role in that part of Tresco. *Phormium tenax*, the New Zealand flax, first introduced to Tresco in 1890 and planted in Lighthouse Walk at the same time as its fellow, *P.colensoi*, was planted in the Old Nursery Garden, is virtually naturalized in Tresco and upwards of twenty varieties are grown there, mostly in the part of the garden called Lower Australia, though a few are scattered elsewhere.

The Chinese hawthorn, *Photinia serrulata*, has white flowers like the English May but there the resemblance ends, as the Chinese shrub is evergreen while our own bush is deciduous. The Chinese plant is a long-standing resident of Tresco, having grown in the Pear Tree Garden since 1856. Specimens of two allied varieties of *Photinia* were planted in the East Orchard and Well Garden in 1973 and 1977 respectively. *Phygelius capensis*, the Cape figwort is represented in the garden by a variety planted in 1859. The small heath-like South African shrub *Phylica ericoides* has been in the garden even longer. Like the *Photinia*, it was planted in 1856 and grows on what is now called the Podalyria Bank. Three species of the ornamental grasses of the genus *Phyllostachys* grow in the Bamboo Garden, *P.nigra* from China having been planted in 1890, *P.aurea* from Japan in 1914 and *P.mitis* from Japan in 1962.

The genus *Pittosporum* is very well represented at Tresco by eleven species and fifteen varieties. The first species introduced was *P.tobira* from Japan, planted in the East Rockery in 1850. This was followed almost immediately by *P.tenuifolium* from New Zealand, which arrived in the Pear Tree Garden in 1851. *P.crassifolium* and *P.eugenioides*, both from New Zealand, were introduced in 1890. These were planted in the Fernery and on the Top Terrace respectively. The remainder were

introduced at various dates from 1914 onwards. The beautiful blue of the flowers of *Plumbago capensis* from South Africa is well known to many people who do not know its name. It has climbed over the Old Abbey ruins since 1851. *Podalyria calyptrata*, an evergreen shrub from South Africa with pale rose flowers, is sufficiently noteworthy to have given its name to the place where it grows, Podalyria Bank, on which it has flourished since 1905. The genus of evergreen trees entitled *Podocarpus* is scattered about the world and the eight species grown at Tresco come from six different countries. *P.totara* from New Zealand and *P.andinus* from Chile were the two earliest to arrive, both being planted in the part of the garden called Lower Australia in 1890. *P.dacrydioides*, the kahikatea from New Zealand, and *P.milanjianus* followed in 1914, finding places in the Abbey Drive. The others have all been added since 1959.

The rich purple of the flowers of the South African shrub *Polygala myrtifolia* 'Grandiflora', which has grown on the Middle Terrace since 1914, is a striking colour. Not so the pale yellow of the Australian *Pomaderris elliptica*, which was planted on the Long Walk in 1856. Another species of *Pomaderris*, *P.rugosa*, was planted in the East Orchard in 1973. Two species of the strongly scented genus *Prostanthera*, the Australian mint- bushes or mint-trees, have been grown in Tresco since 1856. *P.lasianthos*, the Victorian dogwood, whose white flowers are tinged with red, was planted in that year on the Podalyria Bank and the purple-flowered *P.rotundifolia* on the South Africa Flat. *P.incisa* has been grown in the Hop Circle since 1914, and most of the six other species and varieties of *Prostanthera* also grown, all planted in 1981, are to be found in the Hop Circle. Members of the South Africa genus *Protea* are renowned for their striking beauty. Twelve species are grown in Tresco, the first planted there, *P.repens*, having been set on the Moraine in 1856. *P.cynaroides* has grown on the Middle Terrace since 1912, and *P.eximia* (*P.latifolia*) on the Top Terrace West since 1914. All the others except *P.susannae*, planted on the South Africa Flat in 1945, *P.mundi* and *P.lacticolor* (*P.longiflora*)planted on the Top Terrace West in 1950 and 1952 and *P.longiflora* planted in 1959 on the Top Terrace, have been introduced since 1970.

The leaves of the large evergreen shrub *Pseudopanax crassifolius* from New Zealand, which has grown in the area called Higher Australia since 1856, are long, thick and fleshy, with a prominent deep orange mid-rib, the flowers being inconspicuous. In 1914 two other species were planted in the same part of the garden, *P.chathamicus* from the Chatham Islands and *P.ferox* from New Zealand. A variety of *P.lessonii* called 'Gold Splash', a small tree with very stout branches and rather larger flowers, was planted in the East Orchard in 1976, and a variety of *P.crassifolius* called 'Purpureum' in the Duckery in 1981. The pleasant blue-striped flowers of *Psoralea pinnata* from South Africa have adorned the Grassy Walk since 1890. *P.affinis*, also from South Africa, was introduced in 1914 and grows on the Top Terrace.

Raphiolepis umbellata (*Raphiolepis japonica*) from Japan was planted in 1890 in the Long Walk West and a hybrid of this species with *R.indica*, the East Indian Hawthorn, native of China, was established in the same area in 1914. Also planted in 1914 was the palm *Rhapis humilis* from Japan, which arrived in the Pear Tree Garden in that year. The spiny *Rhapithamnus spinosus* (*Volkameria spinosa*) from

Chile has grown in the same area since 1908. The Nikau palm, *Rhopalostylis sapida* from New Zealand, planted in the Long Walk in 1863, is another palm that enhances the exotic air of the garden. *Royena lucida*, the African bladder-nut or snowdrop tree, with white flowers and red fruits, is a rather undistinguished shrub of little beauty which has occupied a place on the Grassy Walk since 1914.

The ornamental evergreen *Semele androgyna* from the Canary Islands, which has white flowers, has been climbing in the Long Walk since 1914, and since 1976 a variety of it called 'Variegata' which originated on Tresco has been growing in the Well Garden. *Smilax aspera*, the prickly ivy from southern Europe, has greenish fragrant flowers which have been seen in the area called Lower Australia since 1890. Two species of the very large showy-flowered genus *Solanum* are grown outdoors on Tresco. *S.jasminoides*, a many-twigged twining shrub from South America, which has bluish-white flowers, grows near the Old Abbey ruins, where it has occupied a place since 1853, and the violet-flowered *S.laciniatum* (*S.aviculare*), the kangaroo apple or bird solanum, an erect shrub from Australia, was planted in the Abbey Woods in 1890. *Sollya fusi formis* is another Australian climber. This has carried its nodding blue flowers and evergreen leaves on the Middle Terrace Wall since 1904. *Sophora microphylla* (*S.tetraptera*), the small-leaved yellow-flowered New Zealand kowhai, has grown in the Lighthouse Walk since 1865. Another species of *Sophora*, *S.macrocarpa* from Chile, an elegant evergreen shrub, was planted in the Grassy Walk in 1959.

The conspicuous white flowers, freely borne, of *Sparmannia africana*, the African hemp, are very beautiful, and the plant is rightly a favourite. At Tresco it has grown in the Abbey Drive since 1865, and the equally handsome double-flowered variety 'Flore-pleno' has ornamented the Lighthouse Walk South since 1890. The Australian tree *Stenocarpus salignus* has small and greenish flowers, and leaves which are willow-like. A specimen may be found on Gardeners' Walk, where it was planted in 1891. The ornamental *Sterculia diversifolia* is another Australian tree with an expressive vernacular name, being known as the bottle tree of Victoria. It has grown since 1973 in the Long Walk. The small shrub *Strobilanthes dyerianus* from Penang, planted in the Old Nursery Garden in 1959, has dark green purple-centred leaves and displays pale-blue flowers in the autumn. *Suttonia australis*, a New Zealand shrub which has grown on the Top Terrace since 1914, has minute white flowers carried in close clusters and its much-veined leaves are studded with rounded glands. The allied species *S.salicina* from New Zealand and *S.chathamica* from the Chatham Islands were planted in the Fernery and the Long Walk respectively in 1945 and 1973. *Swainsonia galegifolia*, the Darling River pea from Australia, whose reddish flowers may be seen in the Well Garden, is a much older inhabitant of Tresco, having been planted in 1851.

The palm *Syagrus campestris*, native of Brazil, is another elegant and highly ornamental palm which adds to the exotic appearance of Tresco. It has been growing in the Pebble Garden since 1914. The small Australian shrub *Templetonia retusa*, the coral bush, has displayed its red flowers by the Old Abbey Wall since 1914. *Trachelospermum jasminoides* from China is a pretty climber with very fragrant white flowers which has grown on the House Terrace since 1914. In 1957 a variety

called 'Variegatum' was planted in the Well House Garden. *Trachycarpus fortunei*, the Chusan palm from China, grown since 1854 in the Hop Circle, is another of the palms that help to create the exotic atmosphere of the Tresco garden. Another species of *Trachycarpus*, *T.martianus* from the Himalayas, was planted in the Long Walk in 1973. The tree *Virgilia capensis*, grown on the Top Terrace since 1914, comes from South Africa and displays its white to rosy-purple flowers in July. A variety of the Californian palm *Washingtonia filifera* called 'Robusta' has grown in the Pebble Garden since 1957 and, like the other palms in that area, imparts an exotic touch to the scene. *Weinmannia racemosa*, established in 1914 in Monument Walk, is another New Zealand tree that finds the climate of Tresco congenial. The specific name *eremicola* of the small rather twiggy Australian shrub *Westringia eremicola* means desert-loving and indicates the kind of milieu in nature where it prefers to display its pale blue rather small flowers. *Widdringtonia cupressoides*, a shrubby conifer from South Africa, was planted in the Gardeners' Walk in 1914. Another species, *W.schwarzii*, known as the Willowmore cedar, also from South Africa, has grown in the West Orchard since 1945.

Do not be daunted by this long list of possible sub-tropical shrubs and trees for your garden. Collectors have been scouring the world for a long time now looking for plants that will grow in gardens in the British Isles, and in similar temperate climates, and their labours have augmented the possibilities year by year, so that there is much within your reach. The horticultural newspapers and journals contain many articles which are helpful in making a choice and they also contain the advertisements of nurseries and individuals who specialize in supplying those who would like to grow something a little out of the common run in their gardens. Like every other subject, if you are going to get the best out of your gardening you must study it. Meanwhile, you can see a few possible choices flourishing at Tresco.

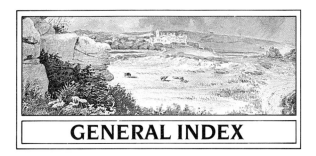

GENERAL INDEX

The Plant Catalogue at the end of the book gives full details of a plant's location in today's garden and its date of introduction.

The photograph on the title page is
reproduced by permission of
Frank Gibson. Photographs on pages
67, 68 and 72 are reproduced by
permission of Frank Naylor, and the
photograph on page 66 by permission
of Roy Cooper. Illustrations from the
library of Tresco Abbey are
reproduced by permission of Robert
Dorrien Smith from the photographs
of Roy Cooper. The flower paintings
by Frances le Marchant are © Robert
Dorrien Smith 1985 and are
reproduced from photographs by
Nick Allen.

LIST OF PLATES

Paintings and prints

TRESCO ABBEY GARDENS
PLANT CATALOGUE

The list contains details of genera, species, sub-species and
cultivars grown in the garden. The family in which a genus occurs is listed
in brackets after the generic name.
Common names are given where possible. Country of origin of species
follows this, unless the plant is of garden origin, where the designation
'Hort.' replaces the country of origin. Hybrid origin is listed where known.
The last two columns give details of the first date that the plant is
recorded as having been present in the gardens, followed by the main site in
the garden where the plant was located at the time the list was compiled.

Abelia (Caprifoliaceae)
A.floribunda	Mexico	1854 Podalyria Bank
A.x grandiflora	*chinensis x uniflora*	1959 Podalyria Bank
A.x grandiflora 'Variegata'	*chinensis x uniflora*	1975 Long Walk
A.x 'Edward Goucher'	*x grandiflora*	
	x schumanii	1975 Podalyria Bank

Abies (Pinaceae)
A.pinsapo (Spanish fir)	Spain	1865 Top Terrace

Abromeitiella (Bromeliaceae)
A.brevifolia	Argentina	1977 Palm Rockery

Abutilon (Malvaceae)
A.megapotamicum	Brazil	1890 Long Walk (North-East)
A.megapotamicum 'Variegatum'	Brazil	1953 Augustus Wall
A.globosum 'Boule de Neige'	Hort.	1890 Pebble Garden
A.globosum 'Canary Bird'	Hort.	1959 Long Walk (North-East)
A.globosum 'Nabob'	Hort.	1959 Long Walk (North-East)
A.striatum	Guatemala	1959 Grassy Walk
A.striatum 'Thompsonii'	Guatemala	1959 Lighthouse Walk
A.x suntense	*ochsenii x vitifolium*	1973 Old Abbey
A.vitifolium	Chile	1853 Long Walk
A.vitifolium 'Album'	Chile	1865 Long Walk

Acacia (Leguminosae)
A.acinacea	South Australia	1904 East Orchard
A.armata (kangaroo thorn)	Australia	1855 Gardeners' Path
A.armata 'Paradoxa'	Australia	1959 Gardeners' Path
A.baileyana (Cootamundra wattle)	Australia	1914 Arcadia
A.buxifolia	Australia	1973 Gardeners' Walk
A.cultriformis	Australia	1865 Nerine Bank
A.cyanophylla	Australia	1894 Toy Greenhouse Bank
A.dealbata (silver wattle)	Australia	1853 Arcadia (East)
A.decurrens (green wattle)	Australia	1914 Arcadia (West)
A.decurrens 'Mollissima' (black wattle)	Australia	1959 Garden Field
A.longifolia 'Sophorae'	Australia	1904 Top Terrace
A.longifolia (Sydney golden wattle)	Australia	1856 Garden Field
A.melanoxylon (blackwood acacia)	Australia	1890 Abbey Drive (West)
A.myrtifolia	Australia	1856 Gardeners' Walk
A.neriifolia	Australia	1959 Arcadia
A.pendula (weeping myall)	Australia	1973 Arcadia (East)
A.polybotrya	Australia	1976 Monument Path (South)
A.pravissima (ovens wattle)	Australia	1973 Arcadia (East)
A. 'President Doumergue'	Australia	1959 Arcadia (West)
A.prominens	Australia	1968 Gardeners' Walk
A.retinoides	Australia	1890 Monument Path (North)

A.retinoides 'Brigitte' and following
A.retinoides 'Brigitte'	Australia	1973 Monument Path (North)
A.riceana	Australia	1856 Arcadia (West)
A.saligna	Australia	1959 Top Terrace
A.x veitchiana	*longifolia x riceana*	1959 Arcadia (East)
A.verticillata	Australia	1890 Arcadia (East)

Acanthus (Acanthaceae)
A.mollis (bear's breeches)	Southern Europe	1890 Hop Circle

Acer (Aceraceae)
A.pseudoplatanua (sycamore)	Europe	1890 Well Covert

Achillea (Compositae)
A.ptarmica 'The Pearl'	Europe	1979 Cut Flower Garden

Acidanthera (Iridaceae)
A.bicolor 'Murielae'	Ethiopia	1932 Citrus Garden

Aconitum (Ranunculaceae)
A.napellus (monkshood)	Europe	1973 Glasshouses

Acorus (Araceae)
A.gramineus 'Variegatus'	Europe	1959 Old Abbey

Acrodon (Aizoaceae)
A.bellidiflorus	South Africa	1914 Middle Terrace

Actinostrobus (Pinaceae)
A.pyramidalis	Australia	1914 Top Terrace

Adiantum (Adiantaceae)
A.capillis-veneris (maidenhair fern)	Britain	1856 Fern Collection
A.capillis-veneris 'Bifidum'	Britain	1978 Fern Collection
A.hispidulum (rosy maidenhair)	New Zealand	1975 Fern Collection
A.pedatum (northern maidenhair)	North America	1865 Fern Collection
A.pedatum 'Japonicum' (rose-fronded maidenhair)	Japan	1975 Fern Collection
A. 'Minus' (dwarf maidenhair)	Japan	1975 Fern Collection
A.raddianum	Brazil	1894 Conservatory
A.raddianum 'Brilliant Else'	Hort.	1975 Fern Collection
A.raddianum 'Elegantissimum'	Hort.	1976 Fern Collection
A.raddianum 'Fragrantissimum'	Hort.	1976 Fern Collection
A.raddianum 'Fritz Luthi'	Hort.	1976 Fern Collection
A.raddianum 'Gracillimum'	Hort.	1976 Fern Collection
A.raddianum 'Pacific Maid'	Hort.	1976 Fern Collection
A.tenerum 'Ghiesbreghtii Roseum'	Bermuda	1975 Fern Collection
A.venustum	Canada	1975 Tree Fern Glade

Adromischus (Crassulaceae)
A.clavifolius	South Africa	1959 Succulent Collection
A.cooperi	South Africa	1959 Succulent Collection

A.cristatus	South Africa	1959 Succulent Collection
A.hemisphaericus	South Africa	1959 Succulent Collection
A.maculatus	South Africa	1959 Succulent Collection
A.poellnitzianus	South Africa	1959 Succulent Collection

Aechmea (Bromeliaceae)

A.fasciata	Rio de Janeiro	1977 Conservatory

Aeonium (Crassulaceae)

A.arboreum	Crete	1890 Cypress Rockery
A.arboreum 'Atropurpureum'	Unknown	1959 Valhalla
A.arboreum 'Folis-purpureus Marnier-Lapostolle'	Unknown	1959 South Africa Cliff
A.balsamiferum	Lanzarote	1914 Cypress Rockery
A.x barbatum	A.caespitosum x spathulatum	1959 Miss Innis' Garden
A.bethencourtianum	Fuerteventura	1914 Cypress Rockery
A.burchardii	Tenerife	1959 Mexico: Middle Terrace
A.canariense	Tenerife	1959 West Rockery
A.castello-paivae	Gomera	1894 Cypress Rockery
A.ciliatum	Tenerife	1894 Middle Terrace
A.ciliatum x palmense	Palma	1975 Cypress Rockery
A.cuneatum	Tenerife	1894 Cypress Rockery
A.decorum	Gomera	1926 Cypress Rockery
A.domesticum	Unknown	1959 Cypress Rockery
A.glandulosum	Madeira	1949 Cypress Rockery
A.glandulosum Perennial form	Porto Santo	1973 Middle Terrace
A.glutinosum	Madeira	1894 Agave Bank East
A.goochiae	Palma	1973 Cypress Rockery
A.haworthii	Tenerife	1894 Old Abbey
A.holochrysum	Hierro	1975 Cypress Rockery
A.lancerottense	Lanzarote	1959 Collection
A.leucoblepharum	Eritrea	1975 Cypress Rockery
A.lindleyi	Palma	1959 Cypress Rockery
A.lindleyi x tabulaeforme	Gran Canaria	1959 Cypress Rockery
A.manriqueorum	Gran Canaria	1959 Cypress Rockery
A.nobile	Palma	1973 Cypress Rockery
A.percarneum	Gran Canaria	1959 Cypress Rockery
A.rubrolineatum	Gomero	1975 Cypress Rockery
A.sedifolium	Tenerife	1925 Agave Bank
A.simsii	Gran Canaria	1924 Cypress Rockery
A.smithii	Tenerife	1925 Collection
A.spathulatum	Hierro	1959 Cypress Rockery
A.spathulatum var. cruentum	Hierro	1959 Cypress Rockery
A.spathulatum x Greenovia aurea:	see Greenonium	
A.subplanum	Gomera	1959 West Rockery
A.tabulaeforme	Tenerife	1890 Top Terrace
A.tortuosum	Lanzarote	1848 Cypress Rockery
A.undulatum	Gran Canaria	1894 Old Abbey
A.valverdense	Hierro	1925 Cypress Rockery
A.velutinum	A.caespitosum x canariense	1959 Cypress Rockery
A.virgineum	Gran Canaria	1959 Cypress Rockery

Aesculus (Hippocastanaceae) horse chestnuts

A.hippocastanum (horse chestnut)	Greece	1959 Abbey Drive
A.indica	Himalaya	1959 Hop Circle East
A.parviflora	South-East U.S.A.	1959 Lighthouse Walk East

Agapanthus (Liliaceae)

A.africanus	South Africa	1959 General
A.campanulatus	South Africa	1959 West Rockery
A.inapertus	South Africa	1962 Mexico: Middle Terrace
A.orientalis	South Africa	1856 General
A.'Albus'	South Africa	1856 General
A.'Hybrids'	South Africa	1959 General
A.'Purple Cloud'	Hort.	1974 East Rockery Entrance

Agathis (Araucariaceae)

A.australis (kauri pine)	New Zealand	1856 Abbey Drive

Agathosma (Rutaceae)

A.imbricata	South Africa	1959 Top Terrace

Agave (Agavaceae)

A.amaniensis	Mexico	1974 Toy Greenhouse Bank
A.americana	Mexico	1886 West Rockery
A.americana 'Marginata aurea'	Mexico	1856 Middle Terrace
A.applanata	Mexico	1890 Agave Bank
A.bergeri	Mexico	1974 Cypress Rockery
A.chloracantha	Mexico	1974 West Rockery
A.deserti	California	1952 Cactus Bank
A.echinoides	Mexico	1973 Miss Innis' Garden
A.ellemeetiana	Mexico	1974 Toy Greenhouse Bank
A.ferox	Mexico	1890 Middle Terrace
A.filifera	Mexico	1890 Mexico: Middle Terrace
A.huachucensis	Arizona	1959 Palm Rockery
A.lophantha	Mexico	1959 West Rockery
A.macroantha	Mexico	1890 Cactus Bed
A.parrasana	Mexico	1973 Cypress Rockery
A.polyacantha	Mexico	1952 West Rockery
A.salmiana	Mexico	1894 Middle Terrace
A.scheuermaniana	Caribbean	1974 Toy Greenhouse Bed
A.schottii	Mexico	1952 Cactus Bed
A.shawii	California	1890 West Rockery
A.stricta	Mexico	1952 Palm Rockery
A.weberi	Mexico	1973 Agave Bank

Agonis (Myrtaceae)

A.flexuosa	Australia	1948 Neptune
A.marginata	Australia	1959 Top Terrace East

Aichryson (Crassulaceae)

A.bollei	Canary Islands	1977 Old Abbey
A.dichotomum	Canary Islands	1959 Palm Rockery
A.dumosum	Canary Islands	1979 Abbey Yard Rockery

Akebia (Lardizabalaceae)

A.trifoliata	China	1950 Old Nursery Garden

Albizia (Leguminosae)

A.julibrissin	Asia	1979 Glasshouses
A.lophantha	Australia	1855 Palm Rockery

Albuca (Liliacreae)

A.sp.	South Africa	1914 Mexico: Middle Terrace

Alectryon (Sapindaceae)

A.excelsus (titoki)	New Zealand	1959 Higher Australia

Allamanda (Apocyanaceae)

A.cathartica	Guyana	1973 Peach House

Allium (Liliacreae)

A.karataviense	Turkestan	1974 Agave Bank
A.ostrowskianum	Turkestan	1974 Avave Bank
A.triquetrum	Native	1834 Throughout garden

Alnus (Betulaceae)

A.glutinosa (common alder)	Britain	1959 Fernery, Well Covert

Aloe (Liliacreae)

A.aculeata	Transvaal	1975 West Rockery
A.africana	Cape Province	1975 West Rockery
A.angelica	Transvaal	1975 Abbey Rock Garden
A.arborescens Early form	Cape Province	1848 South Africa Cliff
A.arborescens Late form	Cape Province	1952 South Africa Cliff
A.aristata	Cape Province	1959 Cypress Rockery
A.brevifolia	Cape Province	1959 Araucaria Rockery
A.ciliaris 'Robusta'	Cape Province	1959 West Rockery
A.ciliaris 'Tidmarshii'	Cape Province	1959 Palm Rockery
A.dichotoma	Cape Province	1959 Cypress Rockery
A.dolomitica	Transvaal	1975 West Rockery
A.dorotheae	Tanganyika	1975 Toy Greenhouse Rockery
A.duckeri	Nyasaland	1975 Cypress Rockery
A.excelsa	Rhodesia	1952 West Rockery
A.ferox	Natal	1952 South Africa Cliff
A.fosteri	Transvaal	1952 Collection
A.glauca	Cape Province	1973 South Africa Cliff
A.globuligemma	Rhodesia	1952 Cypress Rockery
A.jacksonii	Ethiopia	1975 Araucaria Rockery
A.jucunda	Somaliland	1975 Abbey Yard

138

A.kniphofioides	Transvaal	1959 Mexico:
		Middle Terrace
A.lettyae	East Africa	1975 Toy Greenhouse
A.lineata	Cape Province	1973 West Wall:
		Middle Terrace
A.lineata 'Muirii'	Cape Province	1975 Miss Innis' Rockery
A.marlothii	Bechuanaland	1950 Collection
A.melanacantha	Cape Province	1973 West Rockery
A.mitriformis	Cape Province	1894 Conservatory
		Rockery
A.mutabilis	Transvaal	1973 South Africa Cliff
A.plicatilis	Cape Province	1959 West Wall:
		Middle Terrace
A.pluridens	Cape Province	1952 Middle Terrace: Pot
A.rivae	Somaliland	1973 South African
		Rockery
A.rubroviolacea	Arabia	1973 Cypress Rockery
A.saponaria	Cape Province	1890 South Africa Cliff
A.speciosa	Natal	1934 Miss Innis' Rockery
A.spectabilis	Natal	1973 South Africa
		Rockery
A.striata	South-West Africa	1882 West Wall:
		Middle Terrace
A.striatula	Cape Province	1959 Middle Terrace
A.succotrina	Cape Province	1959 West Wall:
		Middle Terrace
A.trichosantha	Eritrea	1973 Mexico:
		Middle Terrace
A.variegata	Cape Province	1977 Palm Rockery

Alstroemeria (Alstroemeriaceae)

A.aurantiaca	Chile	1854 Well Garden
A.aurantiaca 'Yellow Form'	Chile	1854 Well Garden
A.Ligtu hybrids	Chile	1974 Hop Circle

Amaryllis (Amaryllidaceae)

A.belladonna	South Africa	1890 Many places
A.belladonna 'Kewensis'	South Africa	1959 Old Abbey
A.belladonna 'White Form'	South Africa	1952 Mexico:
		Middle Terrace

Amorphophallus (Araceae)

A.rivieri (devil's tongue)	East Indies	1959 West Rockery Bog

Anacampsereos (Portulacaceae)

A.lanceolatum	Cape Province	1974 Collection
A.rufescens	Cape Province	1959 Collection
A.telephiastrum	Cape Province	1959 Collection

Anemone (Ranunculaceae)

A.blanda	Greece	1973 Palm Rockery
A.x fulgens (A.pavonina x hortensis)	Balkans	1973 Top Terrace:
		Agave Bank
A.hupehensis	China	1848 Hop Circle
A.hupehensis 'Alba'	China	1848 Hop Circle

Angophora (Myrtaceae)

A.cordifolia	Australia	1959 Monument Walk
		South

Anigozanthus (Haemodoraceae)

A.flavidus (kangaroo paw)	Australia	1959 South Africa Flat
A.flavidus 'Rubra'	Australia	1959 South Africa Flat

Anopterus (Escalloniaceae)

A.glandulosus	Tasmania	1865 Higher Australia

Antegibbaeum (Aizoaceae)

A.fissoides	South Africa	1959 Abbey Rock Garden

Antholyza (Iridaceae)

A.ringens	South Africa	1978 Collection

Antirrhinum (Aponogetonaceae)

A.distachyon (water hawthorn)	South Africa	1851 Well Covert Pond

Aptenia (Aizoaceae)

A.cordifolia	South Africa	1959 Old Abbey

Aquilegia (Ranunculaceae)

A.vulgaris (Colombo)	Europe	1959 Well Garden

A.vulgaris 'Flore Pleno'	Hort.	1959 Well Garden
A.vulgaris 'McKana Hybrids'	Hort.	1974 Well Garden

Araucaria (Araucariaceae)

A.angustifolia (Parana pine)	Brazil	1959 Long Walk
A.araucana (monkey puzzle)	Chile	1914 Abbey Rock Garden
A.bidwillii (bunya bunya pine)	Australia	1857 Pear Tree Garden
A.excelsa (Norfolk Is. pine)	Norfolk Island	1851 Long Walk

Arbutus (Ericaceae)

A.menziesii (madrona)	North-West America	1856 Grassy Walk
A.unedo (strawberry tree)	Europe	1959 East Rockery

Archontophoenix (Palmaceae)

A.alexandrae	Queensland	1973 Collection
A.cunninghamiana (Illawarra palm)	Queensland	1973 Long Walk

Arctotis (Compositae)

A.aspera	South Africa	1873 Middle Terrace

Argyroderma (Aizoaceae)

A.littorale	South Africa	1974 Conservatory
		Rock Garden

Arisaema (Araceae)

A.speciosum	Himalaya	1979 Well Garden

Aristea (Iridaceae)

A.capitata	South Africa	1959 General
A.compacta	South Africa	1973 Podalyria Bank
A.thyrsiflora	South Africa	1959 Mexico:
		Middle Terrace

Aristotelia (Elaeocarpaceae)

A.serrata (wineberry)	New Zealand	1950 Abbey Drive

Armeria (Plumbaginaceae)

A.pseudoarmeria	Portugal	1974 Middle Terrace

Arthropodium (Liliaceae)

A.cirrhatum	New Zealand	1896 Well Garden
A.millefolium	New Zealand	1959 Well Garden

Arum (Arum)

A.italicum	Native	1834 General

Aruncus (Rosaceae)

A.sylvester	N.Hemisphere	1973 West Rockery

Arundinaria (Gramineae)

A.falconeri	Himalaya	1874 West Orchard
A.fastuosa	Japan	1964 Lighthouse Walk
A.hookeriana	Sikkim	1914 Bamboo Garden
A.japonica	Japan	1914 Bamboo Walk
A.marmorea	Japan	1963 Bamboo Walk
A.nitida	China	1914 Lighthouse Walk
A.pygmaea	Japan	1979 Collection
A.simonii	Japan	1890 Bamboo Garden
A.vagans	Japan	1964 Long Walk
A.variegata	Japan	1959 Long Walk
A.viridistriata	Japan	1973 Bamboo Garden

Arundo (Gramineae)

A.donax (Spanish reed)	South Europe	1851 West Orchard

Asarina (Scrophulariaceae)

A.procumbens	South France	1959 Well Garden

Asclepias (Asclepiadaceae)

A.curassavica (blood flower)	Tropical America	1977 Glasshouse

Asparagus (Liliaceae)

A.crispus	South Africa	1959 Conservatory
A.medeoloides (smilax)	South Africa	1914 Well Garden
A.plumosus (asparagus fern)	South Africa	1894 Augustus Smith
		Wall
A.sprengeri	Natal	1914 Conservatory

Asphodelus (Liliaceae)

A.microcarpus	South Europe	1914 Toy Greenhouse
		Bank

Aspidistra (Liliaceae)		
A.lurida	China	1894 Well Garden

Asplenium (Aspleniaceae)		
A.adiantum-nigrum (black spleenwort)	Native	1855 Rock crevices
A.billotii (lanceolate spleenwort)	Native	1855 Rock crevices
A.bulbiferum (hen and chickens fern)	New Zealand	1894 Fernery
A.marinum (sea spleenwort)	Native	1855 East Rockery Wall
A.nidus var. *australasicum*	Australia	1863 Conservatory
A.scolopendrium (hart's tongue)	Native	1855 Well Covert
A.scolopendrium 'Bifidum'	Native	1973 Well Covert
A.scolopendrium 'Crispum'	Britain	1855 Collection
A.scolopendrium 'Crispum Cristatum'	Britain	1975 Collection
A.scolopendrium 'Crispum Moly'	Britain	1975 Collection
A.scolopendrium 'Cristatum'	Britain	1894 Collection
A.scolopendrium 'Ramo-cristatum'	Britain	1977 Collection
A.trichomanes ssp. *quadrivalens*	Native	1855 Collection
A.trichomanes 'Cristatum'	Britain	1975 Collection
A.trichomanes 'Incisum Moule'	Britain	1976 Collection
A.trichomanes 'Ramo-cristatum'	Britain	1976 Collection

Astelia (Liliaceae)		
A.cunninghamii	New Zealand	1959 Fernery
A.nervosa	New Zealand	1896 Fernery
A.petriei	New Zealand	1977 Tree Ferns: Abbey Drive

Aster (Compositae)		
A.pappei	South Africa	1959 Top Terrace

Astilbe (Saxifragaceae)		
A. x *arendsii* Hybrids	East Asia	1959 East Rockery

Athrotaxis (Pinaceae)		
A.cupressoides	Tasmania	1865 Well Covert

Athyrium (Aspleniaceae)		
A.filix-foemina (lady fern)	Native	1855 Shade throughout
A.filix-foemina 'Corymbiferum'	Britain	1975 Fern Bed: Entrance
A.filix-foemina 'Frizelliae'	Britain	1975 Collection
A.filix-foemina 'Minutissima'	Britain	1975 Collection
A.filix-foemina 'Percristatum'	Britain	1977 Collection
A.filix-foemina 'Regale'	Britain	1975 Collection
A.filix-foemina 'Vernonae'	Britain	1977 Collection

Atriplex (Chenopodiaceae)		
A.halimus	Southern Europe	1896 Top Terrace

Aubrietia (Cruciferae)		
A.deltoidea	Mediterranean	1973 Middle Terrace

Aucuba (Cornaceae)		
A.japonica	Japan	1848 Long Walk
A.japonica 'Variegata'	Japan	1914 Lily Garden

Azara (Flacourtiaceae)		
A.lanceolata	Chile	1959 Grassy Walk
A.microphylla	Chile	1959 Grassy Walk

Azolla (Salviniaceae)		
A.caroliniana	America	1975 Collection

Babiana (Iridaceae)		
B.stricta	S. Africa	1886 Agave Bank

Baccharis (Compositae)		
B.patagonica	Argentina	1894 Collection

Ballota (Labiatae)		
B.pseudodictamnus	Crete	1959 Pear Tree Garden

Banksia (Proteaceae)		
B.baxteri	Australia	1973 South Africa Flat
B.caleyi	Australia	1965 By Neptune
B.coccinea	Australia	1914 Top Terrace East
B.collina	Australia	1973 Top Terrace West
B.ericaefolia	Australia	1904 Puya Bank
B.grandis	Australia	1890 Top Terrace East
B.integrifolia	Australia	1890 Long Walk
B.littoralis	Tasmania	1890 Miss Innis' East
B.marginata	Australia	1914 Grassy Walk

B.quercifolia	Australia	1914 Arcadia: Oak Garden
B.serratifolia (aemula)	Australia	1890 Gardeners' Path West
B.spinulosa	Australia	1914 Arcadia
B.verticillata	Australia	1973 Gardeners' Path East

Barosma (Rutaceae)		
B.lanceolata	South Africa	1914 Agave Bank

Beaufortia (Myrtaceae)		
B.sparsa	Australia	1894 Top Terrace

Bedfordia (Compositae)		
B.salicina	Australia	1973 Old Nursery Garden

Berberidopsis (Flacourtiaceae)		
B.corallina	Chile	1867 Collection

Berberis (Berberidaceae)		
B.darwinii	Chile	1853 Lighthouse Walk

Bergenia (Saxifragaceae)		
B.cordifolia	Siberia	1959 Hop Circle

Beschorneria (Agavaceae)		
B.bracteata	Mexico	1976 By Tea Hut
B.tubiflora	Mexico	1896 Neptune Steps West
B.yuccoides	Mexico	1890 South Africa Flat

Betula (Betulaceae)		
B.pubescens (silver birch)	Britain	1890 Abbey Drive: Tree Fernery

Billbergia (Bromeliaceae)		
B.nutans	Brazil	1959 Cypress Rockery

Blechnum (Polypodiaceae)		
B.capense	New Zealand	1895 Fernery
B.penna-marina	New Zealand	1959 Lapageria Corner
B.spicant (hard fern)	Native	1855 Abbey Drive
B.tabulare	South America	1857 Collection

Bletilla (Orchidaceae)		
B.striata	China	1914 South Africa Rockery

Bomarea (Alstroemeriaceae)		
B.caldasii	Ecuador	1914 Well Garden

Boronia (Rutaceae)		
B.alata	Australia	1903 Agave Bank

Bossiaea (Leguminosae)		
B.linophylla	Australia	1914 Top Terrace

Bougainvillea (Nyctaginaceae)		
B.glabra	Brazil	1914 Conservatory

Boussingaultia (Basellaceae)		
B.baselloides	South America	1890 Collection

Bowiea (Liliaceae)		
B.volubilis	South Africa	1894 Peach House

Bowkeria (Scrophulariaceae)		
B.gerardiana	Natal	1914 Grassy Walk North

Brachyglottis (Compositae)		
B.repanda	New Zealand	1856 Tea Hut
B.repanda 'Rangiora'	New Zealand	1914 Stone Table

Brachychiton (Sterculiaceae)		
B.acerifolia	Australia	1904 Long Walk North-West
B.diversifolia	Australia	1914 Grassy Walk North

Briza (Gramineae)		
B.minor (quaking grass)	Native	1973 Toy Greenhouse etc.

Brodiaea (Liliaceae)		
B.laxa (Ithuriel's spear)	California	1890 Mexico
Buddleia (Loganiaceae)		
B.asiatica	East India	1914 Duckery Lawn
B.auriculata	South Africa	1914 Duckery Entrance
B.colvillei	Himalayas	1914 Lighthouse Walk
B.davidi	China	1914 West Orchard
B.farreri	China	1959 Stone Table
B.globosa	Chile	1856 Duckery
B.madagascariensis	Madagascar	1914 West Orchard
B.officinalis	China	1977 Duckery
B.salvifolia	South Africa	1914 Stone Table
B.x weyeriana	B.davidi	
	x B. globosa	1973 Grassy Walk North
Bupleurum (Umbelliferae)		
B.fruiticosum	Southern Europe	1890 Old Abbey
B.salicifolium	Canary Islands	1974 Well Garden
Bursaria (Pittosporaceae)		
B.spinosa	Australia	1959 Middle Terrace
Caesalpinia (Leguminosae)		
C.gilliesii	Argentina	1851 Conservatory
C.japonica	Japan	1959 Citrus Garden
Calceolaria (Scrophulariaceae)		
C.integrifolia 'Angustifolia'	Chile	1914 Citrus Garden
Callistemon (Myrtaceae) bottle brushes		
C.acuminatus	Australia	1953 Monument Path South
C.brachyandrus	Australia	1914 Top Terrace
C.citrinus	Australia	1959 Pebble Garden
C.citrinus 'Splendens'	Australia	1959 Top Terrace
C.linearis	Australia	1890 Cypress Rockery
C.macropunetata	Australia	1977 Collection
C.pallidus 'Roseus'	Australia	1959 Grassy Walk South
C.pinifolius	Australia	1959 Monument Walk
C.salignus	Australia	1914 Top Terrace
Callitris (Cupressaceae) cypress pines		
C.rhomboides (Oyster Bay pine)	Australia	1894 Gardeners' Walk
Calluna (Ericaceae)		
C.vulgaris (ling)	Native	1852 Top Terrace
Calocephalus (Compositae)		
C.brownii	Australia	1973 Mexico
Calodendrum (Rutaceae)		
C.capense (Cape chestnut)	South Africa	1907 Grassy Walk North
Calothamnus (Myrtaceae)		
C.gilesii	Australia	1973 Top Terrace West
C.homalophyllus	Australia	1973 Top Terrace West
C.quadrifidus	Australia	1959 Miss Innis'
C.sanguineus	Australia	1959 Puya Bank
Caltha (Ranunculaceae)		
C.palustris (marsh marigold)	Britain	1914 Well Covert
Calystegia (Convolvulaceae)		
C.sepium (hedge bindweed)	Native	1852 Weed: Cut Flower Garden
Camassia (Liliaceae)		
C.leichtlinii (quamash)	West North America	1894 Lower Fish Pond
Camellia (Theaceae)		
C.cuspidata	China	1959 Toy Greenhouse Path
C.hongkongensis	Hong Kong	1973 Lily Garden
C.japonica Cultivars	Japan	1890
C. 'Adolphe Audusson'		1959 Long Walk
C. 'Alba Plena'		1959 Citrus Garden
C. 'Althiiflora'		1959 Long Walk
C. 'Anna Grumeau'		1959 Potting Shed Bed
C. 'Chandleri'		1959 Lower Australia
C. 'Contessa Lavinia Maggi'		1959 Long Walk

C. 'Donckelarii'		1959 Old Nursery Garden
C. 'Elegans'		1959 Lower Australia
C. 'Grandiflora Alba'		1959 Long Walk
C. 'Imbricata Rubra'		1959 Long Walk
C. 'Jupiter'		1959 Toy Greenhouse Path
C. 'Lady Clare'		1959 Long Walk
C. 'Lotus'		1959 Long Walk
C. 'Magnoliiflora'		1959 Well Garden
C. 'Montironi'		1959 Potting Shed Bed
C. 'Mrs. D.W. Davis'		1973 Hop Circle
C. 'Nagasaki'		1959 Potting Shed Bed
C. 'Rogetsu'		1973 Hop Circle
C. 'Rubescens Major'		1973 Hop Circle
C. 'Sacco Nova'		1959 Well Garden
C. 'Snow Princess'		1959 Well Garden
C. 'Souvenir de Bahoud Litou'		1959 Potting Shed Bed
C. 'Stella Polaris'		1959 Lower Australia
C. 'Yuki-mi-gurma'		1973 Hop Circle
C.reticulata	China	1902 Well Garden
C.saluenensis	China	1950 Duckery Dell
C.sasanqua	Japan	1973 Duckery Dell
C.sasanqua 'Narumi-gata'	Japan	1973 Lily Garden
C.x williamsii		
(C.saluenensis) x japonica		
C. 'Caerhays'	Hort.	1973 Hop Circle
C. 'Donation'		1973 Hop Circle
C. 'George Blandford'		1973 Hop Circle
C. 'J.C. Williams'		1973 Hop Circle
C. 'Mary Jobson'		1973 Hop Circle
C. 'November Pink'		1973 Hop Circle
C. 'Rosemary Williams'		1973 Hop Circle
C. 'St. Ewe'		1973 Hop Circle
Campanula (Campanulaceae)		
C.carpatica 'Alba'	Europe	1973 Conservatory
C.vidalii	Azores	1854 Collection
Candollea (Dilleniaceae)		
C.cuneiformis	Australia	1973 Old Abbey South
C.tetrandra	Australia	1890 Potting Shed Bed
Canna (Cannaceae)		
C.generalis	Hort.	1890 Old Abbey Citrus Garden
C.generalis 'Flamant Rose'	Hort.	1973 Old Abbey Citrus Garden
C.indica	Trop. America	1890 Lighthouse Walk
C.iridiflora	Peru	1868 Well Garden
Caragana (Leguminosae)		
C.arborescens (bladder senna)	Siberia	1973 Top Terrace
Carex (Cyperaceae) sedges		
C.baccans	India	1973 Collection
C.pendula	Britain	1973 Bamboo Garden
Carmichaelia (Leguminosae)		
C.cunninghamii	New Zealand	1914 Grassy Walk South
Carpobrotus (Aizoaceae)		
C.acinaceforme	South Africa	1853 Toy Greenhouse Bed
C.aequalaterale	Australia	1894 Collection
C.edulis (Hottentot fig)	South Africa	1856 Toy Greenhouse Bed
C.edulis 'Mauve Form'	South Africa	1959 Cypress Rockery
C.fourcadei	South Africa	1974 Neptune Steps
C.muirii	South Africa	1952 Cypress Rockery
Cassia (Leguminosae)		
C.corymbosa	South America	1856 Old Nursery Garden
Cassinia (Compositae)		
C.fulvida	New Zealand	1865 East Orchard
C.leptophylla	New Zealand	1914 Collection
Castanea (Fagaceae)		
C.sativa (sweet chestnut)	Southern Europe	1894 Podalyria Bank
Casuarina (Casuarinaceae)		
C.equisetifolia	Australia	1914 Collection
C.stricta (sheoke)	Australia	1914 South Africa Flat
C.torulosa	Australia	1975 Pear Tree Garden

Ceanothus (Rhamnaceae)
C.arboreus 'Trewithen Blue'	California	1959 Pear Tree Garden
C.impressus	California	1856 Pear Tree Garden

Celmisia (Compositae)
C.bellidioides	New Zealand	1979 Collection
C.coriacea 'Stricta'	New Zealand	1979 Collection
C.coriacea 'Inshriach Hybrid'	Hort.	1979 Collection
C.monroi	New Zealand	1979 Collection
C.ramulosa	New Zealand	1979 Collection

Centaurea (Compositae)
C.arbutifolia	Canary Islands	1973 Long Walk
C.macrocephala	Caucasus	1973 Lily Garden

Cereocarpus (Rosaceae)
C.betuloides	California	1949 Grassy Walk

Cereus (Cactaceae)
C.forbesii	South America	1975 Cactus Bank
C.hexagonus	South America	1973 Cactus Bank
C.jamaracu	Brazil	1973 Toy Greenhouse
C.peruvianus 'Monstrosus'	South America	1854 Cactus Bank

Ceropegia (Aselepiadaceae)
C.fusca	Canary Islands	1973 Conservatory
C.stapeliiformis	South Africa	1974 Conservatory
C.woodii	Natal	1973 Collection

Cestrum (Solanaceae)
C.x newellii	Hort.	1959 Pear Tree Garden
C.parqui	Chile	1933 Pear Tree Garden

Chaenomeles (Rosaceae)
C.speciosa (flowering quince)	Japan	1894 Duckery Gate

Chamaecyparis (Cupressaceae)
C.lawsoniana (Lawson's cypress)	California	1894 Abbey Drive
C.lawsoniana 'Erecta Viridis'	Hort.	1914 Abbey Drive
C.lawsoniana 'Intertexta'	Hort.	1856 Abbey Drive
C.lawsoniana 'Wisselii'	Hort.	1959 Middle Terrace
C.pisifera (Sawara cypress)	Japan	1894 Well Garden

Chamaerops (Palmaceae)
C.humilis	Mediterranean	1856 Hop Circle

Chasmanthe (Iridaceae)
C.aethiopica	South Africa	1959 Top Terrace
C.bicolor	South Africa	1959 Well Covert etc.

Chlidanthus (Amaryllidaceae)
C.fragrans	Andes	1975 Collection

Chlorophytum (Liliaceae)
C.comosum 'Variegatum'	South Africa	1959 Well Garden

Choisya (Rutaceae)
C.ternata (Mexican orange blossom)	Mexico	1890 Lighthouse Walk

Chordospartium (Leguminosae)
C.stevensonii	New Zealand	1922 Grassy Walk

Chrysanthemoides (Compositae)
C.monolifera	South Africa	1959 Top Terrace

Chrysanthemum (Compositae)
C.frutescens (marguerite)	Canary Islands	1856 East Orchard
C.frutescens 'Jamaican Primrose'	Hort.	1959 Old Abbey
C.frutescens 'Mary Wootton'	Hort.	1894 Lighthouse Walk
C.maximum	Pyrenees	1973 Long Walk
C.maximum 'Esther Read'	Hort.	1977 Cut Flower Garden

Chrysocoma (Compositae)
C.coma-aurea	South Africa	1914 Top Terrace

Cinnamomum (Lauraceae)
C.camphora (camphor)	Japan	1890 Long Walk

Cissus (Vitidaceae)
C.antarctica (kangaroo vine)	Australia	1863 Well Garden
C.juttae	South-West Africa	1973 Toy Greenhouse

Cistus (Cistaceae)
C.x aguilari		
(populifolius x ladaniferus)	Spain	1959 Top Terrace
C.albidus	Mediterranean	1914 Top Terrace
C.x corbariensis		
(populifolius x salviifolius)	South France	1973 Top Terrace
C.creticus	Mediterranean	1973 Top Terrace
C.x florentinus		
(salviifolius x monspeliensis)	South Europe	1894 Top Terrace
C.ladaniferus 'Albiflorus'	South Europe	1959 Neptune Steps
C.monspeliensis	South Europe	1914 Top Terrace
C.populifolius	South-West Europe	1959 Top Terrace
C.x pulverulentus 'Sunset'	crispus x albidus	1973 Top Terrace:
		'Miss Innis'
C.x purpureus		
(creticus x ladanifer)	Hort.	1959 Top Terrace
C.salvifolius	Mediterranean	1914 Monument Walk South
C.x skanbergii		
(Monspeliensis x parviflorus)	Greece	1973 Monument Walk

Colchicum (Liliaceae)
C.agrippinum	Greece	1894 Palm Rockery
C.autumnale (Autumn crocus)	Britain	1894 Palm Rockery

Coleonema (Rutaceae)
C.album	South Africa	1894 Top Terrace
C.pulchrum	South Africa	1950 Top Terrace

Colletia (Rhamnaceae)
C.cruciata	Uruguay	1914 Top Terrace

Colutea (Leguminosae)
C.arborescens (bladder senna)	Southern Europe	1959 Top Terrace

Commelina (Commelinaceae)
C.coelestis	Mexico	1890 Pebble Garden

Coniogramme (Adiantaceae)
C.japonica	Japan	1975 Collection

Conophytum (Aizoaceae)
C.species	South Africa	1959 Toy Greenhouse

Convallaria (Liliaceae)
C.majalis (lily of the valley)	Britain	1890 Hop Circle

Convolvulus (Convolvulaceae)
C.cneorum	South Europe	1854 Collection
C.floridus	Canary Islands	1948 Middle Terrace
C.mauritanicus	North Africa	1865 Old Abbey

Coprosma (Rubiaceae)
C.lucida	New Zealand	1890 Pear Tree Garden
		South
C.repens	New Zealand	1890 Long Walk
C.repens 'Variegata'	New Zealand	1978 Collection
C.repens 'Variegata Tresco Form'	Tresco	1890 Long Walk
C.robusta	New Zealand	1914 Higher Australia

Cordyline (Agavaceae)
C.australis (N.Z. cabbage tree)	New Zealand	1856 Long Walk
C.australis 'Atropurpurea'	New Zealand	1914 Hop Circle
C.australis 'Aureo-striata'	New Zealand	1914 Old Abbey
C.banksii	New Zealand	1914 Middle Terrace
C.baueri	Norfolk Island	1890 Podalyria Bank
C.indivisa	New Zealand	1853 Long Walk
C.kaspar	New Zealand	1973 Grassy Walk
C.x scilloniensis	C.australis	
	x C.banksii	1882 Old Abbey
C.stricta	Australia	1959 Top Terrace

Coreopsis (Compositae)
C.mutica	Unknown	1973 Collection

Cornus (Cornaceae)
C.capitata	Nepal	1914 Lighthouse Walk

Corokia (Cornaceae)
C.buddleoides	New Zealand	1856 Abbey Drive
C.cotoneaster	New Zealand	1891 Collection
C.macrocarpa	Chatham Island	1973 Well Covert

Coronilla (Leguminosae)
C.glauca	Southern Europe	1894 Middle Terrace
C.glauca 'Variegata'	Southern Europe	1959 Collection

Correa (Rutaceae)
C.alba	Australia	1850 Top Terrace East
C.backhousiana	Australia	1873 Top Terrace
C.decumbens	Australia	1959 Top Terrace
C.x harrisii	Australia	1856 East Orchard
C.lawrenciana	Australia	1851 Podalyria Bank
C.pulchella	Australia	1850 Middle Terrace
C.reflexa 'Cardinalis'	Australia	1863 East Orchard
C.reflexa 'Dusky Bell'	Australia	1973 East Orchard
C.reflexa 'Mannii'	Australia	1973 Palm Rockery
C.reflexa 'Recurviflora'	Australia	1959 Top Terrace East
C.reflexa 'Rosea'	Australia	1959 Long Walk
C.reflexa 'Viridiflora'	Australia	1959 Miss Innis'
C.schlechtendalii	Australia	1973 Middle Terrace

Cortaderia (Graminae) pampas grass
C.rhendetlerii	Argentina	1977 Cactus Bank Lawn
C.selloana	Argentina	1959 East Rockery
C.'Alba lineata'	Argentina	1977 Limpet Midden
C.'Gold Band'	Argentina	1977 Limpet Midden
C.'Pumila'	Argentina	1977 Limpet Midden
C.'Sunningdale Silver'	Argentina	1959 Middle Terrace

Corynocarpus (Corynocarpaceae)
C.laevigata (karaka)	New Zealand	1856 Long Walk

Cotoneaster (Rosaceae)
C.conspicuus	Tibet	1973 West Rockery
C.horizontalis	China	1914 Middle Terrace West
C.pannosa	China	1973 Agave Bank
C.simonsii	China	1882 Monument

Cotyledon (Crassulaceae)
C.decussata	South Africa	1959 Mexico: Middle Terrace
C.orbiculata	South Africa	1914 Middle Terrace
C.paniculata	South Africa	1973 Collection
C.teretifolia	South Africa	1959 Collection
C.undulata	South Africa	1973 Collection

Crambe (Cruciferae)
C.maritima (sea kale)	Native	1856 Garden Field
C.strigosa	Canary Islands	1976 Higher Australia

Crassula (Crassulaceae)
C.acutifolia	South Africa	1973 Collection
C.albiflora	South Africa	1854 Collection
C.arborescens	South Africa	1959 Middle Terrace
C.cephalophera	South Africa	1959 Collection
C.cooperi	South Africa	1959 Collection
C.cordata	South Africa	1959 Collection
C.cultrata	South Africa	1959 Toy Greenhouse Bed
C.falcata	South Africa	1894 Toy Greenhouse Bed
C.johannis-winkleri	South Africa	1973 Middle Terrace
C.justus-corderoyi	South Africa	1959 Collection
C.lactea	South Africa	1890 Toy Greenhouse Bed
C.lycopodioides	South Africa	1959 Collection
C.lycopodioides 'Turrita'	South Africa	1959 Collection
C.multicava	South Africa	1894 Aeonium Bank
C.multicava 'Variegata'	South Africa	1973 Collection
C.nealeana	South Africa	1973 Collection
C.obliqua 'Foliis Variegata'	South Africa	1973 Collection
C.obvallata	South Africa	1959 Collection
C.perfoliata	South Africa	1959 Toy Greenhouse Bed
C.perforata	South Africa	1890 Collection
C.portulacea	South Africa	1959 Collection
C.portulacea 'Humel's Sunset'	South Africa	1973 Collection
C.radicans	South Africa	1959 Cypress Rockery
C.rosularis	South Africa	1959 Collection
C.rupestris	South Africa	1973 Collection
C.sarcocaulis	South Africa	1914 Collection
C.sarmentosa	South Africa	1959 Collection
C.sladenii	South Africa	1973 Collection
C.spathulata	South Africa	1973 Collection
C.tabularis	South Africa	1959 Collection
C.tetragona	South Africa	1894 Middle Terrace

Crataegus (Rosaceae)
C.monogyna (hawthorn)	Native	1890 Abbey Drive

Crepis (Compositae)
C.incana	Greece	1973 Collection

Crinodendron (Elaeocarpaceae)
C.patagua	Chile	1914 Fernery

Crinum (Amaryllidaceae)
C.bulbispermum	South Africa	1856 Citrus Garden
C.moorei	South Africa	1890 Top Terrace
C.x powellii	C.bulbispermum x C. moorei	1894 Duckery Gate

Crithmum (Umbelliferae)
C.maritimum (rock samphire)	Native	1750 Middle Terrace

Crocosmia (Iridaceae)
C.crocosmiiflora (montbretia)	C.potsii x aurea	1890 Long Walk etc.
C.masonorum	South Africa	1975 East Orchard

Cunninghamia (Pinaceae)
C.lanceolata (Chinese fir)	China	1959 Abbey Drive

Cuphea (Lythraceae)
C.cyanea	Mexico	1959 Old Abbey
C.ignea (cigar plant)	Mexico	1959 Old Abbey

x Cupressocyparis (Cupressaceae)
C.leylandii	Cham. lawsoniana x C.nootkatensis	1953 Abbey Drive
C.leylandii 'Castlewellan'	Hort.	1975 Conifer Lawn

Cupressus (Cupressaceae) cypresses
C.arizonica	U.S.A.	1952 Monument Wood North
C.cashmeriana	India	1914 Abbey Drive
C.funebris	China	1894 Conifer Lawn
C.macrocarpa	California	1894 Abbey Wood etc.
C.macrocarpa 'Lutea'	California	1959 Abbey Drive
C.sempervirens var. sempervirens	Southern Europe	1959 Old Abbey

Curtonus (Iridaceae)
C.paniculatus	South Africa	1890 Top Terrace

Cyanella (Amaryllidaceae)
C.capensis	South Africa	1977 Collection

Cyathea (Cyatheaceae)
C.dealbata (ponga)	New Zealand	1865 Fernery
C.medullaris (mamaku)	New Zealand	1891 Fernery
C.robusta	New Zealand	1959 Tree Ferns: Abbey Drive
C.smithii	New Zealand	1894 Fernery

Cyclamen (Primulaceae)
C.hederaefolium	South Europe	1973 Fernery
C.repandum	Southern Europe	1973 Fernery

Cynara (Compositae)
C.scolymus	Mediterranean	1973 Garden Field

Cyperus (Cyperaceae)
C.alternifolius (umbrella plant)	Madagascar	1894 West Rockery

Cyphomandra (Solanaceae)
C.betacea (tree tomato)	Brazil	1914 Pear Tree Garden

Cyrtanthus (Amaryllidaceae)
C.mackenii	South Africa	1914 Collection

Cyrtomium (Aspleniaceae)
C.falcatum 'Rochfordianum'	Japan	1894 Long Walk

Cystopteris (Aspleniaceae)
C.fragilis (brittle bladder fern)	Britain	1855 Entrance

Cytisus (Leguminosae)
C.fragrans	Southern Europe	1865 West Rockery
C.maderensis 'Magnifoliosus'	Madeira	1914 West Rockery

C.nigricans	Southern Europe	1914 Well Garden	*Doodia* (Blechnaceae)		
C.proliferus	Canary Islands	1914 Long Walk	*D.caudata*	Australia	1974 Collection

Daboecia (Ericaceae)

D.cantabrica (St. Dabeoc's heath)	Europe	1959 Neptune, Top Terrace	*Doryanthes* (Amaryllidaceae)		
			D.excelsa (Queensland rock lily)	Australia	1891 West Rockery

Dacrydium (Taxcaceae)

D.cupressinum (rimu)	New Zealand	1914 Tree Ferns: Abbey Drive	*Dorycnium* (Leguminosae)		
			D.hirsutum	Southern Europe	1973 Collection

Dahlia (Compositae)

D.coccinea	Mexico	1959 Citrus Garden	*Doryopteris* (Adiantaceae)		
			D.pedata	South America	1976 Collection

Daphne (Thymelaceaceae)

D.laureola (spurge laurel)	Native	1890 Old Nursery Garden	*Dracaena* (Agavaceae)		
			D.draco (dragon tree)	Canary Islands	1857 Collection

Daphniphyllum (Euphorbiaceae)

D.macropodum	Korea	1914 Grassy Walk	*Dranunculus* (Araceae)		
			D.vulgaris	Southern Europe	1844 Well Garden

Dasylirion (Agavaceae)

D.acrotrichum	Mexico	1890 Citrus Garden	*Drimys* (Winteraceae)		
D.glaucophyllum	Mexico	1959 Cypress Rockery	*D.winteri* (Winter's bark)	South America	1914 Long Walk

Datura (Solanaceae)

D.arborea (angel's trumpet)	Peru	1894 Collection	*Drosanthemum* (Aizoaceae)		
D.cornigera	Mexico	1914 Lighthouse Walk South	*D.floribundum*	South Africa	1865 Cypress Rockery
D.ferox	Southern Europe	1978 Collection	*Dryandra* (Proteaceae)		
D.sanguinea	Peru	1959 Entrance Gate	*D.formosa*	Australia	1914 Top Terrace
D.stramonium (thorn apple)	Native	1938 Garden Field			
D.suaveolens	Mexico	1978 Collection	*Dryopteris* (Aspleniaceae)		
			D.aemula (hay-scented buckler fern)	Britain	1855 Collection

Davallia (Davalliaceae)

D.bullata (squirrel's foot fern)	Japan	1888 Collection	*D.austriaes* (broad buckler fern)	Native	1855 Abbey Drive
D.canariensis (hare's foot fern)	Canary Islands	1890 By Potting Shed	*D.austriaes* 'Grandiceps'	Britain	1975 Collection
			D.austriaes 'Lepidiota-Cristata'	Britain	1975 Collection
			D.carthusiana	Native	1855 Collection

Delospermum (Aizoaceae)

D.aberdeenensis	South Africa	1974 Pot: Neptune Steps	*D.erythrosora*	China	1975 Tree Ferns: Abbey Drive
D.echinatum	South Africa	1914 Collection	*D.filix-mas* (male fern)	Native	1856 Long Walk
D.lehmannii	South Africa	1974 Collection	*D.filix-mas* 'Crispa Cristata'	Britain	1975 Collection
			D.filix-mas 'Linearis'	Britain	1976 Collection

Delphinium (Ranunculaceae)

*D.*Garden cultivar	Hort.	1973 Pebble Garden	*D.filix-mas* 'Linearis Congesta-Crispa'	Britain	1976 Collection
			D.filix-mas 'Polydactyla'	Britain	1975 Collection

Desfontainea (Loganiaceae)

D.spinosa	Chile	1854 Lighthouse Walk South	*D.filix-mas* 'Robustissima'	Britain	1975 Collection
			D.pseudo-mas (scaly male fern)	Native	1975 Collection
			D.pseudo-mas 'Angustata Cristata'	Britain	1977 Collection

Deutzia (Philadelphaceae)

D.longifolia	China	1959 Citrus Garden	*D.pseudo-mas* 'Cristata'	Britain	1976 Collection
			D.pseudo-mas 'Grandiceps'	Britain	1975 Collection

Dianella (Liliaceae)

D.caerulea	Australia	1890 Higher Australia	*D.pseudo-mas* 'Polydactyla'	Britain	1976 Collection
D.revoluta	Australia	1894 Lower Australia	*D.villarii* (rigid buckler fern)	Britain	1855 Collection
D.tasmanica	Australia	1894 Higher Australia East			

Dudleya (Crassulaceae)

			D.farinosa	California	1973 Mexico

Dicksonia (Cyatheaceae)

D.antarctica (tall tree fern)	Australia	1863 Fernery	*Dyckia* (Bromeliaceae)		
D.fibrosa (wheki-ponga)	New Zealand	1914 Tree Ferns: Abbey	*D.rariflora*	Brazil	1894 Mexico
D.squarrosa (wheki)	New Zealand	1863 Fernery			

Eccremocarpus (Bignoniaceae)

			E.scaber	Chile	1894 Old Abbey

Didymochlaena (Aspleniaceae)

D.truncatula	Pan-tropic	1976 Collection	*Echeveria* (Crassulaceae)		
			E.x derenosa	*derenbergii* x *setosa*	1959 Toy Greenhouse Bed

Dierama (Iridaceae)

D.pulcherrimum	South Africa	1890 Middle Terrace	*E.gibbiflora* 'Caranculata'	Mexico	1973 Collection
			E.gibbiflora 'Metallica'	Mexico	1953 South Africa Cliff

Digitalis (Scrophulariaceae)

D.purpurea (foxglove)	Native	1852 Abbey Drive	*E.rubella*	Mexico	1979 Collection
			E.sedoides	Mexico	1977 Collection

Diaphyma (Aizoaceae)

D.crassifolium	South Africa	1856 Collection	*Echinocactus* (Cactaceae)		
			E.grusonii	Mexico	1959 Limpet Midden

Dodonea (Sapindaceae)

D.viscosa	New Zealand	1890 Collection	*Echinocereus* (Cactaceae)		
D.'Purpurea'	New Zealand	1959 East Orchard	*E.berlandii*	Mexico	1979 Collection

Dolichos (Leguminosae)

D.lignosus (Australian pea)	Australia	1890 Old Abbey	*Echinopsis* (Cactaceae)		
			E.multiplex	Brazil	1973 Limpet Midden
			E.wilkinsonii	Argentina	1979 Collection

Echium (Boraginaceae)

E.callithyrsum	Canary Islands	1894 Limpet Midden
E.pininana	Canary Islands	1913 Entrance etc.
E.x scilloniensis	*webbii* x *pininana*	1948 Middle Terrace
E.webbii	Canary Islands	1915 Middle Terrace
E.webbii 'Tresco Blue'	Canary Islands	1973 Limpet Midden
E.wildpretii	Canary Islands	1914 Higher Australia

Elaeagnus (Elaeagnaceae)

E.macrophylla	Japan	1959 East Rockery
E.pungens 'Frederici'	Japan	1975 Collection
E.pungens 'Maculata'	Japan	1973 Higher Australia
E.x reflexa	pungens x glabra	1851 Long Walk etc.
E.x reflexa 'Inhce Castle'	Tresco	1973 Long Walk etc.
E.umbellata 'Parviflora'	Himalaya	1979 East Rockery

Elinghamita

E.johnsonii	New Zealand	1972 Long Walk

Elodea (Hydrocharidaceae)

E.densa	South America	1975 Ponds

Endymion (Liliaceae)

E.hispanicus (Spanish bluebell)	Spain	1952 Fernery
E.non-scriptus (bluebell)	Native	1834 Woodland, Abbey Drive

Entelea (Liliaceae)

E.arborescens	New Zealand	1914 Old Nursery Garden

Epiphyllum (Cactaceae)

E.'Auger' Hybrids	Hort.	1974 Cypress Rockery
E.oxypetalum	Mexico	1974 Collection

Eremurus (Liliaceae)

E.bungei	South-West Asia	1977 West Orchard
E.robustus	Central Asia	1977 West Orchard

Erepsia (Aizoaceae)

E.inclaudens	South Africa	1894 West Rockery

Erica (Ericaceae)

E.arborea (bruyere)	South Europe	1894 South Africa Flat etc.
E.baccans	South Africa	1882 Top Terrace (West)
E.bauera	South Africa	1959 Top Terrace
E.canaliculata	South Africa	1950 Toy Greenhouse Area
E.carnea 'Springwood White'	Europe	1972 Old Abbey
E.chamissonis	South Africa	1959 South Africa Flat
E.chloroloma	South Africa	1953 South Africa Flat
E.cinerea (bell heather)	Native	1834 Top Terrace
E.cruenta	South Africa	1972 South Africa Flat
E.formosa	South Africa	1972 Top Terrace
E.glandulosa 'Rubra'	South Africa	1914 South Africa Flat etc.
E.lusitanica	South-West Europe	1854 Toy Greenhouse Area
E.mauritanica	South Africa	1972 South Africa Flat
E.mediterranea	South-West Europe	1890 Old Abbey
E.patersonia	South Africa	1953 South Africa Flat
E.peziza	South Africa	1953 South Africa Flat
E.quadrangularis	South Africa	1973 South Africa Flat
E.terminalis	Spain	1959 Old Abbey
E.terminalis 'Thelma Woolner'	Sardinia	1976 Old Abbey
E.transparens	South Africa	1972 Top Terrace Centre
E.vagans	Britain	1894 Old Abbey
E.x veitchii	arborea x lusitanica	1908 Top Terrace
E.versicolor	South Africa	1959 South Africa Flat
E.verticillata	South Africa	1914 South Africa Flat

Erigeron (Compositae)

E.mucronatus	Mexico	1890 Old Abbey Walls etc.

Eriocephalus (Compositae)

E.africanus	South Africa	1959 Middle Terrace
E.sericeus	South Africa	1914 Miss Innis' Garden

Eriogonum (Polygonaceae)

E.giganteum (St. Catherine's lace)	California	1973 Top Terrace
E.latifolium 'Nudum'	California	1973 Top Terrace

Erlangea (Compositae)

E.tomentosa	East Africa	1959 Old Nursery Garden

Eryngium (Umbelliferae)

E.agavifolium	Argentine	1972 Old Nursery Garden

E.amethystinum	Europe	1977 West Rockery
E.bourgatii	Mediterranean	1977 Middle Terrace
	Mexico	
E.planum	East Europe	1977 Puya Bank

Erysimum (Cruciferae)

E.linifolium 'Bowles' Mauve'	Spain	1972 East Orchard

Erythrina (Leguminosae)

E.crista-gallii (coral tree)	Brazil	1853 Middle Terrace

Escallonia (Escalloniaceae)

E.bifida	Brazil	1853 Grassy Walk
E.bifida 'C.F. Ball'	Hort.	1959 Puya Bank
E.bifida 'Crimson Spire'	Hort.	1959 Toy Greenhouse Steps
E.x exoniensis	E.rosea x rubra	1894 Miss Innis'
E.'Gwen Anley'	Hort.	1959 Geranium Bank: Top Terrace
E.x iveyi	E.bifida x exoniens	1914 Abbey Drive Stables
E.laevis	U.S.A.	1856 Old Nursery Garden
E.x langleyensis	E.rubra x virgata	1914 Below Toy Greenhouse
E.paniculata 'Floribunda'	South America	1850 Podalyria Bank
E.'Red Hedger'	Hort.	1973 Hedge Aloe Walk
E.revoluta	Chile	1894 Lighthouse Walk West
E.rosea	Chile	1856 Geranium Bank: Top Terrace
E.rubra 'Glutinosa'	Chile	1959 Below Podalyria Bank
E.rubra 'Macrantha'	Chile	1882 Hedging General

Eucalyptus (Myrtaceae)

E.blakelyi	Australia	1976 East Rockery
E.calophylla	Australia	1904 Gardeners' Walk
E.cinerea	Australia	1952 Arcadia etc.
E.cornuta	Australia	1914 Gardeners' Walk
E.crenulata	Australia	1975 East Orchard
E.diversicolor	Australia	1973 Above Cut Flower Garden
E.ficifolia (red gum)	Australia	1904 Top Terrace etc.
E.globulus (Tasmanian blue gum)	Australia	1848 Long Walk
E.leucoxylon	Australia	1959 Monument North
E.linearis	Australia	1934 Gardeners' Walk
E.maculata	Australia	1959 Arcadia
E.nicholii	Australia	1975 Cut Flower Garden
E.obliqua	Australia	1894 Higher Australia
E.ovata	Australia	1959 Long Walk
E.perriniana	Australia	1976 Abbey Drive West
E.polyanthemos	Australia	1976 Abbey Drive West
E.preissiana	Australia	1924 Top Terrace North
E.regnans	Australia	1959 Long Walk
E.rubida	Australia	1979 Abbey Drive North-West
E.torquata	Australia	1924 Tree Fern Abbey Drive

Eucomis (Liliaceae)

E.bicolor (pineapple flower)	Natal	1973 Citrus Garden Wall
E.comosa	South Africa	1890 Citrus Garden Wall

Eucryphia (Eucryphiaceae)

E.cordifolia (ulmo)	Chile	1959 Mexico

Eugenia (Myrtaceae)

E.paniculata	Puerto Rico	1959 Higher Australia
E.smithii (lilly-pilly)	Australia	1959 Long Walk Centre

Euonymus (Celastraceae)

E.japonicus	Japan	1890 Hedging Valhalla etc.
E.japonicus 'Albo-Marginatus'	Japan	1978 Abbey Drive Kauri Garden
E.japonicus 'Aureo-pictus'	Japan	1890 Puya Bank
E.lucidus	Himalaya	1959 Toy Greenhouse South

Eupatorium (Compositae)

E.micranthum	Mexico	1914 Long Walk

Euphorbia (Euphorbiaceae)

E.aphylla	Canary Islands	1959 Collection
E.atropurpurea	Canary Islands	1974 East Orchard
E.balsamifera	Canary Islands	1978 Collection
E.bergeri	South Africa	1973 Collection
E.canariensis	Canary Islands	1914 Collection
E.caput-medusae	South Africa	1914 Collection
E.decaryi	Madagascar	1978 Collection
E.didieroides	Madagascar	1978 Collection
E.enopla	South Africa	1959 Collection
E.francoisi	Madagascar	1978 Collection
E.heptagona	South Africa	1978 Collection
E.lathyrus (caper spurge)	Britain	1959 Well Garden
E.mellifera	Canary Islands	1934 Well Covert
E.milii 'Splendens'	Madagascar	1959 Collection
E.resinifera	Morocco	1959 Palm Rockery South
E.tridentata	South Africa	1978 Collection

Euryops (Compositae)

E.abrotanifolius	South Africa	1973 South Africa Flat
E.athanasiae	South Africa	1914 Top Terrace
E.pectinatus	South Africa	1959 Palm Rockery
E.virgineus	South Africa	1959 Limpet Midden

Eustephia (Amaryllidaceae)

E.darwinii 'Variegata'	Peru	1978 Collection

Fagus (Fagaceae)

F.sylvatica (beech)	Britain	1894 Fernery

Fascicularia (Bromeliaceae)

F.bicolor	Chile	1959 Middle Terrace
F.pitcairniifolia	Tropical America	1914 Top Terrace

Fatsia (Araliaceae)

F.japonica	Japan	1856 Long Walk etc.
F.'Variegata'	Japan	1890 Higher Australia

Faucaria (Aizoaceae)

F.peersii	South Africa	1959 Collection
F.tigrinum	South Africa	1894 Collection

Feijoa (Myrtaceae)

F.sellowiana	Brazil	1908 Old Abbey South

Felicia (Compositae)

F.amelloides	South Africa	1890 Top Terrace

Ficus (Moraceae)

F.capensis	South Africa	1973 Long Walk
F.crica (fig)	Europe	1914 Glasshouse Wall
F.macrophylla (Moreton Bay fig)	Australia	1914 Well Garden
F.pumila (creeping fig)	Australia	1894 Lapageria Corner

Forsythia (Oleaceae)

F.suspensa	Japan	1894 Pebble Garden

Fragaria (Rosaceae)

F.vesca (wild strawberry)	Britain	1894 Lily Garden

Francoa (Francoaceae)

F.ramosa	Chile	1894 Pear Tree Garden
F.sonchifolia (bridal wreath)	Chile	1959 Pear Tree Garden

Fraxinus (Oleaceae)

F.excelsior (ash)	Britain	1894 Well Covert

Freesia (Iridaceae)

F.refracta	South Africa	1894 Abbey Rockery
F.refracta 'Alba'	South Africa	1894 Abbey Rockery

Freycinetia (Pandanaceae)

F.banksii	New Zealand	1935 Fernery

Freylinia (Scrophulariaceae)

F.lanceolata	South Africa	1953 Long Walk

Fuchsia (Onagraceae)

F.'A.1'	Hort.	1978 Jam Tart
F.'Aintree'	Hort.	1978 Jam Tart
F.'Alaska'	Hort.	1978 Jam Tart
F.'Alfred Rambaud'	Hort.	1978 Jam Tart
F.'Alice Travis'	Hort.	1978 Jam Tart
F.'Ambassador'	Hort.	1978 Collection
F.'Andre Carnegie'	Hort.	1978 Jam Tart
F.'Arabella Improved'	Hort.	1978 Jam Tart
F.arborescens	Mexico	1894 Pebble Garden
F.'Arthur Cope'	Hort.	1978 Jam Tart
F.'Aunt Juliana'	Hort.	1978 Jam Tart
F.'Australia Fair'	Hort.	1978 Jam Tart
F.'Beauty of Clyffe Hall'	Hort.	1978 Jam Tart
F.'Bella Forbes'	Hort.	1978 Jam Tart
F.'Berliner Kind'	Hort.	1978 Jam Tart
F.'Billy Green'	Hort.	1978 Jam Tart
F.'Bishop's Bells'	Hort.	1978 Jam Tart
F.'Blue Beauty'	Hort.	1978 Jam Tart
F.'Blue Bush'	Hort.	1978 Jam Tart
F.'Blue Lagoon'	Hort.	1978 Jam Tart
F.boliviana	Bolivia	1950 Well Garden
F.'Brandt's 500 Club'	Hort.	1978 Jam Tart
F.'Breeder's Dream'	Hort.	1978 Jam Tart
F.'Brigadoon'	Hort.	1978 Jam Tart
F.'Burning Bush'	Hort.	1978 Jam Tart
F.'Buttons and Bows'	Hort.	1978 Jam Tart
F.'Carioca Pale'	Hort.	1978 Jam Tart
F.'Carmel Blue'	Hort.	1978 Jam Tart
F.'Celia Smedley'	Hort.	1978 Jam Tart
F.'Checkerboard'	Hort.	1978 Jam Tart
F.'Chillerton Beauty'	Hort.	1978 Jam Tart
F.'China Lantern'	Hort.	1978 Jam Tart
F.'Cloth of Gold'	Hort.	1978 Jam Tart
F.colensoi	New Zealand	1914 Lily Garden
F.'Coppelia'	Hort.	1978 Jam Tart
F.cordifolia	Mexico	1865 Well Garden
F.cordifolia x splendens	Hort.	1938 Middle Terrace
F.'Core'n Grato'	Hort.	1978 Jam Tart
F.corymbiflora	Peru	1851 Augustus Smith's Wall
F.'Cupid Light'	Hort.	1978 Jam Tart
F.'Curtain Call'	Hort.	1978 Jam Tart
F.'Danish Pastry'	Hort.	1978 Jam Tart
F.'Day Star'	Hort.	1978 Jam Tart
F.'Derby Imp'	Hort.	1978 Jam Tart
F.'Display'	Hort.	1978 Jam Tart
F.'Dollar Princess'	Hort.	1978 Jam Tart
F.'Drame'	Hort.	1978 Jam Tart
F.'Estelle Marie'	Hort.	1978 Jam Tart
F.'Evelyn Steele Little'	Hort.	1978 Jam Tart
F.excorticata	New Zealand	1894 Middle Terrace
F.'Forget-me-not'	Hort.	1978 Jam Tart
F.'Forgotten Dreams'	Hort.	1978 Jam Tart
F.'Frau Hilde Rademacher'	Hort.	1978 Jam Tart
F.'Frances Red'	Hort.	1978 Jam Tart
F.fulgens	Mexico	1856 Augustus Smith's Wall
F.'General Monk'	Hort.	1978 Jam Tart
F.'George Barr'	Hort.	1978 Jam Tart
F.'Giselle'	Hort.	1978 Jam Tart
F.'Golden Treasure'	Hort.	1978 Jam Tart
F.'Green 'n' Gold'	Hort.	1978 Jam Tart
F.'Great Scott'	Hort.	1978 Jam Tart
F.'Guy Dauphine'	Hort.	1978 Jam Tart
F.'Heidi Ann'	Hort.	1978 Jam Tart
F.'Heron'	Hort.	1978 Collection
F.'Hidcote Beauty'	Hort.	1978 Jam Tart
F.'Hindu Belle'	Hort.	1978 Collection
F.'James Lye'	Hort.	1978 Jam Tart
F.'Jenny Hampson'	Hort.	1978 Jam Tart
F.'Lady Boothby'	Hort.	1973 Limpet Midden Hedge
F.'La Rosita'	Hort.	1978 Jam Tart
F.'Laura'	Hort.	1978 Jam Tart
F.'Leanora'	Hort.	1978 Jam Tart
F.'Leverkusen'	Hort.	1978 Jam Tart
F.'Lilac Lustre'	Hort.	1978 Jam Tart
F.'Lord Byron'	Hort.	1978 Jam Tart
F.'Loveliness'	Hort.	1978 Jam Tart
F.'Lynn Ellen'	Hort.	1978 Jam Tart
F.magellanica 'Discolor'	Falkland Islands	1938 Jam Tart
F.magellanica 'Gracilis'	Chile	1865 Old Abbey
F.magellanica 'Gracilis Variegata'	Chile	1978 Jam Tart
F.magellanica 'Macrostemma'	Chile	1914 Abbey Arch

F.magellanica 'Molinae'	Chile	1938 Long Walk
F.magellanica 'Purpurea'	Chile	1980 Collection
F.magellanica 'Pumila'	Chile	1977 East Entrance
F.magellanica 'Riccartonii'	Chile	1856 Lighthouse Walk
F.'Margaret Brown'	Hort.	1978 Jam Tart
F.'Mayfayre'	Hort.	1978 Jam Tart
F.microphylla	Mexico	1856 Jam Tart
F.microphylla	Chile	1978 Jam Tart
F.'Mieke Meursing'	Hort.	1978 Jam Tart
F.'Molesworth'	Hort.	1978 Jam Tart
F.'Moonlight Sonata'	Hort.	1978 Jam Tart
F.'Mrs. L. Swisher'	Hort.	1978 Jam Tart
F.'Pacifica'	Hort.	1978 Jam Tart
F.paniculata	Mexico	1980 Collection
F.'Pauline Rawlings'	Hort.	1978 Jam Tart
F.'Peppermint Stick'	Hort.	1978 Jam Tart
F.perscandens	New Zealand	1977 Stone Table
F.'Personality'	Hort.	1978 Jam Tart
F.'Phyllis'	Hort.	1978 Jam Tart
F.'Pink Ballet Girl'	Hort.	1978 Collection
F.'Pink Pearl'	Hort.	1978 Jam Tart
F.'Pink Temptation'	Hort.	1978 Jam Tart
F.'Prelude'	Hort.	1978 Jam Tart
F.'President Unwin'	Hort.	1978 Jam Tart
F.'Preston Guild'	Hort.	1978 Jam Tart
F.'Prince Charming'	Hort.	1978 Jam Tart
F.'Prosperity'	Hort.	1978 Jam Tart
F.procumbens	New Zealand	1894 Jam Tart
F.'Purple Heart'	Hort.	1978 Jam Tart
F.'Queen Mary'	Hort.	1978 Jam Tart
F.'Query'	Hort.	1978 Jam Tart
F.'R.A.F.'	Hort.	1978 Jam Tart
F.regia	Brazil	1959 Long Walk
F.'Requiem'	Hort.	1978 Jam Tart
F.'Rose Aylett'	Hort.	1978 Jam Tart
F.'Rose of Castille'	Hort.	1938 Jam Tart
F.'Royal Crown'	Hort.	1978 Jam Tart
F.'Royal Purple'	Hort.	1929 Augustus Smith's Wall
F.'Rufus'	Hort.	1978 Jam Tart
F.'Schneeball'	Hort.	1978 Jam Tart
F.'Snowcap'	Hort.	1978 Jam Tart
F.splendens	Mexico	1856 Augustus Smith's Wall
F.'Sunkissed'	Hort.	1978 Jam Tart
F.'Sunny'	Hort.	1978 Jam Tart
F.'Swanley Gem'	Hort.	1978 Jam Tart
F.'Temptation'	Hort.	1978 Jam Tart
F.'Thais'	Hort.	1978 Jam Tart
F.'The Doctor'	Hort.	1978 Jam Tart
F.thymifloia	Mexico	1914 Augustus Smith's Wall
F.'Ting-a-ling'	Hort.	1978 Jam Tart
F.'Tom Thumb'	Hort.	1959 Top Terrace
F.'Topaz'	Hort.	1978 Jam Tart
F.triphylla	West Indies	1914 Collection
F.'Tutone'	Hort.	1978 Jam Tart
F.'Uncle Steve'	Hort.	1978 Jam Tart
F.'Violet Rosette'	Hort.	1978 Jam Tart

Furcraea (Agavaceae)

F.longaeva	Mexico	1894 Lighthouse Walk
F.selloa	Guatemala	1914 Collection
F.selloa 'Marginata'	Guatemala	1963 Collection

Galanthus (Amaryllidaceae)

G.nivalis (snowdrop)	Britain	1890 Well Covert

Galtonia (Liliaceae)

G.candicans (berg lily)	South Africa	1890 Lighthouse Walk

Gasteria (Liliaceae)

G.angulata	South Africa	1848 Collection
G.radulosa	South Africa	1914 Cypress Rockery
G.verrucosa	South Africa	1959 Cypress Rockery
G.v. scaberrima	South Africa	1962 Collection

x **Gastrolea** (Liliaceae)

G.lapaixii	G.maculata x Aloe aristata	1973 Cypress Rockery

Gaultheria (Ericaceae)

G.shallon	Alaska	1973 Abbey Drive

Gazania (Compositae)

G.rigens	South Africa	1914 Middle Terrace
G.splendens	South Africa	1914 Middle Terrace
G.splendens 'Variegata'	South Africa	1914 Old Abbey
G.Unnamed hybrids	South Africa	1914 Middle Terrace

Geranium (Geraniaceae)

G.canariense	Canary Islands	1973 Old Abbey
G.incisum	Oregon	1977 Neptune Steps
G.madarense	Madeira	1929 Middle Terrace
G.palmatum	Madeira	1973 Old Abbey
G.rubescens	Madeira	1959 Old Abbey

Gerbera (Compositae)

G.jamesonii (Barberton daisy)	South Africa	1894 Citrus Garden

Gheissorhiza (Iridaceae)

G.rochea	South Africa	1894 Middle Terrace

Gibbaeum (Aizoaceae)

G.cryptopodium	South Africa	1914 Collection
G.gibbosum	South Africa	1959 Collection
G.petrense	South Africa	1959 Conservatory Rock
G.schwantesii	South Africa	1959 Conservatory Rock

Gladiolus (Iridaceae)

G.byzantinus	Mediterranean	1844 Mexico: Middle Terrace
G.'Corfe Castle'	Hort.	1980 Collection
G.x nanus 'Amanda Mahy'	Hort.	1980 Podalyria Bank
G.x nanus 'Charm'	Hort.	1980 Podalyria Bank
G.x nanus 'Colvillii Albus'	Hort.	1848 Mexico: Middle Terrace
G.x nanus 'Good Luck'	Hort.	1973 Cut Flower Garden
G.x nanus 'Guernsey Glory'	Hort.	1980 Podalyria Bank
G.x nanus 'Impressive'	Hort.	1980 Podalyria Bank
G.x nanus 'Robinetta'	Hort.	1980 Podalyria Bank
G.x nanus 'Spitfire'	Hort.	1973 Mexico: Middle Terrace
G.primulinus Hybrids	Hort.	1977 Cut Flower Garden

Gloriosa (Liliaceae)

G.rothschildiana	Trop. Africa	1973 Collection
G.superba	East Indies	1894 Collection

Glottiphyllum (Aizoaceae)

G.lingueforme	South Africa	1865 Collection
G.regium	South Africa	1959 Collection
G.semicylindricum	South Africa	1959 Collection

Goodenia (Goodeniaceae)

G.ovata	Australia	1972 Podalyria Bank

Goodia (Leguminosae)

G.lotifolia	Australia	1856 Old Abbey

Gordonia (Theaceae)

G.axillaris	China	1932 Long Walk

x **Graptoveria** (Crassulaceae)

G.ivesii	Graptopetalum x Echeveria	1973 Palm Rockery

x **Greenonium** (Crassulaceae)

G.species	Aeonium spauthulatum x Greenovia aurea	1973 Cypress Rockery

Greenovia (Crassulaceae)

G.aurea	Canary Islands	1959 South Africa Cliff
G.dodrentalis	Canary Islands	1978 Beehive Rockery

Grevillea (Proteaceae)

G.alpina	Australia	1905 South Africa Flat
G.biternata	Australia	1973 Top Terrace
G.crithmifolia	Australia	1973 Top Terrace
G.juniperina 'Sulphurea'	Australia	1854 South Africa Flat
G.lanigera	Australia	1973 South Africa Flat

G.robusta	Australia	1856 Top Terrace West
G.rosmarinifolia	Australia	1856 Top Terrace
G.x semperflorens	*G.sulphurea* x *G. thelemanniana*	1959 Top Terrace

Greyia **(Greyiaceae)**

G.radlkolferi	Transvaal	1959 Podalyria Bank
G.sutherlandii	Natal	1914 Middle Terrace

Griselinia **(Griseliniaceae)**

G.littoralis	New Zealand	1857 Scillonian Hedge
G.littoralis 'Variegata'	New Zealand	1914 Long Walk
G.lucida	New Zealand	1890 Top Terrace

Gunnera **(Gunneraceae)**

G.chilensis	Chile	1890 Duckery
G.manicata	Brazil	1890 Duckery

Haemanthus **(Amaryllidaceae)**

H.albiflos	South Africa	1894 Miss Innis' Rockery
H.coccineus	South Africa	1890 Miss Innis' Rockery
H.puniceus	South Africa	1959 Miss Innis' Rockery

Hakea **(Proteaceae)**

H.crassifolium	Australia	1973 Top Terrace Quarry
H.elliptica	Australia	1959 Top Terrace South
H.lissocarpha	Australia	1914 Top Terrace North
H.oleifolia	Australia	1873 Long Walk West
H.suaveolens	Australia	1873 East Rockery, Top Terrace

Halimium **(Cistaceae)**

H.halimifolium	Mediterranean	1959 Top Terrace

Halleria **(Scrophulariaceae)**

H.lucida	South Africa	1890 Long Walk East

Hardenbergia **(Leguminosae)**

H.comptoniana	Australia	1904 Top Terrace Quarry

Hebe **(Scrophulariaceae)**

H.'Alicia Amherst'	Hort.	1959 Collection
H.'Amy'	Hort.	1977 Collection
H.x Andersonii	*H.speciosa* x *H.salicifolia*	1856 Lighthouse Walk
H.x Andersonii 'Aureo-Marginata'	*H.speciosa* x *H.salicifolia*	1978 Collection
H.x Andersonii 'Variegata'	*H.speciosa* x *H.salicifolia*	1854 Lighthouse Walk
H.armstrongii	New Zealand	1978 Conifer Lawn
H.'Blush Wand'	Hort.	1978 Collection
H.brachysiphon	New Zealand	1959 Grassy Walk South
H.'Carl Teschner'	Hort.	1978 Old Abbey
H.chathamica	Chatham Island	1914 Long Walk South
H.colensoi	New Zealand	1914 Old Abbey
H.x Cranleighensis	*parviflora* x *speciosa*	1950 Well Garden
H.cupressoides	New Zealand	1914 Collection
H.dieffenbachii	Chatham Island	1914 Collection
H.edinensis	New Zealand	1978 Higher Australia East
H.elliptica	Falkland Islands	1856 West Orchard
H.elliptica 'Variegata'	Tresco	1978 West Orchard
H.x franciscana	*H.elliptica* x *speciosa*	1959 Hedging throughout
H.x franciscana 'Autumn Glory'	*H.elliptica* x *speciosa*	1973 Conservatory Bridge
H.x franciscana 'Blue Gem'	*H.elliptica* x *speciosa*	1978 Collection
H.x franciscana 'Variegata'	*H.elliptica* x *speciosa*	1978 Collection
H.'Gauntletii'	Hort.	1978 Collection
H.gigantea	Chatham Island	1914 Grassy Walk
H.glaucophylla	New Zealand	1978 Higher Australia East
H.glaucophylla 'Variegata'	New Zealand	1978 Collection
H.'Great Orme'	Hort.	1978 Collection
H.hulkeana	New Zealand	1908 Collection
H.'La Seduisante'	Hort.	1959 Lighthouse Walk
H.x lewisii	*H.elliptica* x *salififolia*	1894 Stone Table
H.macrocarpa		
H.macrocarpa var. 'Headfortii'	New Zealand	1914 Long Walk
H.macrocarpa var. 'Latisepala'	New Zealand	1914 Hop Circle
H.pimelioides	New Zealand	1914 Nerine Bank
H.pinguifolia		
H.pinguifolia var. 'Pagei'	New Zealand	1894 Higher Australia East
H.'Purple Queen'	Hort.	1890 Collection
H.rakaiensis	New Zealand	1978 Nerine Bank
H.salicifolia	New Zealand	1856 Hop Circle
H.'Simon Deleaux'	Hort.	1973 Top Terrace
H.'Spender's Seedling'	Hort.	1978 Higher Australia East
H.'Violet Wand'	Hort.	1978 Collection
H.'Waikiki'	Hort.	1978 Collection

Hedera **(Araliaceae) ivy**

H.canariensis 'Gloire de Marengo'	Canary Islands	1978 Well Garden
H.helix	Britain	1834 Native
H.helix 'Gold Heart'	Hort.	1978 Collection
H.helix 'Ivalace'	Hort.	1978 Well Top

Hedychium **(Zingiberaceae)**

H.coccineum	India	1914 Lighthouse Walk
H.coccineum 'Aurantiacum'	India	1973 East Orchard
H.densiflorum	India	1959 Lighthouse Walk
H.gardnerianum	India	1914 Citrus Garden
H.greenei	India	1959 Well Garden
H.spicatum 'Acuminatum'	India	1914 Well Garden
H.raffilii	India	1973 East Orchard

Helichrysum **(Compositae)**

H.angustifolium	Southern Europe	1973 South Africa Flat
H.costatifructum	South Africa	1973 Lighthouse Walk East
H.felinum	South Africa	1950 South Africa Flat
H.italicum	Mediterranean	1934 Middle Terrace
H.petiolatum	South Africa	1959 Top Terrace East
H.rosmarinifolius	Australia	1959 Lighthouse Walk East
H.setosum	South Africa	1978 Collection

Helleborus **(Ranunculaceae)**

H.corsicus	Sardinia, Corsica	1959 Middle Terrace
H.'Georgina Nightingale'	Hort.	1977 West Rockery Pool
H.'Hazy Dawn'	Hort.	1977 West Rockery Pool
H.'Petsamo'	Hort.	1977 West Rockery Pool
H.'Snow White'	Hort.	1977 West Rockery Pool
H.'Wood Nymph'	Hort.	1977 West Rockery Pool

Hemerocallis **(Liliaceae) day lily**

H.fulva	Asia	1890 Long Walk
H.'Black Prince'	Hort.	1977 East Rockery
H.'Eva Langford'	Hort.	1977 East Rockery
H.'Festivity'	Hort.	1977 East Rockery
H.'Mary Randall'	Hort.	1977 East Rockery
H.'Mary Rippingdale'	Hort.	1977 East Rockery
H.'Peach Amber'	Hort.	1977 East Rockery
H.'Peach Flash'	Hort.	1977 East Rockery
H.'Pink Prelude'	Hort.	1977 East Rockery
H.'Romany'	Hort.	1977 East Rockery

Heteromorpha **(Umbelliferae)**

H.arborescens	Trop. Africa	1953 Old Nursery Garden

Hibbertia **(Dilleniaceae)**

H.volubilis	Australia	1890 Conservatory

Hibiscus **(Malvaceae)**

H.rosa-sinensis	China	1894 Collection
H.'The President'	Hort.	1959 Collection
H.waimeae	Hawaii	1935 Conservatory

Hippeastrum **(Amaryllidaceae)**

Hort. varieties	Hort.	1914 Collection
H.rutilum	Brazil	1978 Collection

Hoheria **(Malvaceae)**

H.populnea	New Zealand	1914 Well Garden
H.sexstylosa	New Zealand	1959 Long Walk

Homalanthus (Euphorbiaceae)		
H.populifolius	Australia	1959 Old Nursery Garden
Homeria (Iridaceae)		
H.collina	South Africa	1932 Top Terrace
H.collina 'Aurantiaca'	South Africa	1890 Top Terrace
Hosta (Liliaceae)		
H.albo-picta	China	1977 East Rockery
H.fortunei	Japan	1959 East Rockery
H.fortunei 'Hyacinthina'	Japan	1977 West Rockery
H.fortunei 'Marginata-Alba'	Japan	1977 East Rockery
H.undulata 'Erronema'	Japan	1977 East Rockery
Hoya (Asclepiadaceae)		
H.bella	India	1959 Collection
H.carnosa	Australia	1894 Collection
Huania (Palmaceae)		
H.australis	Tasmania	1970 Lighthouse Walk
Hydrangea (Hydrangeaceae)		
H.macrophylla Hybrids	China	1851 Lower Parts
H. 'Nigra'	Manchuria	1959 Long Walk
H. 'Variegata'	Japan	1890 Old Nursery Garden
Hylocereus (Cactaceae)		
H.undatus	South America	1959 Collection
Hymenanthera (Violaceae)		
H.chathamica	Chatham Island	1973 Bamboo Walk
Hymenocallis (Amaryllidaceae)		
H.x festalis 'Zwanenburg'	Hort.	1975 West Rockery
Hymenosporum (Pittosporaceae)		
H.flavum	Australia	1904 Pear Tree Garden
Hypericum (Guttiferae)		
H.calycinum	Greece	1894 Old Abbey North
H.canariense	Canary Islands	1914 Lighthouse Walk East
H.grandifolium	Canary Islands	1973 Long Walk Centre
H. 'Hidcote'	Hort.	1973 East Orchard
H.hircinum	Southern Europe	1973 Lighthouse Walk South
H.hookeranum	Nepal	1957 Lighthouse Walk
H.leschenaultii	Malaya	1950 Long Walk Centre
Idesia (Flacourtaceae)		
I.polycarpa	Japan	1959 Grassy Walk
Ilex (Aquifoliaceae) holly		
I.aquifolium	Britain	1890 Duckery Dell
I.x altaclarensis 'Camelliifolia'	Britain	1890 Top Terrace
Illicium (Illiciaceae)		
I.anisatum	Japan	1881 Top Terrace
Idesia (Flacourtaceae)		
I.polycarpa	Japan	1959 Grassy Walk
Ilex (Aquifoliaceae) holly		
I.aquifolium	Britain	1890 Duckery Dell
I.x altaclarensis 'Camelliifolia'	Britain	1890 Top Terrace
Illicium (Illiciaceae)		
I.anisatum	Japan	1881 Top Terrace
Iochroma (Solanaceae)		
I.cyanea	Tropical America	1944 Mulberry Wall
I.fuchsoides	Peru	1959 Pebble Garden
I.grandiflora	Peru	1959 Long Walk North-West
Ipomoea (Convolvulaceae)		
I.learii	Tropical America	1959 Old Abbey
Iris (Iridaceae)		
I. 'Bourne Graceful'	Hort.	1980 West Rockery
I.chameiris	Southern Europe	1980 Palm Rockery

I.chrysographes	Szechwan	1980 West Rockery
I.chrysographes 'Black Form'	Szechwan	1980 Collection
I.chrysographes 'Inshriach Form'	Szechwan	1980 Collection
I.chrysographes 'Rubella'	Szechwan	1980 Collection
I.confusa	West China	1959 Pebble Garden
I.confusa x japonica	Hort.	1980 West Rockery
I. 'Desert Dream'	Hort.	1980 Collection
I.florentina	Southern Europe	1959 Palm Rockery
I.foetidissima	Native	1834 Woodland Shade
I.foetidissima 'Variegata'	Britain	1894 Collection
I.forrestii	Yunnan	1980 West Rockery
I.formosana	Yunnan	1980 West Rockery
I.fulva	S.U.S.A.	1980 West Rockery
I.x fulvala	Hort.	1979 Old Abbey
I.halophila	Asia	1980 West Rockery
I. 'Intermediate Bearded'	Hort.	1961 Pump Garden
I.japonica 'Ledger's Var.'	Hort.	1980 West Rockery
I.kaempferi	Japan	1890 West Rockery
I.kaempferi 'Alba'	Japan	1973 West Rockery
I.kaempferi 'Mandarin Purple'	Hort.	1980 Collection
I.koreana	Korea	1980 West Rockery
I.lactiflora	Asia	1980 West Rockery
I. 'Margot Holmes'	Hort.	1980 Collection
I.monnierii		1973 Middle Terrace
I.munzii Hybrids	Hort.	1980 West Orchard
I.orientalis	Asia	1980 Middle Terrace
I.Pacific Coast Hybrids	Hort.	1973 Old Abbey
'Banbury Beauty'	Hort.	1980 West Orchard
'Banbury Candy'	Hort.	1980 West Orchard
'Banbury Pageant'	Hort.	1980 West Orchard
'Banbury Velvet'	Hort.	1980 West Orchard
'No-name'	Hort.	1980 West Orchard
'Weisser Orient'	Hort.	1980 West Rockery
I.setosa	Asia	1980 Collection
I.sibirica 'Alba'	Asia	1980 Collection
I.sibirica 'Gatineau'	Asia	1980 Collection
I.sibirica 'Helen Astor'	Asia	1980 Collection
I.sibirica 'Perry's Blue'	Hort.	1973 West Rockery
I.unguicularis	Mediterranean	1890 Pebble Garden
I.unguicularis 'Alba'	Mediterranean	1890 Long Walk
I.xiphium	Spain	1894 Top Terrace
Isoplexis (Scrophulariaceae)		
I.canariensis	Canary Islands	1914 Old Nursery Garden
I.sceptrum	Canary Islands	1973 Well Garden
I.x scilloniensis	Tresco *(canariensis x sceptrum)*	1970 Well Garden
Ixia (Iridaceae)		
I.Hort. hybrids	Hort.	1914 Top Terrace etc.
I.viridiflora	South Africa	1844 Neptune Steps
Jasminum (Oleaceae)		
J.angulare	South Africa	1929 Old Abbey
J.azoricum	Azores	1948 Neptune Steps East
J.nudiflorum	Asia	1851 Collection
J.officinale	India	1894 Mulberry Wall
J.polyanthum	China	1959 Middle Terrace
J.x stephanense	*beesianum x officinale*	1959 Lighthouse Walk
J.subhumile 'Glabricymosum'	Asia	1959 Middle Terrace
Jovellana (Scrophulariaceae)		
J.violacea	Chile	1890 Long Walk
Jubaea (Palmae)		
J.spectabilis	Chile	1914 Pebble Garden East
Juniperus (Cupressaceae)		
J.oxycedrus	Europe	1959 North Abbey Drive
J.recurva	China	1959 North Abbey Drive
J.squamata 'Meyeri'	Asia	1979 East Entrance
Kalanchoe (Crassulaceae)		
K.blossfeldiana 'Morning Sun'	South Africa	1976 Collection
K.blossfeldiana 'Vulcan'	South Africa	1976 Collection
K.beharensis	South Africa	1959 Collection
K.fedtschenkoi 'Variegata'	South Africa	1976 Collection
K.grandiflora	East Africa	1890 Collection
K.x kewensis	*teretifolia x flammea*	1973 Collection
K.laxiflora	Madagascar	1976 Collection

K.mangini	Madagascar	1976 Collection
K.marmorata	Ethiopia	1959 Collection
K.marnieriana	Madagascar	1976 Collection
K.prolifera	Madagascar	1973 Collection
K.pumila	Madagascar	1974 Collection
K.rosei var. *rosei*	Madagascar	1974 Collection
K.tomentosa	Madagascar	1959 Collection

Kennedya (Leguminosae)
K.macrophylla	Australia	1914 Old Abbey
K.nigricans	Australia	1904 Old Abbey
K.rubicunda	Australia	1904 Valhalla

Kerria (Rosaceae)
K.japonica var. *pleniflora*	Japan	1894 Collection

Kleinia (Compositae)
K.acaulis	South Africa	1894 Collection
K.aizoides	South Africa	1959 Middle Terrace

Knightia (Proteaceae)
K.excelsa (rewa)	New Zealand	1914 Tree Ferns Abbey Drive

Kniphofia (Liliaceae)
K.'Atlanta'	Hort.	1981 Duckery Bank
K.caulescens	South Africa	1890 Palm Rockery
K.'Limelight'	Hort.	1981 Duckery Bank
K.'Maid of Orleans'	Hort.	1978 Collection
K.sarmentosa	South Africa	1978 Collection
K.uvaria	South Africa	1890 Aloe Walk etc.

Koelreuteria (Sapindaceae)
K.paniculata	China	1959 Collection

Kohlrauschia (Carycphyllaceae)
K.velutina	Europe	1978 Collection

Kunzea (Myrtaceae)
K.ambigua	Australia	1906 West Arcadia
K.baxteri	Australia	1960 Top Terrace
K.ericifolia	Australia	1914 Protea Gully, Top Terrace

Laburnum (Leguminosae)
L.anagyroides	Southern Europe	1894 Collection

Lachenalia (Liliaceae)
L.aloides	South Africa	1890 Top Terrace
L.'Aurea'	South Africa	1973 Top Terrace

Lagunaria (Malvaceae)
L.patersonii	Norfolk Island	1914 Long Walk

Lampranthus (Aizoaceae)
L.aurantiacus	South Africa	1894 Cypress Rockery
L.auratus	South Africa	1951 West Rockery
L.aureus	South Africa	1865 West Rockery
L.blandus	South Africa	1848 West Rockery
L.blandus 'Pallidus'	South Africa	1959 Cypress Rockery
L.blandus 'Roseus'	South Africa	1953 West Rockery
L.brownii	South Africa	1894 Toy Greenhouse
L.emarginatus	South Africa	1914 Agave Bank
L.falciformis	South Africa	1856 Middle Terrace
L.formosus	South Africa	1865 Beehive Rockery
L.glaucus	South Africa	1848 Neptune Steps
L.godmaniae	South Africa	1973 Podalyria Bank
L.haworthii	South Africa	1865 Middle Terrace
L.haworthii 'Silver Pink'	South Africa	1973 Middle Terrace
L.haworthii 'White Form'	South Africa	1973 Middle Terrace
L.littlewoodii	South Africa	1973 Old Abbey Rock
L.roseus	South Africa	1865 Collection
L.saturatus	South Africa	1973 Middle Terrace
L.skinneri	South Africa	1973 Podalyria Bank
L.'Tresco Apricot'	South Africa	1959 South Africa Cliff
L.'Tresco Brilliant'	South Africa	1959 Collection
L.'Tresco Fire'	South Africa	1973 South Africa Cliff
L.'Tresco Hollow'	South Africa	1979 Collection
L.verruculatus	South Africa	1873 Abbey Rockery
L.vredenbergensis	South Africa	1974 Abbey Rockery

L.watermeyeri	South Africa	1948 South Africa Rockery
L.zeyheri	South Africa	1894 Cypress Rockery

Lapageria (Philesiaceae)
L.rosea	Chile	1854 Pebble Garden

Lapeirousia (Iridaceae)
L.laxa	South Africa	1848 Lighthouse Walk

Larix (Pinaceae) (larches)
L.decidua	Central Europe	1959 Long Walk

Lathyrus (Leguminosae)
L.latifolius	Europe	1890 Neptune Steps

Laurelia (Atherospermataceae)
L.serrata	Chile	1959 Podalyria Bank

Laurus (Lauraceae)
L.nobilis (bay)	Mediterranean	1890 Hop Circle
L.nobilis 'Crispa'	Mediterranean	1973 Hop Circle

Lavandula (Labiatae)
L.dentata	Spain	1890 Old Abbey
L.spica	Mediterranean	1890 Middle Terrace
L.stoechas	Mediterranean	1914 Duckery Bank

Lavatera (Malvaceae)
L.olbia 'Rosea'	Mediterranean	1973 Old Abbey

Leonotis (Labiatae)
L.leonurus	South Africa	1890 Stone Table

Leptospermum (Myrtaceae)
L.'Big Red'	New Zealand	1981 Gardeners' Walk
L.'Blossom'	New Zealand	1981 Gardeners' Walk
L.'Elizabeth Jane'	New Zealand	1981 Gardeners' Walk
L.ericoides	New Zealand	1914 Gardeners' Walk
L.flavescens	Australia	1914 Gardeners' Walk
L.'Gaiety Girl'	New Zealand	1981 Gardeners' Walk
L.'Hoia'	New Zealand	1981 Gardeners' Walk
L.'Kiwi'	New Zealand	1981 Gardeners' Walk
L.lanigerum	Australia	1904 Monument Walk
L.liversedgei	Australia	1959 Gardeners' Walk
L.'Martenii'	Australia	1981 Gardeners' Walk
L.prostratum	Australia	1980 Top Terrace
L.'Red Ensign'	New Zealand	1981 Gardeners' Walk
L.rodwayanum	Tasmania	1959 Miss Innis' Garden
L.'Rosy Morn'	New Zealand	1981 Gardeners' Walk
L.'Ruda'	New Zealand	1981 Gardeners' Walk
L.scoparium	New Zealand	1890 Lighthouse Walk
L.scoparium 'Album'	New Zealand	1973 Podalyria Bank
L.scoparium 'Keatleyi'	New Zealand	1950 West Orchard
L.scoparium 'Nichollsii'	New Zealand	1908 Neptune Steps
L.scoparium 'Red Damask'	New Zealand	1959 Gardeners' Walk
L.sericeum	New Zealand	1973 Gardeners' Walk
L.'Snow Flurry'	New Zealand	1981 Gardeners' Walk
L.'Sunraisia'	New Zealand	1981 Gardeners' Walk
L.'Winter Cheer'	New Zealand	1981 Gardeners' Walk

Leucadendron (Proteacae)
L.argenteum (silver tree)	South Africa	1914 South Africa Flat
L.comosum	South Africa	1973 South Africa Rockery
L.discolor	South Africa	1959 Top Terrace
L.eucalyptifolium	South Africa	1973 Top Terrace
L.gandogeri	South Africa	1973 Top Terrace
L.laureolum	South Africa	1973 Top Terrace
L.microcephalum	South Africa	1973 Toy Greenhouse
L.platyspermum	South Africa	1973 Toy Greenhouse
L.salicifolium	South Africa	1973 South Africa Rockery
L.sessile	South Africa	1973 South Africa Rockery
L.uliginosum	South Africa	1973 Top Terrace
L.tinctum	South Africa	1973 Top Terrace
L.xanthoconus	South Africa	1973 South Africa Flat

Leucojum (Amaryllidaceae)
L.aestivum	Britain	1890 West Orchard

Leucospermum (Proteaceae)

L.conocarpodendron	South Africa	1914 Cypress Rockery
L.cordifolium	South Africa	1959 Cannon Rockery
L.ellipticum	South Africa	1973 Top Terrace
L.reflexum	South Africa	1954 Top Terrace East
L.tottum	South Africa	1973 Podalyria Bank

Leucothoe (Ericaceae)

L.catesbaei	U.S.A.	1914 Higher Australia

Lewisia

Hort. Hybrids	North America	1978 Old Abbey

Libertia (Iridaceae)

L.caerulescens	Chile	1959 Well Garden
L.formosa	Chile	1979 Well Garden
L.grandiflora	New Zealand	1856 Well Garden
L.ixioides	New Zealand	1959 Well Garden

Ligustrum (Oleaceae)

L.ovalifolium 'Aureum'	Japan	1959 Hop Circle

Lilium (Liliaceae)

L.'African Queen'	Hort.	1975 Collection
L.auratum	Japan	1894 Long Walk
L.auratum 'Platyphyllum'	Japan	1914 Well Garden
L.'Brampford Gold'	Hort.	1978 Collection
L.'Bright Star'	Hort.	1975 Collection
L.candidum (Madonna lily)	Syria	1844 Middle Terrace
L.'Fire King'	Hort.	1979 Well Garden
L.henryi	China	1979 Well Garden
L.pyrenaicum	Southern Europe	1978 Collection
L.regale	China	1959 Well Garden
L.regale 'Sylvia'	Hort.	1980 Collection
L.speciosum	Japan	1959 Lily Garden
L.tigrinum	China	1844 Long Walk
L.wallichianum	Himalayas	1978 Collection

Limoniastrum (Plumbaginaceae)

L.articulatum	Mediterranean	1865 Tea Hut Bank

Limonium (Plumbaginaceae)

L.latifolium (sea lavender)	Europe	1978 Higher Australia

Lippia (Verbenaceae)

L.citriodora (lemon verbena)	Chile	1890 Pear Tree Garden

Lithocarpus (Fagaceae)

L.edulis	Japan	1959 Grassy Walk

Lithospermum (Boraginaceae)

L.diffusum 'Heavenly Blue'	Pyrenees	1865 Palm Rockery

Litsea (Lauraceae)

L.japonica	Japan	1914 Long Walk

Livistonia (Palmae)

L.australis (fountain palm)	Australia	1860 Pebble Garden

Lobelia (Campanulaceae)

L.aberdarica	Central Africa	1979 Long Walk
L.cardinalis	North America	1914 West Rockery
L.erinus	South Africa	1959 Cypress Rockery
L.excelsa	Central Africa	1980 Hop Circle
L.gibberoa	Central Africa	1929 Long Walk
L.laxiflora 'Angustifolia'	Mexico	1959 Citrus Garden
L.telekii	Central Africa	1953 Long Walk
L.tupa	Chile	1914 Pear Tree Garden

Lobularia (Cruciferae)

L.maritimum (alyssum)	Mediterranean	1890 West Rockery

Lomatia (Proteaceae)

L.ferruginea	Chile	1857 Lighthouse Walk
L.illicifolia	Australia	1974 Lighthouse Walk
L.tinctoria	Australia	1912 Pear Tree Garden

Lonicera (Caprifoliaceae) honeysuckle

L.henryi	China	1914 Well Garden
L.hildebrandiana	Burma	1903 Middle Terrace
L.japonica 'Aureo-reticulata'	Japan	1959 Citrus Garden

L.periclymenum	Native	1834 Abbey Woods
L.periclymenum 'Belgica' (Dutch honeysuckle)	Europe	1959 Old Abbey
L.x purpusii	L.standishii x fragrantissima	1973 Grassy Walk
L.xylosteum (fly honeysuckle)	Europe	1952 Puya Bank

Lotus (Leguminosae)

L.berthelotii	Canary Islands	1914 Collection

Luculia (Rubiaceae)

L.gratissima	Himalaya	1863 Long Walk
L.pinceana	Assam	1934 Pear Tree Garden

Lunaria (Cruciferae)

L.biennis (honesty)	Europe	1914 Long Walk

Lupinus (Leguminosae)

L.arboreus (tree lupin)	California	1894 Middle Terrace

Luzula (Juncaceae) woodrushes

L.canariensis	Canary Islands	1978 Fernery
L.sylvatica 'Variegata'	Britain	1981 Lower Australia

Lycium (Solanaceae)

L.barbarum (Chinese box thorn)	China	1973 Old Abbey

Lycopodium (Lycopodiales) club-mosses

L.selago	Britain	1979 Collection

Lycoris (Amaryllidaceae)

L.albiflora	South America	1981 Collection
L.radiata	China	1981 Collection
L.sanguinea	Japan	1905 Collection

Lygodium (Schizaeaceae)

L.japonicum	Japan	1863 Collection

Lyonothamnus (Rosaceae)

L.floribundus 'Aspleniifolius'	California	1979 Long Walk

Lythrum (Lythraceae) loosestrifes

L.salicaria 'Roseum superbum'	Europe	1854 Abbey Pool

Macropiper (Piperaceae)

M.excelsum	New Zealand	1907 Well Garden
M.excelsum 'Aureum-pictum'	New Zealand	1959 Old Nursery Garden

Macrozamia (Cycadaceae)

M.communis	Australia	1980 Lower Australia

Magnolia (Magnoliaceae)

M.campbellii ssp. campbellii	Sikkim	1914 Long Walk
M.grandiflora	South-Eastern U.S.A.	1848 Well Garden

Mahonia (Berberidaceae)

M.aquifolium	North America	1850 Long Walk
M.bealei	China	1973 Long Walk
M.japonica	Japan	1890 Long Walk
M.lomariifolia	Burma	1973 Old Nursery Garden
M.x media	lomariifolia x japonica	1973 Long Walk
M.napaulensis	Sikkim	1856 Mexico

Malephora (Aizoaceae)

M.lutea	South Africa	1973 Middle Terrace

Malva (Malvaceae) mallows

M.moschata (musk mallow)	Europe	1973 Toy Greenhouse

Malvastrum (Malvaceae)

M.puniceum	South Africa	1959 Old Abbey

Mammillaria (Cactaceae)

M.bocosana	South-Western U.S.A.	1978 Collection

Mandevilla (Apocyanaceae)

M.suaveolens	Argentina	1854 Old Abbey

Matteuccia (Aspidiaceae)

M.struthiopteris	U.S.A.	1978 Collection

Medicago (Leguminosae)		
M.arborea	Italy	1890 Long Walk
Melaleuca (Myrtaceae)		
M.armillaris	Australia	1890 Arcadia
M.diosmifolia	Australia	1973 Gardeners' Walk
M.hypericifolia	Australia	1865 Monument Walk
M.linariifolia	Australia	1856 Long Walk
M.nesophila	Australia	1950 Monument Walk
M.preissiana	Australia	1896 West Rockery
M.pubescens	Australia	1973 Below Toy Green-house Path
M.rhaphiophylla	Australia	1952 Toy Greenhouse Path
M.squamea	Australia	1943 West Rockery
M.squarrosa	Australia	1914 Gardeners' Walk
M.styphelioides	Australia	1914 Grassy Walk
M.violacea	Australia	1973 Middle Terrace
Melasphaerula (Iridaceae)		
M.graminea	South Africa	1973 Beehive Rockery
Melia (Meliaceae)		
M.azedarach	China	1974 Collection
Melianthus (Melianthaceae)		
M.major	South Africa	1890 Old Nursery Garden
Melicope (Rutaceae)		
M.ternata	New Zealand	1959 Long Walk
Melicytus (Violaceae)		
M.ramiflorus	New Zealand	1914 Long Walk
Meryta (Araliaceae)		
M.sinclairii	New Zealand	1914 Long Walk
Metrosideros (Myrtaceae)		
M.carminea (climbing rata)	New Zealand	1959 Middle Terrace
M.diffusa	New Zealand	1914 Lapageria corner
M.excelsa (pohutukawa)	New Zealand	1851 Below Mexico
M.'Hallii'	New Zealand	1950 Grassy Walk
M.kermadecensis	Kermadec Island	1965 Limpet Midden
M.kermadecensis 'Variegata'	Kermadec Island	1977 East Rockery
M.robusta (northern rata)	New Zealand	1856 Long Walk
M.umbellata (southern rata)	New Zealand	1914 Lighthouse Walk
M.villosus	New Zealand	1914 Neptune Steps
Michelia (Magnoliaceae)		
M.doltsopa	Himalaya	1953 Well Garden
M.figo	China	1851 Well Garden
Microcitrus (Rutaceae)		
M.australasica	Australia	1914 Pear Tree Garden
Microlepia (Dennstaedtiaceae)		
M.speluncae	Asia	1975 Collection
Microsorium (Polypodiaceae)		
M.diversifolium	New Zealand	1863 Fernery
Mimosa (Leguminosae)		
M.pudica (sensitive plant)	Brazil	1894 Collection
Mirabilis (Nyctaginaceae)		
M.jalapa (marvel of Peru)	Peru	1959 Citrus Garden
Mitraria (Gesneriaceae)		
M.coccinea	Chile	1856 Mexico
Monanthes (Crassulaceae)		
M.polyphylla	Canary Islands	1959 Collection
Monotoca (Epacridaceae)		
M.elliptica	Australia	1959 South Africa Flat
Moraea (Iridaceae)		
M.glaucopsis	South Africa	1973 Top Terrace
M.iridioides	South Africa	1973 Miss Innis'
M.'Johnstonii'	South Africa	1896 Middle Terrace
M.robinsoniana	Lord Howe's Island	1890 Middle Terrace

M.spathacea	South Africa	1914 Middle Terrace
M.spathulata	South Africa	1973 Top Terrace
M.tricuspis	South Africa	1914 Middle Terrace
Morus (Moraceae)		
M.nigra (mulberry)	Italy	1890 Middle Terrace
Muehlenbeckia (Polygonaceae)		
M.complexa	New Zealand	1890 Top Terrace
Musa (Musaceae)		
M.basjoo	Japan	1914 Well Garden
M.ensete	Abyssinia	1894 Collection
Muscari (Liliaceae) grape hyacinths		
M.botryoides	Italy	1865 Old Abbey
M.comosum 'Monstrosum'	Italy	1890 Citrus Garden
Musschia (Campanulaceae)		
M.aurea	Madeira	1973 Collection
M.wollastonii	Madeira	1890 Lighthouse Walk
Myoporum (Myoporaceae)		
M.laetum (ngaio)	New Zealand	1890 Duckery
Myosotidium (Boraginaceae)		
M.hortensia (Chatham Island forget-me-not)	Chatham Island	1914 West Rockery
Myrica (Myricaceae)		
M.faya	Canary Islands	1890 Long Walk
Myrsine (Myrsinaceae)		
M.africana	South Africa	1890 Long Walk
Myrtus (Myrtaceae)		
M.apiculata	Chile	1856 Long Walk
M.apiculata 'Glanleam Gold'	Chile	1981 Collection
M.apiculata 'Penwith'	Chile	1981 Collection
M.bullata	New Zealand	1857 Grassy Walk
M.communis	Southern Europe	1894 Long Walk
M.communis 'Tarentina'	Southern Europe	1959 House Terrace
M.communis 'Variegata'	Southern Europe	1973 Lower Australia
M.'Gloriosa'	Hort.	1980 Collection
M.'Katherine'	Hort.	1980 Collection
M.lechleriana	Chile	1953 Pebble Garden
M.x ralphii	New Zealand	1914 Lighthouse Walk
M.'Traversii'	Hort.	1980 Collection
M.ugni (murtillo)	Chile	1854 Aloe Walk
Nandina (Nandinaceae)		
N.domestica (heavenly bamboo)	China	1914 Pear Tree Garden
N.'Nana'	China	1981 Old Nursery Garden
N.'Wood's Dwarf'	China	1981 Old Nursery Garden
Narcissus (Amaryllidaceae)		
N.'Actea'	Div.9	Hort. All in collections
N.'Admiration'	Div.9	Hort.
N.'Aflame'	Div.3B	Hort.
N.'Aigle d'Or'	Div.8	Hort.
N.asturiensis	Div.10	Mediterranean
N.'Avalanche'	Div.8	Hort.
N.'Beryl'	Div.10	Hort.
N.x biflorus	Div.9	N.poeticus x tazetta
N.'Ann Abbott'	Div.2B	Hort.
N.'Arbar'	Div.3B	Hort.
N.'Beersheba'	Div.1C	Hort.
N.'Binkie'	Div.1B	Hort.
N.'Brunswick'	Div.2B	Hort.
N.bulbocodium 'Conspicuus'	Div.10	Mediterranean
N.bulbocodium 'Tenuifolius'	Div.10	Mediterranean
N.canaliculatus	Div.8	Mediterranean
N.'Canary Bird'	Div.8	Hort.
N.'Cantabile'	Div.9	Hort.
N.'Capricious'		Hort.
N.'Carn Lough'	Div.2B	Hort.
N.'Celestial'		Hort.
N.'Chalice'		Hort.
N.'Cheerfulness'	Div.9	Hort.
N.'Chinita'	Div.8	Hort.
N.'Compressus'	Div.8	Hort.

N.'Courage'	Div.1C	Hort.	
N.cyclamineus	Div.10	Mediterranean	
N.'Cypri'	Div.8	Mediterranean	
N.'Dallas'	Div.3C	Hort.	
N.'Desire'		Hort.	
N.'Double Ming'	Div.4	Hort.	
N.'Dulcimer'	Div.9	Hort.	
N.'Dutch Master'	Div.1	Hort.	
N.'Early Bride'	Div.2B	Hort.	
N.'Erlicheer'	Div.8	Hort.	
N.'February Gold'	Div.10	Hort.	
N.'Frilled Beauty'		Hort.	
N.'Gift'	Div.10	Hort.	
N.'Golden Dawn'	Div.8	Hort.	
N.'Golden Ducat'	Div.4	Hort.	
N.'Golden Raid'	Div.8	Hort.	
N.'Gloriosus'	Div.8	Hort.	
N.'Grande Monarque'	Div.8	Hort.	
N.'Grande Primo Citroniere'	Div.8	Hort.	
N.x Hawera	Div.10	Hort.	
N.'Hexameter'	Div.9	Hort.	
N.'Hollywood'	Div.2A	Hort.	
N.'Hunter's Moon'	Div.1	Hort.	
N.'Ice Follies'	Div.2C	Hort.	
N.'Indian Summer'	Div.2A	Hort.	
N.italicus	Div.8	Italy	
N.johnstonii 'Queen of Spain'	Div.10	Hort.	
N.'Kansas'		Hort.	
N.'Krelage's Victoria'	Div.8	Hort.	
N.lacticolor	Div.8	Mediterranean	
N.'Lough Maree'	Div.2B	Hort.	
N.'Magnificence'	Div.1	Hort.	
N.'Matador'	Div.8	Hort.	
N.'Medusa'	Div.9	Hort.	
N.'Milan'	Div.9	Hort.	
N.monspeliensis	Div.8	Mediterranean	
N.'Mrs. R.O. Backhouse'	Div.2B	Hort.	
N.'Mulatto'	Div.1	Hort.	
N.'Mystic'	Div.3C	Hort.	
N.'Newton'	Div.8	Hort.	
N.'Nora'	Div.8	Hort.	
N.odoratus	Div.8	Mediterranean	
N.papyraceus	Div.8	Mediterranean	
N.'Pallidus Plenus'	Div.4	Mediterranean	
N.'Peshawar'	Div.8	Hort.	
N.poeticus 'Hellenicus'	Div.9	Greece	
N.poeticus 'Ornatus'	Div.9	Greece	
N.poeticus 'Recurvus'	Div.9	Greece	
N.'Polar Ice'	Div.3C	Hort.	
N.'Polindra'	Div.2B	Hort.	
N.polyanthos 'White Pearl'	Div.8	Hort.	
N.pseudonarcissus	Div.10	Europe	
N.'Obvallaris'	Div.10	Britain	
N.'Red Hackle'		Hort.	
N.'Ripple'	Div.10	Hort.	
N.'Romeo'	Div.8	Hort.	
N.'Samite'	Div.1C	Hort.	
N.'Scilly White'	Div.8	Hort.	
N.x 'Silver Chimes'	Div.8	Hort.	
N.'Silver Wedding'	Div.1C	Hort.	
N.'Soleil d'Or'	Div.8	Hort.	
N.'Sonata'	Div.9	Hort.	
N.'St. Agnes'	Div.9	Hort.	
N.'St. Keyne'	Div.9	Hort.	
N.'Stadium'	Div.2B	Hort.	
N.'Tain'	Div.10	Hort.	
N.x 'Thalia'	Div.10	Hort.	
N.'Trevithian'	Div.7B	Hort.	
N.triandrus 'Albus'	Div.10	Mediterranean	
N.'White Lion'	Div.4	Hort.	
N.'White Marvel'	Div.4	Hort.	
N.'White Sail'	Div.4	Hort.	

Nasturtium (Tropaeoleaceae)

N.officinale	Europe	1890 Palm Rockery	

Neopanax (Araliaceae)

N.arboreum	New Zealand	1914 Grassy Walk	
N.laetum	New Zealand	1952 Long Walk	

Neohenricia (Crassulaceae)

N.sibbettii	South Africa	1959 Beehive Rockery	

Nephrolepis (Davalliaceae)

N.exaltata (sword fern)	New Zealand	1976 Collection	

Nerine (Amaryllidaceae)

N.bowdenii	South Africa	1914 Cut Flower Garden	
N.corusca 'Major'	South Africa	1973 Toy Greenhouse	
N.masonorum	South Africa	1973 Toy Greenhouse	
N.'Pink Triumph'	Hort.	1978 Nerine Bank	
N.sarniensis	South Africa	1890 Middle Terrace	
N.undulata 'Alba'	South Africa	1914 Citrus Garden	

Nerium (Apocynaceae)

N.oleander (oleander)	Southern Europe	1890 Miss Innis'	

Nicotiana (Solanaceae)

N.californica	California	1978 Hop Circle	

Nolina (Agavaceae)

N.bigelovii	Arizona	1914 Mexico	
N.erumpens	Mexico	1975 Tea Hut Bank	
N.recurvata	Mexico	1914 West Rockery	

Notelaea (Oleaceae)

N.excelsa	Canary Islands	1914 Lower Australia	
N.ligustrina	Australia	1959 Arcadia	

Nothofagus (Fagaceae) southern beeches

N.cunninghamii	Tasmania	1856 Tree Ferns	
N.dombeyi	Chile	1973 Tree Ferns	
N.menziesii	New Zealand	1912 Tree Ferns	
N.obliqua	Chile	1912 Collection	
N.procera	Chile	1980 Collection	
N.solandri	New Zealand	1914 Tree Ferns	

Nothoscordium (Alliaceae)

N.inodorum	Mexico	1890 Path edges	

Notospartium (Leguminosae)

N.carmichaeliae	New Zealand	1914 Collection	

Nymphaea (Nymphaeaceae)

N.alba	Europe	1890 Well Covert	
N.'Escarboucle'	Hort.	1959 West Rockery	

Odontospermum (Compositae)

O.sericeum	Canary Islands	1959 Middle Terrace	

Olea (Oleaceae)

O.europaea (olive)	Southern Europe	1890 Top Terrace	
O.lanceolata	Asia	1974 Long Walk	

Olearia (Compositae)

O.adenophora	Australia	1974 Lighthouse Walk	
O.albida	New Zealand	1959 Grassy Walk	
O.angustifolia	New Zealand	1914 Stone Table	
O.arborescens	New Zealand	1914 Stone Table	
O.argyrophylla	Australia	1853 Well Covert	
O.avicennifolia	New Zealand	1914 Nerine Bank	
O.capillaris	New Zealand	1959 Collection	
O.colensoi	New Zealand	1914 Old Nursery Garden	
O.coriacea	New Zealand	1973 East Orchard	
O.erubescens	Australia	1914 East Orchard	
O.erubescens 'Ilicifolia'	Australia	1978 Collection	
O.furfuracea	New Zealand	1914 Grassy Walk	
O.x haastii	New Zealand	1890 Stone Table	
O.ilicifolia	New Zealand	1914 East Rockery	
O.insignis	New Zealand	1914 Lighthouse Walk	
O.lacunosa	New Zealand	1914 Stone Table	
O.lirata	New Zealand	1959 Top Terrace South	
O.macrodonta	New Zealand	1873 Stone Table	
O.macrodonta 'Minor'	New Zealand	1914 East Entrance	
O.megalophylla	Australia	1973 Grassy Walk	
O.x mollis	O.ilicifolia x lacunosa	1959 Collection	
O.mollis 'Zennorensis'	O.ilicifolia x lacunosa	1949 Lighthouse Walk	
O.moschata	New Zealand	1914 Stone Table	
O.moschata x ilicifolia	Hort.	1973 Stone Table	

O.nummularifolia	New Zealand	1914 Abbey Rock Garden
O.nummularifolia 'Cymbifolia'	New Zealand	1973 Podalyria Bank
O.odorata	New Zealand	1914 Collection
O.oleifolia	New Zealand	1959 Old Nursery Garden
O.pachyphylla	New Zealand	1962 Grassy Walk
O.paniculata	New Zealand	1890 Top Terrace
O.paniculata 'Major'	New Zealand	1978 Collection
O.phlogopappa	New Zealand	1914 East Orchard
O.phlogopappa 'Splendens Master Michael'	Tasmania	1973 East Entrance
O.phlogopappa 'Splendens Rosea'	Tasmania	1973 Long Walk
O.ramulosa	Tasmania	1914 Stone Table
O.rani	New Zealand	1978 Collection
O.rossii	Unknown	1978 Collection
O.rotundifolia	Australia	1873 East Orchard
O.x scilloniensis	O.phlogopappa x lirata	1948 Long Walk
O.semidentata	New Zealand	1914 Lighthouse Walk
O.solandri	New Zealand	1914 Grassy Walk
O.stellulata	Australia	1873 Lighthouse Walk
O.sub-repanda	Australia	1973 West Orchard
O.traversii	Chatham Island	1914 Grassy Walk
O.virgata 'Lineata'	New Zealand	1959 Grassy Walk
O.viscosa	Australia	1978 Collection
O.x waikariensis	Hort.	1978 Collection

Onoclaea (Polypodiaceae)

O.sensibilis (sensitive fern)	North America	1865 Collection

Opuntia (Cactaceae)

O.aurantiaca	Chile	1894 Cactus Bed
O.basilaris	Arizona	1979 Collection
O.boliviensis	Bolivia	1973 Cactus Bed
O.cochinellifera	Central America	1973 Toy Greenhouse
O.compressa	Central America	1978 Collection
O.cylindrica	Ecuador	1959 Collection
O.dejecta	Central America	1973 Toy Greenhouse
O.excelsa	Central America	1978 Collection
O.grahamii	Central America	1978 Cactus Bed
O.herrpeltii	Central America	1978 Toy Greenhouse
O.imbricata 'Ruthei'	Central America	1973 Toy Greenhouse
O.leptoclada	Mexico	1959 Cactus Bed
O.microdasys 'Rufida'	Mexico	1959 Toy Greenhouse
O.missouriensis	Missouri	1894 Toy Greenhouse
O.mojavensis	California	1978 Toy Greenhouse
O.monocantha 'Variegata'	California	1978 Toy Greenhouse
O.paraguayensis	Paraguay	1976 Cactus Bed
O.phaecantha	Paraguay	1978 Cactus Bed
O.puberula	Paraguay	1978 Cactus Bed
O.rafinesquei	Missouri	1894 Collection
O.robusta	Central America	1978 Cactus Bed
O.salmiana	Central America	1978 Cactus Bed
O.scheeri	Mexico	1959 Toy Greenhouse
O.spinosa	Central America	1978 Cactus Bed
O.subulata	Central America	1973 Collection
O.subulata 'Minor'	Central America	1973 Cactus Bed
O.tunicata	Central America	1973 Cactus Bed
O.undulata	Central America	1978 Collection
O.vaseyi	Central America	1978 Collection
O.velutina	Central America	1978 Cactus Bed
O.verschaffeltii	Central America	1978 Collection
O.vulgaris	Central America	1894 Collection

Orepanax (Araliaceae)

O.epremesnilianum	Hort.	1959 Old Nursery Garden

Ornithogalum (Liliaceae)

Species	South Africa	1894 West Rockery

Orthrosanthus (Iridaceae)

O.multiflorus	Australia	1934 Middle Terrace

Oscularia (Aizoaceae)

O.deltoides	South Africa	1865 Middle Terrace

Osmanthus (Oleaceae)

O.x burkwoodii	O.delavayi x O.decorus	1959 Lily Garden
O.x fortunei	O.ilicifolius x O.aquifolius	1914 Grassy Walk

Osmaronia (Rosaceae)

O.cerasiformis	California	1959 Higher Australia

Osmunda (Osmundaceae)

O.claytoniana (interrupted fern)	North America	1975 Long Walk
O.regalis (royal fern)	Native	1856 Well Covert
O.regalis 'Crispa'	Britain	1975 Long Walk
O.regalis 'Cristata'	Britain	1975 Long Walk
O.regalis 'Purpurescens'	Britain	1975 Long Walk

Osteospermum (Compositae)

O.barberiae	South Africa	1973 Middle Terrace
O.'Compacta'	South Africa	1976 Middle Terrace
O.ecklonis	South Africa	1973 Middle Terrace
O.ecklonis 'Blue Streak'	South Africa	1973 South Africa Rockery
O.ecklonis 'Compacta'	South Africa	1977 Podalyria Bank
O.ecklonis 'Pink'	South Africa	1973 South Africa Rockery
O.hyloserioides	South Africa	1973 Middle Terrace
O.'Tresco Peggy'	South Africa	1973 South Africa Rockery

Othonna (Compositae)

O.capensis	South Africa	1894 Collection

Oxalis (Oxalidaceae)

O.articulata	South America	1854 General
O.deppei	Mexico	1973 Toy Greenhouse
O.exilis	Cosmopolitan	1959 General
O.megalorrhiza	Chile	1894 Toy Greenhouse
O.pes-caprae (Bermuda buttercup)	Bermuda	1894 General

Oxylobium (Leguminosae)

O.ellipticum 'Angustifolium'	Tasmania	1959 Lighthouse Walk
O.lineare	Tasmania	1973 Grassy Walk

Ozothamnus (Compositae)

O.diosmifolius	Australia	1950 Lighthouse Walk
O.thyrsoides	Australia	1959 Lighthouse Walk

Pachycereus (Cactaceae)

P.pringlei	Mexico	1974 Cactus Bed

Pachyphytum

P.compactum	Mexico	1965 Collection
P.heterosepalum	Mexico	1973 Collection
P.oviferum	Mexico	1959 Collection

Pancratium (Amaryllidaceae)

P.maritimum	Europe	1844 Conservatory Rockery

Pandorea (Bignoniaceae)

P.jasminoides 'Rosea-superba'	Australia	1973 Well Garden

Parthenocissus (Vitadaceae)

P.quinquefolia	Japan	1890 Collection

Passiflora (Passifloraceae) passion flower

P.antioquiensis	Columbia	1914 Collection
P.caerulea	Peru	1894 Mexico Pergola
P. x caerulea-racemosa	Hort.	1973 Augustus Smith's Wall
P. x exoniensis	P.antioquiensis x P.mollissima	1894 Middle Terrace
P.quadrangularis	South America	1981 Collection

Paulownia (Scrophulariaceae)

P.tomentosa	China	1959 Long Walk

Pelargonium (Geraniaceae)

Generally distributed throughout the garden, but often replaced for rejuvenation purposes. All material is held in a collection in the Peach House, so no garden site is given.

P.acetosum	South Africa	1981
P.albescens	South Africa	1959
P. x ardens	P.fulgidum x P. lobatum	1894
P.asperum	South Africa	1971

P. 'Aurore's Unique'	Hort. Unique	1971
P.australe	Australia	1962
P.betulinum	Tropical Africa	1914
P.capitatum	South Africa	1914
P. 'Carisbrooke'	Hort. Regal	1962
P.caudatum	South Africa	1973
P.citriodorum 'Prince of Orange'	Hort. Scented-leaved	1865
P.crispum	South Africa	1914
P.crispum 'Minor'	South Africa	1914
P.cucullatum	South Africa	1914
P.cucullatum 'Flore Pleno'	South Africa	1914
P.cucullatum x *citriodorum*	Hort. Scented-leaved	1973
P.dasycaule	South Africa	1959
P.echinatum	South Africa	1914
P.echinatum 'Album'	South Africa	1971
P.echinatum 'Miss Stapleton'	South Africa	1914
P. 'Elizabeth Cartwright'	Hort. Zonal	1962
P.exstipulatum	Africa	1980
P.ficifolium	South Africa	1953
P. 'Flower of Spring'	Hort. Zonal	1959
P. x *fragrans*	*P.exstipulatum*	
	x *odoratissimum*	1890
P. 'Friesdorf'	Hort. Zonal	1978
P.fulgidum	South Africa	1959
P. 'Galilee'	Hort. Ivy-leaved	1959
P.gibbosum	Africa	1914
P.glaucifolium	Africa	1973
P.glaucifolium 'Black and Yellow Form'	Africa	1959
P.glutinosum	South Africa	1914
P.glutinosum 'Viscosissimum'	South Africa	1971
P.graveolens	South Africa	1962
P. 'Happy Thoughts'	Hort. Zonal	1962
P.hirsutum 'Melananthum Carneum'	South Africa	1977
P.inodorum	South Africa	1971
P.inquinans	South Africa	1929
P. 'Jessel's Unique'	Hort. Unique	1971
P. 'Joy Lucille'	Hort. Scented-leaved	1962
P. 'Lady Plymouth'	Hort. Scented-leaved	1914
P. 'La France'	Hort. Ivy-leaved	1959
P. 'L'Elegante'	Hort. Ivy-leaved	1959
P. 'Mabel Grey'	Hort. Scented-leaved	1971
P. 'Madame Ninon'	Hort. Unique	1977
P. 'Monsieur Norin'	Hort. Unique	1914
P. 'Moore's Victory'	Hort. Unique	1914
P. 'Mrs. Kingsbury'	Hort. Unique	1914
P. 'Mrs. Strang'	Hort. Zonal	1962
P. 'Mrs. W.A.R. Clifton'	Hort. Ivy-leaved	1971
P.odoratissimum	South Africa	1914
P. 'Paddy'	Hort. Unique	1959
P.papilionaceum	South Africa	1980
P. 'Paul Crampel'	Hort. Zonal	1973
P. 'Pretty Polly'	Hort. Unique	1914
P.quercifolium	South Africa	1890
P.quercifolium 'Denticulatum'	South Africa	1890
P.quercifolium 'Denticulatum Filicifolium'	South Africa	1914
P.quercifolium 'Fair Ellen'	Hort. Scented-leaved	1914
P.quercifolium 'Mrs. Douglas'	Hort. Scented-leaved	1914
P.quercifolium 'Royal Oak'	Hort. Scented-leaved	1971
P.radula	South Africa	1953
P. 'Red Rambler'	Hort. Zonal	1962
P. 'Red Rosebud'	Hort. Zonal	1980
P.reniforme	South Africa	1959
P. 'Ringo Salmon'	Hort. Zonal	1981
P. 'Rollinson's Unique'	Hort. Unique	1890
P. 'Rosebud Supreme'	Hort. Zonal	1962
P. 'Rouletta'	Hort. Ivy-leaved	1979
P.salmoneum	South Africa	1949
P.salmoneum 'The Boar'	South Africa	1962
P. 'Scarlet Unique'	Hort. Unique	1856
P. 'Smith's Supreme'	Hort. Zonal	1865
P. 'Snowstorm'	Hort. Zonal	1977
P. 'Stella'	Hort. Zonal	1962
P.stenopetalum	Zululand	1959
P.tomentosum	South Africa	1914
P.tricolor	South Africa	1973
P.triste	South Africa	1977
P.umbellatum	South Africa	1980
P. 'Verite'	Hort. Zonal	1973
P.vitifolium	South Africa	1973

P. 'White Unique'	Hort. Unique	1973
P. 'Winter White'	Hort. Zonal	1975
P.zonale	South Africa	1980

Pellaea (Adiantaceae)
P.rotundifolia	New Zealand	1975 Tree Ferns

Penstemon (Scrophulariaceae)
P.hartwegii Hybrids	Hort.	1890 Higher Australia

Pentaglottis (Boraginaceae)
P.sempervirens	Southern Europe	1959 Citrus Garden

Persea (Lauraceae)
P.americana (avocado pear)	North America	1973 Below Toy Greenhouse
P.ichangensis	China	1973 Grassy Walk

Petasites (Compositae)
P.fragrans (winter heliotrope)	Southern Europe	1890 Limpet Midden

Phaedranassa (Amaryllidaceae)
P.viridiflora	Peru	1973 Collection

Phalaris (Gramineae)
P.arundinacea 'Picta' (ribbon grass)	Northern hemisphere	1959 West Rockery
P.communis (common reed)	Established alien	1890 Well Covert

Philadelphus (Philadelphaceae)
P.mexicanus 'Rose Syringa'	Mexico	1853 Grassy Walk

Philageria (Philesiaceae)
P.veitchii	*Lapageria rosea* x	
	Philesia magellanica	1959 Well Garden

Phlomis (Labiatae)
P.cashmeriana	Kashmir	1973 Middle Terrace
P.fruticosa (Jerusalem sage)	Greece	1894 Middle Terrace

Phoenix (Palmae)
P.canariensis (Canary Island palm)	Canary Islands	1894 Lighthouse Walk
P.dactylifera (date palm)	North Africa	1856 Old Abbey West
P.reclinata	South Africa	1914 Pear Tree Garden
P.theophrastii	Canary Islands	1978 Collection

Phormium (Agavaceae)
P. 'Brodick Corkscrew'	Hort.	1981 Lower Australia
P. 'Bronze Baby'	Hort.	1981 Lower Australia
P.colensoi	New Zealand	1890 Old Nursery Garden
P. x *cookianum*	New Zealand	1959 Monument
P. 'Cream Delight'	Hort.	1981 Lower Australia
P. 'Dark Delight'	Hort.	1981 Lower Australia
P. 'Dark Reward'	Hort.	1980 Collection
P. 'Dazzler'	Hort.	1980 Lower Australia
P. 'Duet'	Hort.	1981 Lower Australia
P. 'Emerald Green'	Hort.	1981 Lower Australia
P. 'Gold Wave'	Hort.	1980 Collection
P. 'Gold Spike'	Hort.	1981 Lower Australia
P. 'Maori Maiden'	Hort.	1981 Lower Australia
P. 'Maori Sunrise'	Hort.	1980 Lower Australia
P. 'Purpureum'	New Zealand	1890 East Orchard
P. 'Radiance'	Hort.	1974 Lower Australia
P. 'Red Robin'	Hort.	1980 Duckery
P. 'Sundowner'	Hort.	1980 Lower Australia
P. 'Sunset'	Hort.	1980 Duckery
P. 'Surfer'	Hort.	1981 Lower Australia
P.tenax (New Zealand flax)	New Zealand	1890 Lighthouse Walk
P. 'Thumbelina'	Hort.	1980 Duckery
P. 'Tricolor'	Hort.	1978 West Rockery
P. 'Variegatum'	New Zealand	1890 Lower Australia
P. 'Veirchii'	Hort.	1890 Lower Australia
P. 'Yellow Wave'	Hort.	1981 Lower Australia

Photinia (Rosaceae)
P. x *fraseri* 'Coates Crimson'	Hort.	1977 Well Garden
P. x *fraseri* 'Red Robin'	Hort.	1973 East Orchard
P.serrulata	China	1856 Pear Tree Garden

Phygelius (Scrophulariaceae)
P.aequalis 'Green Form'	South Africa	1981 Collection
P.capensis 'Coccineus'	South Africa	1859 Middle Terrace

Phylica (Rhamnaceae)		
P.ericoides	South Africa	1856 Podalyria Bank

Phyllostachys (Graminae)		
P.aurea	Japan	1914 Bamboo Garden
P.mitis	China	1962 Bamboo Garden
P.nigra	China	1890 Bamboo Garden

Phytolacca (Phytolaccaceae)		
P.decandra (pokeweed)	Yunnan	1973 Hop Circle

Pieris (Ericaceae)		
P.taiwanensis	Taiwan	1973 Duckery Dell

Pileostegia (Hydrangaceae)		
P.viburnoides	China	1977 Well Garden

Pinus (Pinaceae)		
P.ayacuhuite	Mexico	1979 Collection
P.canariensis	Canary Islands	1914 Abbey Drive
P.caribaea	Caribbean	1973 Gardeners' Walk
P.contorta 'Latifolia' (lodgepole)	U.S.A.	1973 Windbreaks
P.halepensis (Aleppo pine)	Southern Europe	1959 East Rockery
P.laricio (Corsican pine)	Southern Europe	1894 Aloe Walk
P.leiophylla	Mexico	1973 Gardeners' Walk
P.montezumae	Mexico	1959 New Lawn
P.muricata (Bishop pine)	U.S.A.	1977 Windbreaks
P.oocarpa	Guatemala	1979 Collection
P.pinaster (maritime pine)	Southern Europe	1894 Long Walk
P.pinea (stone pine)	Southern Europe	1894 Middle Terrace
P.radiata (Monterey pine)	California	1874 Windbreaks
P.thunbergii	Japan	1980 Windbreaks
P.torreyana (Torrey pine)	California	1932 Monument Walk

Pittosporum (Pittosporaceae)		
P.bicolor	Australia	1914 Grassy Walk
P.colensoi	New Zealand	1896 Grassy Walk
P.cornifolium	New Zealand	1914 Fernery
P.crassifolium	New Zealand	1890 Fernery
P.dallii	New Zealand	1925 Old Nursery
P.daphniphylloides	West China	1972 West Orchard
P.eugenoides	New Zealand	1890 Top Terrace
P.eugenoides 'Variegatum'	New Zealand	1959 Well Garden
P.fairchildii	New Zealand	1894 Grassy Walk
P.ralphii	New Zealand	1914 Aloe Walk
P.tenuifolium	New Zealand	1851 Pear Tree Garden
P.tenuifolium 'Abbotsbury Gold'	Hort.	1980 Collection
P.tenuifolium 'Frosty Morn'	Hort.	1975 East Orchard
P.tenuifolium 'Garnetii'	Hort.	1973 Long Walk
P.tenuifolium 'Golden King'	Hort.	1980 Collection
P.tenuifolium 'Irene Patterson'	Hort.	1980 Collection
P.tenuifolium 'Purpureum'	Hort.	1975 West Orchard
P.tenuifolium 'Silver Queen'	Hort.	1978 Well Garden
P.tenuifolium 'James Stirling'	Hort.	1978 Tree Ferns
P.tenuifolium 'Sunburst'	Hort.	1981 Collection
P.tenuifolium 'Tom Thumb'	Hort.	1981 Collection
P.tenuifolium 'Warnham Gold'	Hort.	1980 Collection
P.tobira	Japan	1850 East Rockery
P.tobira 'Variegatum'	Hort.	1890 Collection
P. 'Tresederi'	Hort.	1981 Collection
P. 'Wendle Channon'	Hort.	1981 Collection

Plantago (Plantaginaceae)		
P.palmata	Canary Islands	1976 Lily Garden

Pleiospilos (Aizoaceae)		
P.magnipunctatus	South Africa	1973 Conservatory Rockery
P.willowmorensis	South Africa	1959 Collection

Plumbago (Plumbaginaceae)		
P.capensis	South Africa	1851 Old Abbey

Podalyria (Leguminosae)		
P.calyptrata	South Africa	1905 Podalyria Bank

Podocarpus (Podocarpaceae)		
P.andinus	Chile	1890 Lower Australia
P.dacrydioides (Kahikatea)	New Zealand	1914 Abbey Drive
P.falcatus	South Africa	1977 Collection
P.macrophyllus	Japan	1977 West Orchard

	P.milanjianus	Tanzania	1914 Abbey Drive
	P.neriifolius	China	1959 Abbey Drive
	P.nubigenus	Chile	1959 Tree Ferns
	P.totara	New Zealand	1890 Lower Australia
	P.totara 'Aurea'	New Zealand	1981 Collection

Poellnitzia (Liliaceae)		
P.rubrifolia	South Africa	1959 Collection

Polianthes (Liliaceae)		
P.tuberosa	South Africa	1890 Well Garden

Polygala (Polygalaceae)		
P.myrtifolia 'Grandiflora'	South Africa	1914 Middle Terrace
P.virgata	South Africa	1931 Collection

Polygonatum (Liliaceae)		
P.multiflorum (Solomon's seal)	Britain	1890 Lighthouse Walk

Polygonum (Polygonaceae)		
P.cuspidatum (Japanese knotweed)	Japan	1973 Toy Greenhouse

Polypodium (Polypodiaceae)		
P.australe (southern polypody)	Native	1834 East Rockery
P.australe 'Cambricum'	Britain	1855 West Rockery
P.australe 'Cambricum Barrowii'	Britain	1975 Collection
P.interjectum	Native	1971 Monument Hill
P.vulgare (polypody)	Native	1834 Walls
P.vulgare 'Bifidum'	Britain	1975 Collection
P.vulgare 'Cornubiense'	Britain	1975 Collection
P.vulgare 'Cornubiense Multifidum'	Britain	1975 Collection
P.vulgare 'Longicaudatum'	Britain	1975 Collection
P.vulgare 'Pulcherrimum'	Britain	1975 Collection

Polystichum (Aspleniaceae)		
P.aculeatum (prickly shield fern)	Britain	1855 Collection
P.aculeatum 'Grandiceps'	Britain	1976 Collection
P.setiferum (soft shield fern)	Native	1834 Old Nursery
P.setiferum 'Acutilobum'	Britain	1975 Collection
P.setiferum 'Perserrautum'	Britain	1976 Collection
P.tsus-sinense	Japan	1976 Collection

Pomaderris (Rhamnaceae)		
P.elliptica	Australia	1856 Long Walk
P.rugosa	Australia	1973 East Orchard

Pontederia (Pontederiaceae)		
P.cordata (Pickerel weed)	North America	1959 West Rockery

Populus (Salicaceae) poplars		
P.alba (white poplar)	Britain	1890 Pool Road
P.balsamifera	Europe	1980 Collection
P.generosa	Japan	1980 Collection
P.serotina	Europe	1980 Collection
P.trichocarpa	Europe	1912 Collection
P.nigra 'Italica' (Lombardy poplar)	Europe	1980 Collection
P.nigra 'Casale'	Hort.	1980 Collection
P.robusta	Europe	1980 Collection
P.robusta 'Vereekkon'	Hort.	1980 Collection

Portulacaria (Portulacaceae)		
P.afra	South Africa	1959 Collection
P.afra 'Foliis Variegatus'	South Africa	1973 Collection

Primula (Primulaceae)		
P.denticulata	Himalaya	1857 West Rockery
P.japonica	Japan	1890 Fernery
P.veris (cowslip)	Britain	1975 West Rockery
P.vulgaris (primrose)	Native	1834 Lily Garden
P.vulgaris x *veris* (polyanthus)	Hort.	1959 Pear Tree Garden

Prostanthera (Labiatae)		
P.cuneata	Australia	1981 Hop Circle
P.denticulata	Australia	1981 Hop Circle
P.incisa	Australia	1914 Hop Circle
P.lasianthos	Australia	1856 Podalyria Bank
P.melissifolia 'Parviflora'	Australia	1981 Hop Circle
P.rotundifolia	Australia	1856 South Africa Flat
P.rotundifolia 'Purpurea'	Australia	1981 Hop Circle
P.rotundifolia 'Rosea'	Australia	1981 South Africa Flat
P.sieberi	Australia	1981 South Africa Flat

Protea (Proteaceae)
P.compacta	South Africa	1980 Collection
P.cynaroides	South Africa	1912 Middle Terrace
P.eximia	South Africa	1914 Top Terrace West
P.grandiceps	South Africa	1970 Top Terrace West
P.lacticolor	South Africa	1952 Top Terrace West
P.lepidocarpodendron	South Africa	1972 Toy Greenhouse
P.longiflora	South Africa	1959 Top Terrace
P.longiflora Deep-pink form	South Africa	1973 South Africa Flat
P.mundi	South Africa	1950 Top Terrace West
P.nerifolia	South Africa	1944 Collection
P.prepens	South Africa	1856 Moraine
P.speciosa	South Africa	1973 Top Terrace
P.susannae	South Africa	1945 South Africa Flat

Prunus (Rosaceae)
P.domestica (plum)	Europe	1890 Orchard
P.persica (peach)	Iran	1890 Peach House
P.persica 'Laevis' (nectarine)	Iran	1890 Peach House

Pseudodrynaria (Polypodiaceae)
P.coronans		1976 Tree Ferns

Pseudopanax (Araliaceae)
P.chathamicum	Chatham Island	1914 Higher Australia
P.crassifolium	New Zealand	1856 Higher Australia
P.crassifolium 'Purpureum'	New Zealand	1981 Duckery
P.ferox	New Zealand	1914 Higher Australia
P.lessonii 'Gold Splash'	New Zealand	1976 East Orchard

Pseudowintera (Winteraceae)
P.colorata	New Zealand	1914 Pear Tree Garden

Psoralea (Leguminosae)
P.affinis	South Africa	1914 Top Terrace
P.pinnata	South Africa	1890 Grassy Walk

Pteris (Adiantaceae)
P.cretica	Crete	1863 Fernery
P.cretica 'Everghemensis'	Hort.	1980 Collection
P.cretica 'Roweri'	Hort.	1980 Collection
P.tremula	New Zealand	1894 Collection

Puya (Bromeliaceae)
P.alpestris	Chile	1951 Mexico
P.alpestris Hybrid	Hort.	1970 Neptune Steps
P.berteroniana	Chile	1959 Opposite Palm Rockery
P.chilensis	Chile	1848 Puya Bank
P.coerulea	Chile	1894 Toy Greenhouse area
P.mirabilis	Chile	1974 Collection
P.spathacea	Argentina	1952 Cypress Rockery
P.venusta	Chile	1959 Middle Terrace

Pyrus (Rosaceae)
P.communis (pear)	Europe	1890 Orchard
P.communis 'Olivier de Serre'	Hort.	1914 Pear Tree Garden

Quercus (Fagaceae)
Q.ceris (Turkey oak)	Southern Europe	1890 Hop Circle
Q.ilex (holm oak)	Southern Europe	1890 General
Q.leucotrichophora	Northern India	1959 Grassy Walk
Q.petraea (sessile oak)	Britain	1960 Abbey Drive
Q.robur (common oak)	Britain	1890 Abbey Drive

Raphiolepis (Rosaceae)
R.x delacourii	R.umbellata x R.indica	1914 Long Walk West
R.umbellata	Japan	1890 Long Walk West

Restio (Restionaceae)
R.subverticillatus	South Africa	1914 Pear Tree Garden

Rhaphis (Palmae)
R.humilis	Japan	1914 Pear Tree Garden

Rhaphithamnus (Verbenaceae)
R.spinosus	Chile	1908 Pear Tree Garden

Rhododendron (Ericaceae)
R.arboreum (series Arboreum)	Himalaya	1894 Abbey Drive
R.arboreum 'Blood Red Form'	Himalaya	1914 Abbey Drive
R.arboreum 'Limbatum'	Hort.	1959 Abbey Drive
R.augustinii (series Triflorum)	China	1914 Abbey Drive
R.augustinii 'Lavender Form'	China	1967 Abbey Drive
R. 'Blue Ribbon'	R.augustinii x 'Blue Tit'	1973 Well Covert
R.burmanicum (series Maddenii)	Burma	1973 Duckery Dell
R.charitopes	Yunnan	1959 Abbey Drive
R. 'Chrysomanicum'	R.burmanicum x R.chrysodoron	1973 Abbey Drive
R.cinnabarinum 'Roylei' x maddenii	Hort.	1945 Abbey Drive
R.concatenans (series Cinnabarinum)	Tibet	1959 Abbey Drive
R. 'Countess of Haddington'	R.ciliatum x R.dalhousei	1894 Duckery Dell
R.crassum (series Maddenii)	China	1914 Abbey Drive
R.cubittii 'Ashcombe' (series Maddenii)	North Burma	1973 Duckery Dell
R. 'Endsleigh Pink'	Hort.	1974 Abbey Drive
R. 'Eric Stockton'	'Fabia' x 'Tally-Ho'	1971 Well Covert
R.falconeri (series Falconeri)	Himalaya	1894 Abbey Drive
R. 'Fragrantissimum'	R.edgeworthii x formosum	1959 Abbey Drive
R.grande (series Grande)	Sikkim	1894 Abbey Drive
R. 'Greenway'	Hort.	1975 Duckery Dell
R.griffithianum (series Fortunei)	Himalaya	1894 Abbey Drive
R. 'Hinomayo' (Kurume azalea)	Japan	1976 Duckery Dell
R.johnstoneanum (series Maddenii)	Manipur	1973 Duckery Dell
R.johnstoneanum 'Double Diamond'	Assam	1973 Well Covert
R.johnstoneanum 'Rubro-tinctum'	Assam	1973 Abbey Drive
R. 'Lady Alice Fitzwilliam'	Hort.	1959 Abbey Drive
R. 'Lady Chamberlain'	R.cinnabarinum x R.maddenii	1973 Duckery Dell
R. 'Loderi King George'	R.fortunei x R.griffithianum	1959 Abbey Drive
R.lutescens (series Triflorum)	China	1914 Abbey Drive
R.luteum (series Azalea)	Caucasus	1973 Middle Terrace
R.macabeanum (series Grande)	Assam	1973 Well Covert
R.maddenii (series Maddenii)	Sikkim	1894 Well Covert
R.micranthum (series Micranthum)	Szechwan	1914 Abbey Drive
R. 'Mollis Hybrids'	R.molle x japonicum	1973 Well Covert
R.neriiflorum (series Neriiflorum)	China	1914 Abbey Drive
R.obtusum (series Azalea)	Japan	1970 East Rockery
R.obtusum 'Album'	Japan	1959 Miss Innis'
R.obtusum 'Amoenum'	Japan	1959 Nerine Bank
R.ponticum (series Ponticum)	Caucasus	1894 Abbey Drive
R.racemosum (series Scabrifolium)	China	1914 Abbey Drive
R. 'Saffron Queen'	R.burmanicum x R.xanthostephanum	1973 Duckery Dell
R. 'Sappho'	Hort	1914 Monument Walk
R. 'Selig'	R.calophytum x cinnabarinum	1959 Abbey Drive
R.siderophyllum (series Triflorum)	Yunnan	1970 Well Covert
R.supranubium (series Maddenii)	Yunnan	1973 Well Covert
R.taggianum (series Maddenii)	Yunnan	1970 Abbey Drive
R.taronense (series Maddenii)	China	1973 Duckery Dell
R.x tyermannii	R.nuttallii x R.formusum	1959 Well Covert
R.veitchianum (series Maddenii)	Burma	1959 Abbey Drive
R.zeylanicum (series Arboreum)	Ceylon	1959 Abbey Drive

Rhopalostylis (Palmae)
R.sapida (nikau palm)	New Zealand	1863 Long Walk

Rhus d(Anacardiaceae)
R.lucida	North America	1949 Grassy Walk
R.typhina (stag's horn sumach)	North America	1979 Collection

Robinia (Leguminosae)
R.pseudacacia (locust tree)	North America	1890 Long Walk

Rochea (Crassulaceae)
R.albiflora x coccinea	Hort.	1973 Top Terrace
R.coccinea	South Africa	1890 Top Terrace

Rosa (Rosaceae)
R.arkansana	North America	1978 Collection
R.iberica	Spain	1981 Collection
R.rugosa	China	1894 Middle Terrace

Rosmarinus (Labiatae) rosemary

R.corsicus 'Prostratus'	Mediterranean	1981 Duckery Bank
R.officinalis	Mediterranean	1894 Puya Bank
R.officinalis 'Aurea'	Mediterranean	1981 Collection
R.officinalis 'Prostratus'	Mediterranean	1959 Middle Terrace
R.officinalis 'Jackman's Prostrata'	Mediterranean	1981 Duckery Bank
R.officinalis 'Miss Jessup'	Mediterranean	1981 Collection
R.officinalis 'Severn Sea'	Mediterranean	1981 Collection
R.officinalis 'Tuscan Blue'	Mediterranean	1914 Palm Rockery

Royena (Ebenaceae)

R.lucida	South Africa	1914 Grassy Walk

Rubus (Rosaceae)

R.ulmifolius (bramble)	Native	1834 Native Weed

Ruschia (Aizoaceae)

R.caroli	South Africa	1959 West Rockery

Ruscus (Liliaceae)

R.aculeatus (butcher's broom)	Native	1959 Nerine Bank

Sabal (Palmae)

S.palmetto	Carolina	1860 Collection

Salix (Salicaceae) willows

S.alba 'Britzensis'	Europe	1980 Collection
S.alba 'Caerulea'	Europe	1980 Collection
S.alba 'Vitellina'	Europe	1980 Great Pool
S.aquatica 'Gigantea'	Europe	1980 Great Pool
S. 'Bowles' Hybrid'	Hort.	1980 Collection
S.canariensis	Canary Islands	1959 Old Nursery Garden
S.cinerea 'Oleifolia'	Britain	1890 Great Pool
S.daphnoides	Europe	1980 Great Pool
S.dasyclados	Europe	1980 Collection
S.'Drakenburg'	Hort.	1980 Collection
S.'Foreman Essex'	Hort.	1980 Collection
S.irrorata	Europe	1980 Collection
S.japonica	Japan	1980 Collection
S.'Liempde'	Hort.	1980 Collection
S.'Lockinge'	Hort.	1980 Collection
S.'Polsdonk'	Hort.	1980 Collection
S.rosmarinifolia	Europe	1980 Great Pool
S.'St. Oedenrode'	Hort.	1980 Collection
S.'Vries'	Hort.	1980 Collection
S.'Wantage Hall'	Hort.	1980 Collection

Salvia (Labiatae) sages

S.aurea	South Africa	1890 South Africa Flat
S.broussonetii	Canary Islands	1973 Salvia Garden
S.fulgens	Mexico	1973 Salvia Garden
S.grahami	Mexico	1894 Top Terrace
S.involuvcrata 'Bethellii'	Mexico	1973 Old Abbey
S.leucantha	Mexico	1914 Salvia Garden
S.neurepia	Mexico	1973 Salvia Garden
S.officinalis	Southern Europe	1973 Salvia Garden
S.officinalis 'Tricolor'	Southern Europe	1973 West Orchard
S.patens	Mexico	1856 Salvia Garden
S.rutilans	Unknown	1914 Salvia Garden

Sambucus (Sambucaceae) elders

S.nigra (common elder)	Native	1834 Well Covert
S.nigra 'Albo-Variegata'	Britain	1979 Well Covert
S.nigra 'Lacinata'	Britain	1979 Well Covert

Santolina (Compositae)

S.chamaecyparissus 'Corsica'	Corsica	1890 Old Abbey

Sasa (Graminae)

S.palmata 'Nebulosa'	Japan	1914 Aloe Walk

Saurauja (Actinidiaceae)

S.subspinosa	Upper Burma	1950 Pebble Garden

Schefflera (Araliaceae)

S.digitata	New Zealand	1979 Collection

Schinus (Anacardiaceae)

S.latifolius	South America	1972 East Orchard

Schizostylis (Iridaceae)

S.coccinea	South Africa	1865 Lily Garden

Scilla (Liliaceae)

S.peruviana	Portugal	1844 Top Terrace
S.peruviana 'Alba'	Portugal	1973 Top Terrace
S.siberica	Russia	1848 Fernery
S.violacea	South Africa	1973 Collection
S.violacea 'Alba'	South Africa	1973 Collection

Sedum (Crassulaceae)

S.album	Europe	1848 Middle Terrace
S.allantoides	Mexico	1959 Collection
S.hintonii	Europe	1978 Collection
S.hirsutum 'Baeticum'	Spain	1973 Collection
S.morganianum	Mexico	1959 Collection
S.nussbaumeri	Mexico	1959 Collection
S.pachyphyllum	Mexico	1959 Collection
S.prealtum	Mexico	1959 Collection
S.rubrotinctum (guatemalense)	Mexico	1959 Collection
S.spathulifolium 'Purpureum'	California	1894 Collection

Selaginella (Selaginellaceae)

S.apus	North America	1857 Collection
S.krausseana	Azores	1953 East Orchard
S.krausseana 'Aurea'	Azores	1981 Collection
S.martensii	Unknown	1981 Collection

Selago (Scrophulariaceae)

S.serrata	South Africa	1959 South Africa Flat
S.thunbergii	South Africa	1959 South Africa Flat

Selenicereus (Cactaceae)

S.grandiflorus	Jamaica	1974 Peach House

Semele (Liliaceae)

S.androgyna	Canary Islands	1914 Long Walk
S.androgyna 'Variegata'	Tresco	1976 Well Garden

Sempervivum (Crassulaceae)

S.arachnoideum 'Grandiflorum'	Caucasus	1977 Collection
S.ballsii	Caucasus	1977 Collection
S.caucasicum	Caucasus	1977 Collection
S.x fimbriatum	S.arachnoideum var. doellianum x S.wulfeni	1977 Collection
S.x funckii	Hort.	1977 Collection
S.grandiflorum	Switzerland	1977 Collection
S.grandiflorum x montanum	Hort.	1977 Collection
S.guiseppii	Spain	1977 Collection
S.'Jubilee'	Hort.	1977 Collection
S.'Malby Hybrid'	Hort.	1977 Collection
S.montanum 'Stiriacum'	Austria	1977 Collection
S.octopodes	Greece	1977 Collection
S.'Apetalum'	Greece	1977 Collection
S.schlehanii	Caucasus	1977 Collection
S.tectorum 'Alanum'	Europe	1977 Collection
S.tectorum 'Alpinum'	Europe	1977 Collection
S.tectorum 'Nigrum'	Europe	1977 Collection

Senecio (Compositae)

S.aizoides	South Africa	1973 Collection
S.articulatus	South Africa	1973 Collection
S.cineraria Hybrids	Hort.	1894 Mulberry etc.
S.compactus	New Zealand	1914 East Orchard
S.cruentus	Canary Islands	1959 Middle Terrace
S.elaeagnifolius 'Buchananii'	New Zealand	1914 Collection
S.elegans	South Africa	1914 Collection
S.ficoides	South Africa	1973 Collection
S.glastifolius	South Africa	1959 Cypress Rockery
S.grandiflorus	Mexico	1912 Old Nursery Garden
S.greyii	New Zealand	1914 Old Nursery Garden
S.heritieri	Canary Islands	1973 Well Garden
S.herreanus	South Africa	1978 Collection
S.huntii	Chatham Islands	1909 Lighthouse Walk East
S.laxiflorus 'Sunshine'	New Zealand	1973 West Rockery
S.longiflorus 'Violaceus'	Abyssinia	1978 Collection
S.macroglossus 'Variegatus'	South Africa	1976 Well Garden
S.mikanioides	South Africa	1948 Valley
S.monroi	New Zealand	1914 West Rockery

Name	Origin	Year / Location
S.perdicioides	New Zealand	1914 Long Walk North
S.petasites	Mexico	1890 Old Nursery Garden
S.reinoldii	New Zealand	1959 East Entrance
S.rowleyanus	South Africa	1973 Collection
S.sempervivus	Arabia	1973 Collection

Sideritis (Labiatae)
S.gomerae	Canary Islands	1977 Podalyria Bank

Sinningia (Gesneriaceae)
S.speciosa Hybrids (gloxinia)	Hort.	1894 Collection

Sisyrinchium (Iridaceae)
S.bermudiana	Bermuda	1959 Old Abbey
S.brachypus		1977 Palm Rockery
S.grandiflorum 'Album'	North America	1980 Palm Rockery
S.striatum	Chile	1959 Lily Garden

Skimmia (Rutaceae)
S.x foremannii	*S.japonica* x *S.reevesiana*	1959 Long Walk
S.japonica	Japan	1890 Long Walk

Smilax (Liliaceae)
S.aspera	Southern Europe	1890 Lower Australia

Solanum (Solanaceae)
S.jasminoides	South America	1853 Old Abbey
S.laciniatum	Australia	1890 Abbey Woods
S.wendlandii	Costa Rica	1914 Peach House

Sollya (Pittosporaceae)
S.fusiformis	Australia	1904 Middle Terrace Wall

Sonchus (Compositae)
S.pinnatifidus	Canary Islands	1959 Well Garden
S.platylepis	Canary Islands	1959 Bamboo Garden

Sophora (Leguminosae)
S.'Little Baby'	Hort.	1977 Collection
S.macrocarpa	Chile	1959 Grassy Walk
S.microphylla	New Zealand	1865 Lighthouse Walk
S.secundiflora	Mexico	1974 Collection

Sparaxis (Iridaceae)
S.grandiflora	South Africa	1865 West Rockery
S.tricolor	South Africa	1959 Middle Terrace

Sparmannia (Tiliaceae)
S.africana	South Africa	1865 Abbey Drive
S.africana 'Flore-pleno'	South Africa	1890 Lighthouse Walk South

Spartium (Leguminosae)
S.junceum	Mediterranean	1890 Podalyria Bank

x Sprekanthus (Amaryllidaceae)
S.cagii	*Sprekelia x Habranthus*	1980 Collection

Sprekelia (Amaryllidaceae)
S.formosissima	Mexico	1914 Collection

Stapelia (Asclepiacaceae)
S.asterias 'Lucinda'	South Africa	1979 Collection
S.verrucosa	South Africa	1979 Collection

Stenocarpus (Proteaceae)
S.salignus	Australia	1891 Gardeners' Walk

Sterculia (Sterculiaceae)
S.diversifolia	Australia	1973 Long Walk

Stomatium (Aizoaceae)
S.agnimum	South Africa	1865 Collection

Strelitzia (Strelitziaceae)
S.parviflora	South Africa	1959 Abbey Rock Garden
S.parviflora 'Juncea'	South Africa	1914 Mexico
S.reginae	South Africa	1890 Middle Terrace

Streptocarpus (Gesneriaceae)
S.x hybridus 'Constant Nymph'	Hort.	1976 Collection
S.'White Form'	Hort.	1976 Collection

Strobilanthes (Acanthaceae)
S.dyerianus	Penang	1959 Old Nursery Garden

Stylidium (Stylidiaceae)
S.graminifolium	Australia	1856 South Africa Flat

Suttonia (Myrsinaceae)
S.australis	New Zealand	1914 Top Terrace
S.chathamica	Chatham Island	1973 Long Walk
S.salicina	New Zealand	1945 Fernery

Swainsonia (Leguminosae)
S.galegifolia	Australia	1851 Well Garden

Syagrus (Palmaceae)
S.campestris	Brazil	1914 Pebble Garden

Tamarix (Tamaricaceae)
T.gallica (tamarisk)	Southern Europe	1834 Windbreaks

Taxus (Taxaceae)
T.baccata (yew)	Britain	1959 Lighthouse Walk

Tecomaria (Bignoniaceae)
T.capensis (Cape honeysuckle)	South Africa	1959 Middle Terrace

Tellima (Saxifragaceae)
T.grandiflora	California	1980 Lower Australia

Telopea (Proteaceae)
T.speciosissima (waratah)	Australia	1856 Collection

Templetonia (Leguminosae)
T.retusa	Australia	1914 Old Abbey Wall

Tetrapanax (Araliaceae)
T.papyrifera (rice-paper tree)	China	1857 Old Nursery Garden

Teucrium (Labiatae)
T.fruticans (shrubby germander)	Southern Europe	1890 East Orchard

Thalia (Larantaceae)
T.dealbata	U.S.A.	1976 Middle Terrace Pond

Thalictrum (Ranunculaceae)
T.minus 'Adiantifolia'	Europe	1890 Citrus Garden

Thapsia (Umbelliferae)
T.decipiens	Madeira	1974 Old Nursery Garden

Thujopsis (Pinaceae)
T.dolabrata (hiba)	Japan	1890 Abbey Drive
T.dolabrata 'Hondai'	Japan	1959 Abbey Drive

Thymus (Labiatae)
T.vulgaris (thyme)	Europe	1890 Collection

Tibouchina (Melastomataceae)
T.semidecandra	Brazil	1914 Peach House

Tigridia (Iridaceae)
T.pavonia (peacock flower)	Mexico	1890 Middle Terrace

Trachelium (Campanulaceae)
T.caeruleum	Mediterranean	1959 Middle Terrace

Trachelospermum (Apocyanaceae)
T.jasminoides	China	1914 House Terrace
T.jasminoides 'Variegatum'	China	1959 Well Garden

Trachycarpus (Palmae)
T.fortunei (Chusan palm)	China	1854 Hop Circle
T.martianus	Himalaya	1973 Long Walk

Tradescantia (Commelinaceae)
T.navicularis	Peru	1914 Collection
T.virginiana	North America	1890 Old Nursery Garden

Trichocereus (Cactaceae)

Species	Origin	Year/Location
T.candicans	South America	1973 Collection
T.candicans 'Robustior'	South America	1973 Cactus House
T.chiloensis	Chile	1973 Collection
T.huascha	South America	1973 Outdoor Cactus
T.lamprochlorus x Echinopsis Species	Hort.	1973 Cactus Bed
T.macrogonus	South America	1973 Collection
T.pachanoi	South America	1973 Cactus Bed
T.pasacana	South America	1973 Cactus Bed
T.spachianus	South America	1973 Cactus House
T.terscheckii	South America	1973 Cactus Bed

Trichodiadema (Aizoaceae)

T.densum	South Africa	1959 Collection

Tritonia (Iridaceae)

T.crocata	South Africa	1973 East Orchard

Tropaeolum (Tropaeoleaceae)

T.majus (nasturtium)	Peru	1890 Old Abbey
T.peregrinum (Canary creeper)	Peru	1977 Old Abbey
T.tuberosum	Peru	1890 Long Walk East

Tulbaghia (Liliaceae)

T.violacea	South Africa	1848 Middle Terrace

Tulipa (Liliaceae)

T.clusiana (lady tulip)	Persia	1844 Abbey Rockery
T.eichleri	Transcaucasia	1975 Agave Bank West
T.saxatilis	Crete	1959 Middle Terrace

Ulex (Leguminosae)

U.europaeus (gorse)	Native	1852 Garden weed

Ulmus (Ulmaceae)

U.angustifolia 'Cornubiensis' (Cornish elm)	Britain	1890 Bamboo Garden
U.glabra (wych elm)	Britain	1973 Well Covert
U.procera (common elm)	Britain	1864 Lower Garden

Umbilicus (Crassulaceae)

U.rupestris	Native	1852 Walls

Vallea (Elaeocarpaceae)

V.stipularis	Andes	1973 Toy Greenhouse Path

Vallota (Amaryllidaceae)

V.speciosa	South Africa	1848 South Africa Rockery
V.speciosa 'Delicata'	South Africa	1959 Collection

Veltheimia (Liliaceae)

V.capensis	South Africa	1894 Collection

x Venidio-Arctotis (Compositae)

V.'Bacchus'	Venidium x Arctotis	1959 Middle Terrace
V.'China Pink'	Venidium x Arctotis	1978 Middle Terrace
V.'Flame'	Venidium x Arctotis	1959 Middle Terrace
V.'Mahogany'	Venidium x Arctotis	1959 Middle Terrace
V.'Tangerine'	Venidium x Arctotis	1978 Middle Terrace
V.'Torch'	Venidium x Arctotis	1978 Middle Terrace
V.'White Form'	Venidium x Arctotis	1978 Middle Terrace

Verbascum (Scrophulariaceae)

V.thapsus	Native	1852 Podalyria Bank

Verbena (Verbenaceae)

V.rigida	Argentina	1959 Pebble Garden

Viburnum (Caprifoliaceae)

V.farreri	China	1959 Pear Tree Garden
V.odoratissimum	Japan	1853 Grassy Walk
V.tinus (laurustinus)	Southern Europe	1894 Top Terrace

Vinca (Apocynaceae)

V.difformis	Mediterranean	1890 Limpet Midden
V.major (periwinkle)	Britain	1890 Lower Garden
V.major 'Variegata'	Britain	1977 Limpet Midden

Viola (Violaceae)

V.hederacea (Australian violet)	Australia	1978 Well Garden
V.odorata (sweet violet)	Britain	1967 Higher Australia
V.riviniana (dog violet)	Native	1864 Shade and walls

Virgilia (Leguminosae)

V.capensis	South Africa	1914 Top Terrace

Viscum (Loranthaceae)

V.album (mistletoe)	Britain	1973 East Orchard

Vitex (Verbenaceae)

V.agnus-castus (chaste tree)	Southern Europe	1980 Collection
V.lucens	New Zealand	1851 Long Walk West

Wachendorfia (Haemodoraceae)

W.paniculata	South Africa	1959 Pear Tree Garden
W.thyrsiflora	South Africa	1914 East Entrance

Washingtonia (Palmae)

W.filifera 'Robusta'	California	1959 Pebble Garden

Watsonia (Iridaceae)

W.ardernei	South Africa	1914 South Africa Flat
W.beatricis	South Africa	1951 Jam Tart
W.galpinii	South Africa	1950 West Rockery
W.marginata	South Africa	1959 Mexico
W.'Tresco Hybrids'	South Africa	1890 Middle Terrace
W.versfeldii	South Africa	1977 Palm Rockery

Weigela (Caprifoliaceae)

W.florida	Japan	1856 Abbey Drive
W.florida 'Variegata'	Japan	1978 Hop Circle

Weinmannia (Cunoniaceae)

W.racemosa	New Zealand	1914 Monument Walk

Westringia (Labiatae)

W.eremicola	Australia	1973 Podalyria Bank

Widdringtonia (Cupressaceae)

W.cedarburgensis	South Africa	1973 Gardeners' Walk
W.cupressoides	South Africa	1914 Gardeners' Walk
W.schwarzii (Willowmore cedar)	South Africa	1945 West Orchard

Wisteria (Leguminosae)

W.floribunda	Japan	1890 Old Abbey

Woodwardia (Blechnaceae)

W.radicans	Madeira	1865 Fernery

Yucca (Agavaceae)

Y.aloifolia 'Variegata'	Mexico	1854 Mexico
Y.brevifolia	South-Eastern U.S.A.	1973 Cactus Bed
Y.elata	South-Western U.S.A.	1969 Cactus Bed
Y.filamentosa	South-Western U.S.A.	1865 Cactus Bed
Y.gloriosa	South-Western U.S.A.	1857 East Rockery
Y.guatemalensis	Guatemala	1959 Toy Greenhouse
Y.schoigera	South-Western U.S.A.	1973 Cactus Bed
Y.whipplei	California	1894 Middle Terrace

Zantedeschia (Araceae)

Z.aethiopica (arum lily)	South Africa	1890 Well Covert
Z.aethiopica 'Green Jade'		1975 Well Covert

Zebrina (Commelinaceae)

Z.pendula	Mexico	1894 Collection

Zygocactus (Cactaceae)

Z.truncatus	Brazil	1959 Cypress Rockery